the ARCHITECTURE of FEAR

"SUPERIOR!"   *Library Journal*
"FASCINATING!"   *Twilight Zone*
"WONDERFUL!"   *Publishers Weekly*

"A volume that
should stand the test of time
as a cornerstone in
the development of dark fantasy"
Dennis Etchison, editor of *Cutting Edge*

"A milestone in the development
of contemporary horror fiction"
Mystery News

More Chilling Tales from Avon Books

14 VICIOUS VALENTINES
edited by Rosalind M. Greenberg,
Martin Harry Greenberg, and Charles G. Waugh

HAUNTING WOMEN
edited by Alan Ryan

13 HORRORS OF HALLOWEEN
edited by Carol-Lynn Rössel Waugh,
Martin Harry Greenberg, and Isaac Asimov

TROPICAL CHILLS
edited by Tim Sullivan

THE TWELVE FRIGHTS OF CHRISTMAS
edited by Isaac Asimov, Charles G. Waugh,
and Martin Harry Greenberg

^the ARCHITECTURE of FEAR

edited by
Kathryn Cramer
and Peter D. Pautz

AVON BOOKS ◆ NEW YORK

AVON BOOKS
A division of
The Hearst Corporation
105 Madison Avenue
New York, New York 10016

ACKNOWLEDGMENTS

Publishing any book these days is a committee effort, and an anthology even more so. Without exaggeration this volume would not have been possible without the following good people's advice, care, concern, and patience: Michael Bishop, Lloyd Currey, Bruce & Debbie Dalland, Jack Dann, Patrick X. Gallagher, Charles L. Grant, Kirby McCauley, Marta Randall, Karl Edward Wagner, Gene Wolfe, and the entire Arbor House staff.

Contents

INTRODUCTION
  by Peter D. Pautz..........................ix
IN THE HOUSE OF GINGERBREAD
  by Gene Wolfe...............................1
WHERE THE HEART IS
  by Ramsey Campbell 19
ELLEN, IN HER TIME
  by Charles L. Grant 29
NESTING INSTINCT
  by Scott Baker..............................39
ENDLESS NIGHT
  by Karl Edward Wagner 79
TRUST ME
  by Joseph Lyons 89
THE FETCH
  by Robert Aickman 93
VISITORS
  by Jack Dann...............................135
GENTLEMEN
  by John Skipp and Craig Spector............147
DOWN IN THE DARKNESS
  by Dean R. Koontz..........................173
HAUNTED
  by Joyce Carol Oates 197
IN THE MEMORY ROOM
  by Michael Bishop..........................217
TALES FROM THE ORIGINAL GOTHIC
  by John M. Ford 229
THE HOUSE THAT KNEW NO HATE
  by Jessica Amanda Salmonson................247
AFTERWORD: HOUSES OF THE MIND
  by Kathryn Cramer 273
A GUIDE TO SIGNIFICANT WORKS
  OF ARCHITECTURAL HORROR 277

Introduction

PETER D. PAUTZ

I want to talk a little about horror as an emotional experience. Not shock, not fear, but horror.

As I wrote this, it is a week after the Eleventh World
Fantasy Convention held in Providence, Rhode Island.
Guests of Honor were Ramsey Campbell, Charles L. Grant,
and J. K. Potter. The Master of Ceremonies was Douglas E.
Winter, who, in his introductions and opening remarks to the
awards banquet, brought up the archetypal interviewer who
asks: "Just why is horror so popular?" We who knew it was
unanswerable could be amused.

Pain, fear, and horror. This is not the stuff of ordinary
literary discussion. These are the warning signs of human
existence. Without pain we would never learn to avoid fire,
sharp instruments, physical confrontation. Without fear we
would be unconscionably reckless, following (and worse,
leading) with blind abandon instead of reasoned caution.
And without horror—what?

Complacency. The grand killer of justice, the mangler of
innocence. The television viewer munching a TV dinner over
a Beirut execution, an infant's remains in a New York garbage can, a fish-eyed, famished eight-year-old singing "Jesus
loves me, this I know."

Horror is what Harlan Ellison wrote about so terrifyingly
in "The Whimper of Whipped Dogs." Kitty Genovese experienced the fear, the shock, but it was the reader who felt the
horror as Ellison made us watch that eternity of suffering
once again. Horror is what Stephen King wrote about in *The
Shining,* as we watched a marriage and a mind dissolve from
overwork and failure.

Religious ferocity, betrayal, callousness. We're forced to
watch them all, to feel the horror of sitting in a comfortable
chair or bouncing along Forty-Second Street in a crosstown
bus. Forced to watch and *to do nothing.* It is, after all, only a
book, a story, a movie; the news.

Horror is an experience of the "out there." It is not par-
ticipatory; it's a voyeur's reaction. We watch, we are drawn
in, we are repulsed by the horror of what is happening to

another, even if that other is unaware of the surrounding events.

And what can we do to avoid the horror? Where do we hide? In our houses, our private offices and hospital rooms, our churches and toilet stalls. But even there the horror invades. In fact, it is only in these safe, strangling confines that it begins to touch us, to finally become personalized.

Yi-Fu Tuan's insightful work *Landscapes of Fear* brings this home: "We draw boundaries and protect their apertures. Nonetheless security is not absolute. Horror is the sudden awareness of betrayal and death in the inner sanctum of our refuge."

We come back to the stories. Always the stories. I hope they horrify you. I hope they awaken you, help you do something about the horror. Call a cop, protect a child, vote, read another book. *But do something!* For without action, and the thought that gives birth to action, we become part of the evil ourselves—and in the end, lie helpless and broken like Kurtz in Joseph Conrad's *Heart of Darkness* (or Coppola's *Apocalypse Now*), muttering on our deathbeds, "the horror, the horror." And it will go on.

November 1986

In the House of Gingerbread

by GENE WOLFE

Gene Wolfe, author of the extraordinary four-volume The
Book of the New Sun, went to Edgar Allan Poe Elementary
School in Houston, Texas, and claims that the experience has
influenced all his work since. He is one of the most interesting,
complex, and admired writers in the science fiction and fantasy field. Much of his work has horrific overtones, drawing
upon the myth structures of Western civilization, an engineer's
technical know-how, and a facility for frighteningly accurate
psychological observation. "In the House of Gingerbread,"
one of his rare stories entirely within the horror genre, is a
middle-class fairy tale in the brutal tradition of the Brothers
Grimm.

The woodcutter came up the walk, and the ornate old house
watched him through venetian-blinded eyes. He wore a red-
brown tweed suit; his unmarked car was at the curb. The
house felt his feet on its porch, his quick knock at its door. It
wondered how he had driven along the path through the
trees. The witch would split his bones to get the marrow; it
would tell the witch.

It rang its bell.

Tina Heim opened the door, keeping it on the chain but
more or less expecting a neighbor with coleslaw. She had
heard you were supposed to bring chicken soup for Death;
here it seemed to be slaw, though someone had brought Wal-
dorf salad for Jerry.

"I'm Lieutenant Price," the woodcutter said, unsmiling. He held out a badge in a black leather case. "You're Mrs. Heim? I'd like to talk to you."

She began, "Have the children—"

"I'd like to talk to you," he repeated. "It might be nicer if we did it in the house and sitting down."

"All right." She unhooked the chain and opened the door.

He stepped inside. "You were busy in the kitchen."

She had not seen him glance at her apron, but apparently he had. "I was making gingerbread men for school lunches," she explained. "I like to put a few cookies in their lunches every day."

He nodded, still unsmiling. "Smells good. We can talk in there, and you can watch them so they don't burn."

"They're out already, it only takes a few minutes in the microwave. Can you—" It was too late; he had slipped by her and was out of sight. She hurried through the dark foyer and shadowy dining room, and found him sitting on a dinette chair in her kitchen. "Can you just barge into someone's home this way?"

He shook his head. "You know, I didn't think you could bake in a microwave oven."

"It's hard to get cakes to rise, but nice for cookies." She wavered between hospitality and anger, and decided on the former. It seemed safer, and she could always get angry later. "Would you care for one?"

He nodded.

"And some coffee? Or we have milk if you'd prefer that."

"Coffee will be okay," he told her. "No, Mrs. Heim, we can't just barge into somebody's house; we have to get a search warrant. But once you let us in, you can't stop us from going wherever we want to. I could go up to your bedroom now, for example, and search your bureau."

"You're not—"

He shook his head. "I was just giving you an example. That's the way the law is, in this state."

She stared down uncomprehendingly at the little mug with the smiley face on its side. It was full of black coffee. She had poured it without thinking, like an automaton. "Do you want cream? Sugar?"

"No, thanks. Sit down, Mrs. Heim."

Tina sat. He had taken the chair she usually used. She took the one across from him, Jerry's chair, positioning it carefully and feeling as though she had gone somewhere for a job interview.

"Now then," he said. He made a steeple of his fingers. It seemed an old man's gesture, though he looked no older than she. This is *my* house, she thought. If this is an interview, then *I'm* interviewing *him*. She knew it was not true.

"Mrs. Heim, your husband died last year. In November." She nodded guardedly.

"And the cause of death was—?"

"Lung cancer. It's on the death certificate." The covers of a thousand paperbacks flashed past in her imagination: *Murder on the Orient Express, Fletch, The Roman Hat Mystery.* "You said you were a lieutenant—are you on the Homicide Squad? My god, I'm in a mystery novel!"

"No," he said again. "This isn't fiction, Mrs. Heim. Just a little inquiry. Your late husband was a heavy smoker?"

She shook her head. "Jerry didn't smoke."

"Maybe he'd been a heavy smoker, and quit?"

"No," she said. "Jerry never smoked at all."

Price nodded as though to himself. "I've read that sidewise smoke gets people sometimes." He sipped his coffee. "Are you a smoker, Mrs. Heim? I didn't see any ashtrays."

"No. No, I don't smoke, Lieutenant. I never have."

"Uh huh." His right hand left the handle of the smiley mug and went to his shirt pocket. "As it happens I smoke, Mrs. Heim. Would it bother you?"

"Of course not," she lied. The ashtrays for guests were put away in the cabinet. She brought him one.

He got out a cigarette and lit it with a disposable plastic lighter. "I'm trying to quit," he told her. He drew smoke into his lungs. "Was your husband a chemist, Mrs. Heim? Did he work in a chemical plant?"

She shook her head. "Jerry was an attorney." Surely Price knew all this.

"And his age at death was—?"

"Forty-one."

"That's very young for a nonsmoker to die of lung cancer, Mrs. Heim."

"That's what Jerry's doctor said." Not wanting to cry again, Tina poured coffee for herself, adding milk and diet sweetener, stirring until time enough had passed for her to get her feelings once more under control.

When she sat down again he said, "People must have

wondered. My wife died about three years ago, and I know I got a lot of questions."

She nodded absently, looking at the little plate on the other side of the dinette table. The gingerbread man had lain there, untouched. Now it was gone. She said, "They X-rayed Jerry's lungs, Lieutenant. The X-rays showed cancer. That's what we were told."

"I know," he said.

"But you don't believe Jerry died of cancer?"

He shrugged. "And now your little boy. What was his name?"

Tina tried to keep all emotion from her voice, and felt she succeeded. "It was Alan."

"Just last month. Must have been pretty hard on you."

"It was. Lieutenant, can't we be honest with each other? What are we talking about?"

"All right." He took another sip of coffee. "Anyhow, you've still got two more. A boy and a girl, isn't that right?"

Tina nodded. "Henry and Gail. But Henry and Gail aren't actually mine."

For the first time, he looked surprised. "Why's that?"

"They're stepchildren, that's all. Of course, I love them as if they were my own, or anyway I try to."

"I didn't know that," he told her. "But Alan was—?"

"Our child. Jerry's and mine."

"Your husband had been married before. Divorce?"

"Yes. Jerry got full custody. Rona doesn't—didn't—even have visiting rights."

"Like that," he said.

"Yes, like that, Lieutenant."

"And now that your husband's dead?" Price flicked ashes into the salad plate that had held the gingerbread man.

"I don't know. If Rona tries to take them, I'll go to court; then we'll see. Won't you tell me what this is about?"

He nodded. "It's about insurance, really, Mrs. Heim. Your husband had a large policy."

She nodded guardedly. "They paid."

Price was no longer listening, not to her. "Did Henry or Gail stay home from school, Mrs. Heim? It's only one-thirty."

"No, they won't be back until after three. Do you want to speak to them?"

He shook his head. "I heard footsteps upstairs. A kid's, I thought."

"Henry's eighteen, Lieutenant, and Gail's sixteen. Believe me, they don't sound like kids stamping around up there. Do you want to go up and see? You don't need an excuse—so you said."

He ground out his cigarette in the salad plate. "That's right, I don't need an excuse. Alan was poisoned, wasn't he, Mrs. Heim? Lead poisoning?"

She nodded slowly, pretending there was a lovely clay mask on her face, a mask that would be dissolved by tears, broken by any expression. "He ate paint chips, Lieutenant. In his closet there was a place where the old paint was flaking off. We had repainted his room, but not in there. He was only two, and ... And ..."

"It's okay," he told her. "I've got two kids of my own."

"No, it will never be okay." She tore off a paper towel and stood in a corner, her back to him, blowing her nose and dabbing at her tears. She hoped that when she turned around, he would be gone.

"Feeling better now?" he asked. He had lit another cigarette.

"A little. You know, it's not fair."

"What isn't?"

"You smoking like that. But you're still alive, and Jerry never smoked, but Jerry's gone."

"I'm trying to quit." He said it mechanically, toying with his cigarette. "Actually, some insurance people pretty much agree with you, Mrs. Heim."

"What do you mean by that?"

"Your husband had a policy with Attica Life. A hundred thousand dollars."

Automatically she shook her head. "Two hundred thousand. That was what they paid."

He inhaled smoke and puffed it from his nostrils. "It was a hundred thousand, but it had a double indemnity provision for cancer. A lot of them do now, because people are so worried about it. Cancer generally means big hospital bills."

This was it. She waited, fists clenched in her lap.

"Not with your Jerry, of course. Or anyway, not so much. He was dead in what? Three weeks?"

"Yes," she said. "Three weeks after he went into the hospital."

"And anyway he had hospitalization insurance, didn't he? With his law firm?"

She nodded.

"And you'd taken out policies on the kids too, and on you, naturally. Twenty-five thousand on each kid, wasn't it?"

"It still is. We have a very good agent, Lieutenant; I'll introduce you."

"It still is on Henry and Gail, right. Twenty-five thousand with double indemnity for accidental death. When little Alan died, that was accidental death. A little kid, a baby, swallows paint chips—they call that accidental poisoning."

"You think I killed him." If only my eyes could blast, she thought, he'd be frying like bacon. He'd be burning in Hell. "You think I killed my husband and my son to get that money, don't you, Lieutenant?" She tried to picture it, his brown suit blazing, his face seared, his hair on fire.

"No," he said. "No, I don't, Mrs. Heim. Not really."

"Then why are you here?"

He ground out the new cigarette beside the last. "Your insurance company's making waves."

He paused, but she said nothing.

"Do you blame them? Two claims, big claims, double indemnity claims, in less than two years."

"I see." She felt drained now; the fire had gone out. "What do you want me to do—take a lie detector test and say that I didn't murder my husband? That I didn't poison Alan? All right, I will."

"I want you to sign something, that's all. This will most likely be the end of it." The hand that had fumbled for his cigarettes was fumbling again, this time in the breast pocket of his tweed jacket. "You can read it if you want to. Or I'll tell you. Either way."

It was fine print on legal-length paper. Her eyes caught the word *exhumation*. "Tell me," she said.

"This will let them—the coroner's office—check out your husband's body. They'll check his lungs, for example, to see if there really was cancer."

Gravediggers working at night, perhaps; men with shovels methodically, stolidly, resurrecting those same lumps of earth. Yes, surely by night. They would not want the funeral parties to see that—*Rest in Peace*. They would have lights with long, orange cords to help them work, or maybe only battery torches. "Can they do that?" she asked. "Can they actually tell anything?" She remembered the woman in the Bible: *Lord, it has been four days now; surely there will be a stench.* She said, "It's been more than a year, Lieutenant."

He shrugged. "Maybe yes, maybe no. Your husband was embalmed, wasn't he?"

"Yes. Yes, he was."

"Then there's a good chance. It depends on how good a job they did on him, the soil temperature, and how tight the box is. It depends on a lot of things, really, but there's a good chance. Then there are some tests they can always run—like for arsenic or lead. You can look at a body a hundred years later and still find those things."

"I understand. Do you have a pen?"

"Sure," he said. He took it from the same pocket and handed it to her, first pressing the little plastic thing at the top to extend the point. Like a salesman, she thought. He's just like a salesman who's made the sale.

She took the pen and signed, and he smiled and relaxed. "You know, I didn't think they used those lead-based paints any more."

"They don't." She pushed the paper back. "This is an old house, and that was old paint. One doctor said it might be from the twenties. Do you want to see it? The closet, I mean, not the paint. I repainted it, so that . . ."

"So that it couldn't happen to somebody else's kid," he finished for her. "Sure, let's go up and have a look."

As they went up the stairs, he said, "From outside I wasn't really sure this was an old house, even if it does have all that fancy millwork. It looks like it might have been built new in the old style, like they do at Disneyworld."

"It was built in eighteen eighty-two," she told him. "We had a contractor paint the exterior; we were doing the interior ourselves."

She led the way down the upstairs hall and opened the door. "I haven't gone in here since I painted the closet. I think it's time I did."

He nodded, looking appreciatively at the walls and the oak moldings. "This was a maid's room, I guess, in the old days."

"No, this has always been the nursery. The maid's rooms were upstairs under the eaves."

She fell silent. Newspapers daubed with dark paint were still spread over the floor. A can stood where she had left it, its interior hard and cracked. The caked brush lay beside it. She began to say, *"I didn't clean up. I suppose it shows."*

Before the first word had left her lips, there was a sound. It was a faint sound, yet in the stillness it seemed unnaturally loud—a scraping and shuffling that might have been a small dog scrambling to its feet, or merely some small, hard object sliding from a collection of similar objects, a baby's rattle leaving the top of a careless pile of toys.

So that in place of what she had intended, Tina said, "There's a child in there!"

"There's *something* in there," Price conceded. He went to the closet and twisted the old-fashioned china knob, but the door did not open. "It's locked."

"I didn't lock it." Though she had not been conscious of moving them, her right hand had clasped her left arm, her left hand her right arm. It was cold in the nursery, surely colder than it was outside. Had she shut the vent?

"Sure, you locked it," he told her. "It's a very natural thing to do. That's okay, I don't have to see it."

He's looking at the evidence as a favor to me, she thought. Aloud she said, "I don't even have a key, but we've got to get it open. There's a child inside."

"There's something in there. I doubt if it's a kid." He glanced at the keyhole. "Just an old warded lock. Shouldn't be any trouble."

The paint can had a wire handle. He pulled it off, bending it with strong, blunt fingers.

"I suppose you're right—there *can't* be a child in there. I mean, who would it be?"

He squatted before the keyhole. "You want my guess? You've got a possum in the wall. Or maybe a squirrel. This place doesn't have rats, does it?"

"We've tried to get rid of them. Jerry set traps in the basement—" There was a faint scrabbling from the closet; she spoke more rapidly to cover the sound: "He even bought a ferret and put it down there, but it died. He thought Henry'd killed it."

"Oh?" Price said. The lock squeaked, clicked back, and he rose, smiling. "Probably never been oiled. It was a little stiff."

He twisted the knob again. This time it turned, but the door did not open. "Stuck too. Did you paint the frame?"

She nodded wordlessly.

"Well, you locked it before the paint was dry, Mrs. Heim." He took a big utility knife from the right pocket of his jacket and opened the screwdriver blade.

"Call me Tina," she said. "We don't have to be so formal."

Only a moment before, she had seen him smile for the first time; now he grinned. "Dick," he said. "No Dick Tracy jokes, please. I get enough at the station."

She grinned back. "Okay."

The screwdriver blade slipped between the door and the jamb. He turned the knob again as he pried with the blade, and the door popped open. For an instant it seemed to her that there were eyes near the floor.

He swung the door wide on squealing hinges. "Nothing in here," he said. "Jerry didn't believe in lubrication."

"Yes, he did—he was always oiling things. He said he was no mechanic, but an oil can was half a mechanic."

Price grunted. He had a penlight, its feeble beam playing over the closet walls. "Something's been in here," he said. "It was bigger than a rat; a coon, maybe."

"Let me see," she said. She had been picking up the paint-smeared newspapers and stuffing them into the can. Now she came to the closet to look. There were scratches on the walls, tiny scratches that might have been made by little claws or fingernails. Flakes of plaster and paint lay on the closet floor.

Price snapped off the penlight and glanced at his watch. "I ought to be going. Thanks for signing the permission. I'll phone you and let you know how the tests came out."

She nodded. "I'd appreciate that."

"Okay, I will. What's that book you've got?"

"This?" She held it up. "Just an old children's book. Jerry found it when he was exploring the attic and brought it down for Alan. It was under the newspapers."

She led the way back down the narrow hall. The new, bright paper she and Jerry had hung decked its walls but could not make its way into her mind. When she took her eyes from it, the old, dark paper returned.

Behind her Price said, "Careful on those stairs."

"We were going to get them carpeted," she told him. "Now it hardly seems worth all the trouble. I'm trying to sell the house."

"Yeah, I noticed the sign outside. It's a nice place, but I guess I can't blame you."

"It is *not* a nice place," she muttered; but her words were so soft that only the house heard them. She opened the door.

"Good-bye," he said. "And thanks again, Tina. It was nice meeting you." Solemnly, they shook hands.

She said, "You'll telephone me, Dick?" She knew how it sounded.

"That's a promise."

She watched him as he went down the walk. A step or two before he reached his car, he patted the side pocket of his jacket—not the right-hand pocket, where he had put his knife, but the left one. For the laboratory, she thought to herself. He's taking it to some police lab, to see if it's poisoned.

She did not look down at the book in her hand, but the verses she had read when she lifted the newspaper that had covered it sang in her ears:

> *"You may run, you may run, just as fast as you can,*
> *But you'll never catch ME," said the gingerbread man.*

That evening the house played Little Girl. The essence, the ectoplasm, the soul of the child seeped from the cracked old plaster that had absorbed it when new. Watching television in the family room that had once been the master bedroom, Henry did not hear or see it; yet he stirred plumply, uncomfortably, on the sofa, unable to concentrate on the show or anything else, cursing his teachers, his sister, and his stepmother—hoping the phone would ring, afraid to call anyone and unable to say why he was afraid, angry in his misery and miserable in his rage.

Bent over her schoolbooks upstairs, Gail heard it. Quick steps, light steps, up the hall and down again: *Gioconda is the model of the brilliant young sculptor, Lucio Settala. Although he struggles to resist the fascination that she exercises over him, out of loyalty to his witch, Sylvia, he feels Gioconda is the true inspiration of his art. During Lucio's illness, Sylvia arouses Gioconda's fury and is horribly burned by the model and her brother.*

I'll remember *that,* Gail thought. She wanted to be a model herself, like her real mother; someday she would be. She balanced the book on her head and walked about her bedroom, stopping to pose with studied arrogance.

Tina, drying herself in the bathroom, saw it. Steam left it behind as it faded from the mirror: the silhouette of a child with braids, a little girl whose head and shoulders were almost the outline of a steeply pitched roof. Tina wiped the mirror with her towel, watched the phantom re-form, then thrust it out of her mind. Jerry should have put a ventilating fan in here, she thought. I'll have to tell him.

She remembered Jerry was dead, but she had known that all along. It was not so much that she had forgotten, as that she had forgotten she herself was still living and that the living cannot communicate with the dead, with the dead who neither return their calls nor answer their letters. She had felt for a moment that, though dead, Jerry was merely *gone*, gone to New York or New Orleans or New Mexico, to some-place new to see some client, draft some papers, appear before some Board. Soon she would fly there to join him, in the new place.

He had given her perfumed body powder and a huge puff with which to apply it. She did so now because Jerry had liked it, thinking how long, how very long, it had been since she had used it last.

The steam specter she had been unable to wipe away had disappeared. She recalled its eyes and shuddered. They had been (as she told herself) no more than holes in the steam, two spots where the steam, for whatever reason, would not condense; that made it worse, since if that were the case they were there still, watching her, invisible.

She shivered again. The bathroom seemed cold despite the steam, despite the furnace over which Jerry had worked so hard. She knew she should put on her robe but did not, standing before the mirror instead, examining her powdered breasts, running her hands along her powdered hips. Fat, she was too fat, she had been too fat ever since Alan was born.

Yet Dick Price had smiled at her; she had seen the way he had looked at her in the nursery, had felt the extra moment for which he held her hand.

"Then it was cancer after all, Lieutenant?" Gail asked a few days later. "Don't stand, please." She crossed the wide, dark living room that had once been the parlor and sat down, very much an adult.

Price nodded, sipping the drink Henry had mixed for him. It was Scotch and water, with too much of the first and not enough of the second; and Price was determined to do no more than taste it.

Henry said, "I didn't think it could go that fast, sir."

"Occasionally it does," Price told him.

Gail shook her head. "She killed Dad, Lieutenant. I'm

sure she did. You don't know her—she's a real witch some-times."

"And you wrote those letters to the insurance company." Price set his drink on the coffee table.

"What letters?"

Henry grinned. "You shouldn't bite your lip like that, Goony-Bird. Blows your cover."

Price nodded. "Let me give you a tip, Gail. It's better not to tell lies to the police; but if you're going to, you've got to get your timing right and watch your face. Just saying the right words isn't enough."

"Are you—?"

"Besides, a flat lie is better than a sidestep. Try, 'I never wrote any letters, Lieutenant.' "

"They were supposed to be confidential!"

Henry was cleaning his nails with a small screwdriver. "You think confidential means they won't even show them to the police?"

"He's right." Price nodded again. "Naturally they showed them to us. They were in a feminine hand, and there were details only somebody living here would know; so they were written by you or your stepmother. Since they accused her, that left you. Once in a while we get a nut who writes accus-ing herself, but your stepmother doesn't seem like a nut, and when she signed and dated the exhumation papers for me the writing was different."

"All right, I sent those letters."

The screwdriver had a clip like a pen. Henry replaced it in his shirt pocket. "I helped her with a couple of them. Told her what to say, you know? Are you going to tell her?"

"Do you want me to?" Price asked.

Henry shrugged. "Man, I don't care."

"Then why ask me about it?" Price stood up. "Thanks for the hospitality, kids. Tell Tina I'm sorry I missed her."

Gail rose too. "I'm sure she's just been delayed some-where, Lieutenant. If you'd like to stay a little longer—"

Price shook his head.

Henry said, "Just one question, sir, if you know. How did Dad get lung cancer?"

"His lungs were full of asbestos fibers. It's something that usually happens only to insulators."

In the kitchen, Tina pictured the furnace—its pipes spreading upward like the branches of a long-dead tree, tape peeling from them like bark, white dust sifting down like rotten wood, falling like snow upon Jerry's violated grave.

It's the gingerbread house, she thought, recalling the grim paper they had painted over in the nursery. It doesn't eat you, you eat it. But it gets you just the same.

She tried to move, to strike the floor with her feet, the wall with her shoulders, to chew the dishtowel Gail had stuffed into her mouth, to scrape away the bright new duct tape Jerry had bought when he was rebuilding the furnace.

None of it worked. The door of the microwave gaped like a hungry mouth. Far away the front door opened and closed. "She Used to Be My Girl" blasted from the stereo in the family room.

Fatly, importantly, Henry came into the kitchen on a wave of rock, carrying an almost-full glass of dark liquid. "Your boyfriend's gone. Could you hear us? I bet you thought he was going to save you." He took a swallow of the liquid—whiskey, she could smell it—and set the glass on the drainboard.

Gail followed him. When the door had shut and she could make herself heard, she asked, "Are we going to do it now?"

"Sure, why not?" Henry knelt, scratching at the tape.

"I think it would be better to leave that on."

"I told you, the heat would melt the adhesive. You want to have to swab her face with paint thinner or something when she's dead?" He caught the end of the duct tape and yanked it away." Besides, she won't yell, she'll talk. I know her."

Tina spit out the dish towel. It felt as though she had been to the dentist, as though the receptionist would want to set up a new appointment when she got out of the chair.

Gail snatched the damp towel away. "You fixed up the microwave?"

"Sure, Goony-Bird. It wasn't all that hard."

"They'll check it. They'll check it to see what went wrong."

Tina tried to speak, but her mouth was too dry. Words would not come.

"And they'll find it." Henry grinned. "They'll find a wire that came unsoldered and flipped up so it shorted the safety interlock. Get me an egg out of the fridge."

She knew she should be pleading for her life; yet somehow she could not bring herself to do it. I'm brave, she thought, surprised. This is courage, this silly reluctance. I never knew that.

"See the egg, stepmother dear?" Gail held it up to show her. "An egg will explode when you put it in a microwave."

She set it inside, and Henry shut the door.

"It'll work now whether it's open or closed, see? Only I've got it closed so we don't get radiation out here." He pressed a button and instinctively backed away.

The bursting of the egg was a dull thud, like an ax biting wood or the fall of a guillotine blade.

"It makes a real mess. We'll leave it on for a while so it gets hard."

Gail asked, "Is the music going to run long enough?"

"Hell, yes."

Tina said, "If you *want* to go back to Rona, go ahead. I've tried to love you, but nobody's going to stop you."

"We don't want to live with Rona," Henry told her. "We want to get even with you, and we want to be rich."

"You got a hundred thousand for Dad," Gail explained. "Then all that for the baby."

Henry said, "Another fifty thou."

"So that's a hundred and fifty thousand, and when you're dead, we'll get it. Then there's another fifty on you, double for an accident. We get that too. It comes to a quarter of a million."

The oven buzzed.

"Okay." Henry opened it. "Let's cut her loose." He got the little paring knife from the sink.

"She'll fight," Gail warned him.

"Nothing I can't handle, Goony-Bird. We don't want rope marks when they find her."

The little knife gnawed at the rope behind Tina's back like a rat. After a moment, her lifeless hands dropped free. The rat moved to her ankles.

Gail said, "We'll have to get rid of the rope."

"Sure. Put it in the garbage—the tape too."

A thousand needles pricked Tina's arms. Pain came with them, appearing out of nowhere.

"Okay," Henry said. "Stand up."

He lifted her. There was no strength in her legs, no feeling.

"See, you're cleaning it. Maybe you stick your head in so you can see what you're doing." He thrust her head into the oven. "Then you reach for the cleaner or something, and your arm hits a button."

Gail screamed, shrill and terror-stricken. *I won't*, Tina

told herself. *I won't scream.* She set her lips, clenched her teeth.

The screaming continued. Henry yelled and released her, and she slid to the floor. Flames and thick, black smoke shot from the microwave.

She wanted to laugh. So Hansel, so little Gretel, cooking a witch is not quite so easy as you thought, *nicht wahr?* Henry jerked a cord from the wall. Tina noted with amusement that it was the cord of the electric can-opener.

Gail had filled a pan with water from the sink. She threw it on the microwave and jerked backward as if she had been struck. The flames caught the kitchen curtains, which went up like paper.

On half-numb legs, Tina tried to stand. She staggered and fell. The kitchen cabinets were burning over the microwave, flames racing along dark, varnished wood that had been dry for a century.

The back door burst inward. Henry fled through it howling, his shirt ablaze. Stronger, harder hands lifted her. She thought of Gretel—of Gail—but Gail was beside them, coughing and choking, reeling toward the open doorway.

As though by magic, she was outside. They were all outside, Henry rolling frantically on the grass as Dick beat at the flames with his jacket. Sirens and wolves howled in the distance, while one by one the dark rooms lit with a cheerful glow.

"My house!" she said. She had meant to whisper but found she was almost screaming. "My home! Gone . . . No—I'll always, always remember her, no matter what happens."

Dick glanced toward it. "It doesn't look good, but if you've got something particularly valuable—"

"Don't you dare go back in there! I won't let you."

"My God!" He gripped her arm. "Look!" For an instant (and only an instant) a white face like a child's stared from a gable window; then it was gone, and the flames peered out instead. An instant more and they broke through the roof; the house sighed, a phoenix embracing death and rebirth. Its wooden lace was traced with fire before its walls collapsed and the fire engines arrived.

Later the fire captain asked whether everyone had escaped.

Tina nodded thankfully. "Dick—Lieutenant Price—

thought he saw a face at one of the attic windows, but we're all here."

The captain looked sympathetic. "Probably a puff of white smoke—that happens sometimes. You know how it started?"

Suddenly Henry was silent, though he had voiced an unending string of puerile curses while the paramedics treated his burns. Now the string was broken; he watched Tina with terrified eyes. More practical, Gail edged toward the darkness under the trees.

Tina nodded. "But what I want to know is how Dick came just in time to save us. That was like a miracle."

Price shook his head. "No miracle. Or if it was, it was the kind that happens all the time. I'd come at eight, and the kids said you were still out. Somebody I'd like to talk to about a case I'm on lives a couple of blocks from here, so I went over and rang the bell; but there was nobody home. I came back and spotted the fire through a side window as I drove up."

The captain added, "He radioed for us. You say you know how it started, ma'am?"

"My son Henry was cooking something—eggs, wasn't that what you said, Henry?"

Henry's head moved a fraction of an inch. He managed to answer, "Yeah."

"But the oven must have been too hot, because the eggs, or whatever they were, caught fire. The kitchen was full of smoke by the time Gail and I heard him yell and ran in there."

The captain nodded and scribbled something on his clipboard. "Cooking fire. Happens a lot."

"I called Henry my son a moment ago," Tina corrected herself, "and I shouldn't have, Captain. Actually I'm just his stepmother, and Gail's."

"She's the best mother in the whole world!" Henry shouted. "Isn't that right, Goony-Bird?"

Nearly lost among the oaks and towering hemlocks, Gail nodded frantically.

"Henry, you're a dear." Tina bent to kiss his forehead. "I hope those burns don't hurt too much." Gently, she pinched one of his plump cheeks. He's getting fat, she reflected. But I'll have to neuter him soon, or his testicles will spoil the meat. He'll be easier to manage then.

(She smiled, recalling her big, black-handled dressmaker's

shears. That would be amusing—but quite impossible, to be sure. What was it that clever man in Texas had done, put some sort of radioactive capsule between his sleeping son's legs?)

Dick said loudly, "And I'm sure Henry's a very good son."

She turned to him, still smiling. "You know, Dick, you've never talked much about your own children. How old are they?"

Where the Heart Is

by RAMSEY CAMPBELL

Ramsey Campbell is emerging as a significant force in the development of contemporary horror fiction, especially the novel form. He is a writer of nearly mathematical precision whose story herein is reminiscent of the graphics of M. C. Escher. Through each individual twist and turn, "Where the Heart Is" seems a familiar tale of a man driven mad by the death of his wife. But as with Escher's visions of interlocking architectural realities, for example his print "The Belvedere Terrace," the whole is vastly more unsettling than the sum of its parts.

I've just walked through your house. I lay on your bed and tried to see my wife's face looming over me, the way I used to. I spent longest in your baby's room, because that was where I began to die. Before I do, I want to tell you who I am and why I'm here, and so I'm writing this.

I'm at your dining table now, but I won't be when you find me. You'll have found me, or you couldn't be reading this. There may not be much of me for you to recognize, so let me introduce myself again. I'm the man whose house you bought. This is my house, and you'll never get rid of me now.

I've nothing against you personally. It wasn't your fault that the two of you nearly destroyed my wife and me—you weren't to know what you were doing. I can't let that stop me, but at least I can tell you my reasons. The truth is, I never should have let you or anyone else into my house.

Maybe you remember coming to view it, in the rain. I was

19

sitting in the front room, hearing the rain shake the windows and knowing it couldn't touch me. I was feeling peaceful and secure at last. As a matter of fact, I was wondering if the rain might be the last thing I ever heard, if I could sink into that peace where my wife must be, when your car drew up outside the house.

By the time you got out of your car and ran up the path, you were drenched. I may as well be honest: I took my time about answering the doorbell. Only I heard you saying you'd seen someone in the front room, and that made me feel discovered. So I took pity on you out there in the storm.

I don't suppose you noticed how I drew back as you came in. As you trod on the step, I had the feeling that you meant the house to be yours. Did you realize you hung your wet coats as if it already was? Maybe you were too drenched to wait for me to tell you, but you made me feel redundant, out of place.

That's one reason why I didn't say much as I showed you over the house. I didn't think you would have listened anyway—you were too busy noticing cracks in the plaster and where damp had lifted the wallpaper and how some of the doors weren't quite straight in their frames. I really thought when we came downstairs that you'd decided against the house. Perhaps you saw how relieved I was. I wondered why you asked if you could be alone for a few minutes. I let you go upstairs by yourselves, though I must say I resented hearing you murmuring up there. And all I could do when you came down and said you were interested in the house was make my face go blank, to hide my shock.

You must have thought I was trying to get you to raise your offer, but it wasn't that at all. I was simply feeling less and less sure that I ought to leave the house where my wife and I had spent our marriage. I told you to get in touch with the estate agent, but that was really just a way of saving myself from having to refuse you outright. I should have told you about my wife. You knew I was selling because she'd died, and you'd made sympathetic noises and faces, but I should have told you that she'd died here in the house.

When you'd left, I went upstairs and lay on the bed where she'd died. Sometimes when I lay there and closed my eyes to see her face, I could almost hear her speaking to me. I asked her what I ought to do about you, and I thought I heard her telling me not to let my feelings get the better of me, to think more and feel less, as she often used to say. I thought she was saying that I shouldn't let the house trap me, that so long as I took the bed with me we'd still be together. So I accepted your offer and signed the contract to sell you the house, and the moment I'd finished signing I felt as if I'd signed away my soul.

It was too late by then, or at least I thought it was. I'd already agreed to move out so that you could start the repairs and get your mortgage. When the removal van was loaded, I walked through the house to make sure I hadn't left anything. The stripped rooms made me feel empty, homeless, as if my wife and I had never been there. Even the removal van felt more like home, and I sat on our couch in there as the van drove to my new flat.

I'd bought it with the insurance my wife had on herself, you remember. We'd always been equally insured. What with our bed and the rest of the furniture we'd chosen together being moved to the flat and her insurance money buying it, she should have been there with me, shouldn't she? I thought so that first night when I turned off the lamp and lay in the bed and waited to feel that she was near me.

But there was nothing, just me and the dark. The heating was on, yet the bed seemed to get colder and colder. All I wanted was to feel that I wasn't totally alone. But nights went by, and the bed grew colder, until I felt I'd die of the chill in a place I'd let myself be evicted to, that was nothing like home.

You must be wondering why, if I wanted to be with my wife so much, I didn't consult a medium. My wife was a very private person, that's why—I couldn't have asked her to communicate with me in front of a stranger. Besides, I didn't trust that sort of thing much any more. I hadn't since I'd thought we'd been given a sign that we were going to have a child.

We'd started a child when it was really too late. That was one time my wife let her feelings get the better of her. We'd been trying for years, and then, when she'd given up expecting to be able, she got pregnant. I was afraid for her all those months, but she said I mustn't be: whatever was going to happen would happen, and we'd be prepared for it, whatever it was. She didn't even make the guest room into a nursery, not that we ever had guests.

She went into hospital a month before we thought she would. The first I knew of it was when the hospital phoned me at the bank. I visited her every evening, but I couldn't see her on weekdays—too many of my colleagues were on their summer holidays. I became afraid I wouldn't be with her at the birth.

Then one evening I saw something that made me think I'd no reason to be anxious for her. I was going upstairs to bed in the dark when I saw that I'd left the light on in the guest room. I opened the door and switched off the light, and just as I did so I saw that it wasn't a guest room any longer, it was a nursery with a cot in it and wallpaper printed with teddy bears dancing in a ring. When I switched on the light again it was just a guest room, but I didn't care—I knew what I'd seen. I didn't know then what I know now.

So when they called me to the hospital urgently from work, I felt sure the birth would be a success, and when I learned that the baby had been born dead, I felt as if the house had cheated me, or my feelings had. I felt as if I'd killed the baby by taking too much for granted. I almost couldn't go in to see my wife.

She tried to persuade me that it didn't matter. We still had each other, which was pretty well all that we'd had in the way of friendship for years. But she must have thought it was dangerous to leave me on my own, because she came home before she was supposed to, to be with me. That night in bed we held each other more gently than we ever had, and it seemed as if that was all we needed, all we would ever need.

But in the middle of the night I woke and found her in agony, in so much pain she couldn't move or speak. I ran out half naked to phone for an ambulance, but it was too late. I got back to her just in time to see the blood burst out of her face—I wasn't even there to hold her hand at the end. I just stood there as if I didn't have the right to touch her, because it was my feelings that had killed her, or her concern for them had.

You see now why I didn't tell you where she died. It would have been like admitting I hoped she was still in the house. Sometimes I thought I sensed her near me when I was falling asleep. But once I'd moved to the flat I couldn't sleep, I just lay growing colder as the nights got longer. I thought she might have left me because she'd had enough of me. She still had to be alive somewhere, I knew that much.

By then you'd started work on the house, and I felt as if it didn't belong to me, even though it still did. Sometimes I walked the two miles to it late at night, when I couldn't sleep. I told myself I was making sure nobody had broken in.

I remember one night I looked in the front window. The streetlamp showed me you'd torn off the wallpaper and hacked away the plaster. The orange light from outside blackened everything, made it seem even more ruined, made the room look as if it hadn't been lived in for years. It made me feel I hardly existed myself, and I walked away fast, walked all night without knowing where, until the dawn came up like an icy fog and I had to huddle in my flat to keep warm.

After that I tried to stay away from the house. The doctor gave me pills to help me sleep, the old kind that aren't addictive. I didn't like the sleep they brought, though. It came too quickly and took away all my memories, didn't even leave me dreams. Only I knew I had to sleep or I'd be out of a job for making too many mistakes at the bank. So I slept away the nights until you got your mortgage and were able to buy the house.

I expected that to be a relief to me. I shouldn't have felt drawn to the house, since it wasn't mine any longer. But the day I had to hand over my last key I felt worse than I had when I'd signed the contract, and so I made a copy of the key to keep.

I couldn't have said why I did it. Every time I thought of using the key I imagined being caught in the house, taken away by the police, locked up in a cell. Whenever I felt drawn back to the house I tried to lose myself in my work, or if I was in the flat I tried to be content with memories of the time my wife and I had in the house. Only, staying in the flat so as not to be tempted to go to the house made me feel as if I'd already been locked up. I went on like that for weeks, telling myself I had to get used to the flat, the house was nothing to do with me now. I took more of the pills before going to bed, and the doctor renewed the prescription. And then one morning I woke up feeling cold and empty, hardly knowing who I was or where, feeling as if part of me had been stolen while I was asleep.

At first I thought the pills were doing that to me. It was snowing as I walked to work; it looked as if the world were flaking away around me, and I felt as if I were. Even when I leaned against the radiator in the bank I couldn't stop shivering. I made myself sit at the counter when it was time for the manager to open the doors, but he saw how I was and insisted I go home, told me to stay there till I got better. He ordered me a taxi, but I sent it away as soon as I was out of sight of the bank. I knew by then I had to come to the house.

You see, I'd realized what was missing. There was part of the house I couldn't remember. I could still recall making love to my wife, and the way we used to prepare alternate courses of a meal, but I couldn't call to mind how we'd spent our evenings at home. I fought my way to the house, the snow scraping my face and trickling under my clothes, and then I saw why. You'd torn down a wall and made two rooms into one.

We must have had a front room and a dining room. Presumably we moved from one room to the other when we'd finished dinner, but I couldn't recall any of that, not even what the rooms had looked like. Years of my life, of all I had left of my marriage, had been stolen overnight. I stood there with the snow weighing me down until I felt like stone, staring at the wound you'd made in the house, the bricks gaping and the bare floor covered with plaster dust, and I saw that I had to get into the house.

I'd left the key under my pillow. I might have broken in—the street was deserted, and the snow was blinding the houses—if you hadn't already made the house burglar-proof. I struggled back to the flat for the key. I fell a few times on the way, and the last time I almost couldn't get up for shivering. It took me five minutes or more to open the front door of my new building; I kept dropping the key and not being able to pick it up. By the time I reached my flat I felt I would never stop shivering. I was barely able to clench my fist around the key to the house before I crawled into bed.

For days I thought I was dying. When I lay under the covers I felt hot enough to melt, but if I threw them off, the shivering came back. Whenever I awoke, which must have been hundreds of times, I was afraid to find you'd destroyed more of my memories, that I'd be nothing by the time I died. The fever passed, but by then I was so weak that it was all I could do to stumble to the kitchen or the toilet. Sometimes I had to crawl. And I was only just beginning to regain my strength when I felt you change another room.

I thought I knew which one. It didn't gouge my memories the way the other had, but I had to stop you before you did worse. I knew now that if my wife was anywhere on this earth, she must be at the house. I had to protect her from you, and so I put on as many clothes as I could bear and made myself go out. I felt so incomplete that I kept looking behind me, expecting not to see my footprints in the snow.

I was nearly at the house when I met one of my old neighbors. I didn't want to be seen near the house, I felt like a burglar now. I was trying desperately to think what to say to her when I realized that she hadn't recognized me after all—she was staring at me because she wondered what someone who looked like I looked now was doing in her street. I walked straight past and round the corner, and once the street was deserted I came back to the house.

I was sure you were out at work. There was such a confusion of footprints in the snow on the path that I couldn't see whether more led out than in, but I had to trust my feelings. I let myself into the house and closed the door, then I stood there feeling I'd come home.

You hadn't changed the hall. It still had the striped Regency wallpaper, and the dark brown carpet my wife had chosen still looked as if nobody had ever left footprints on it, though you must have trodden marks all over it while you were altering the house. I could almost believe that the hall led to the rooms my wife and I had lived in, that the wall you'd knocked down was still there, except that I could feel my mind gaping where the memories should be. So I held my breath until I could hear that I was alone in the house, then I went up to the guest room.

Before I reached it I knew what I'd see. I'd already seen it once. I opened the door, and there it was: the nursery you'd made for the child you were expecting, the cot and the wallpaper with teddy bears dancing in a ring. My feelings when my wife was in hospital hadn't lied to me after all, I'd just misinterpreted them. As soon as I realized that, I felt as if what was left of my mind had grown clearer, and I was sure I could sense my wife in the house. I was about to search for her when I heard your car draw up outside.

I'd lost track of time while I was ill. I thought you'd be at work, but this was Saturday, and you'd been out shopping. I felt like smashing the cot and tearing off the wallpaper and waiting for you to find me in the nursery, ready to fight for the house. But I ran down as I heard you slam the car doors, and I hid under the stairs, in the cupboard full of mops and brushes.

I heard you come in, talking about how much better the house looked now you'd knocked the wall down and put in sliding doors so that you could have two rooms there or one as the mood took you. I heard you walk along the hall twice,

laden with shopping, and then close the kitchen door. I
inched the door under the stairs open, and as I did so I noticed what you'd done while you were putting in the central
heating. You'd made a trapdoor in the floor of the cupboard
so that you could crawl under the house.

I left the cupboard door open and tiptoed along the hall. I
was almost blind with anger at being made to feel like an
intruder in the house, but I managed to control myself, because I knew I'd be coming back. I closed the front door by
turning my key in the lock and almost fell headlong on the
icy path. My legs felt as if they'd have melted, but I held
onto garden walls all the way to the flat and lay down on my
bed to wait for Monday morning.

On Sunday afternoon I felt the need to go to church,
where I hadn't been since I was a child. I wanted to be reassured that my wife was still alive in spirit and to know if I was
right in what I mean to do. I struggled to church and hid at
the back, behind a pillar, while they were saying mass. The
church felt as if it was telling me yes, but I wasn't sure which
question it was answering. I have to believe it was both.

So this morning I came back to the house. The only thing
I was afraid of was that one of the neighbors might see me,
see this man who'd been loitering nearby last week, and call
the police. But the thaw had set in and was keeping people
off the streets. I had to take off my shoes as soon as I'd let
myself in, so as not to leave footprints along the hall. I don't
want you to know I'm here as soon as you come home.
You'll know soon enough.

You must be coming home now, and I want to finish this.
I thought of bolting the front door so that you'd think the
lock had stuck and perhaps go for a locksmith, but I don't
think I'll need to. I haven't much more to tell you. You'll
know I'm here long before you find me and read this.

It's getting dark here now in the dining room with the
glass doors shut so that I can't be seen from the street. It
makes me feel the wall you knocked down has come back,
and my memories are beginning to. I remember now, my
wife grew house plants in here, and I let them all die after
she died. I remember the scents that used to fill the room—I
can smell them now. She must be here, waiting for me.

And now I'm going to join her in our house. During the
last few minutes I've swallowed all the pills. Perhaps that's
why I can smell her flowers. As soon as I've finished this I'm
going through the trapdoor in the cupboard. There isn't

enough space under the house to stretch your arms above your head when you're lying on your back, but I don't think I'll know I'm there for very long. Soon my wife and I will just be in the house. I hope you won't mind if we make it more like ours again. I can't help thinking that one day you may come into this room and find no sliding doors any longer, just a wall. Try and think of it as our present to you and the house.

Ellen, in Her Time

by CHARLES L. GRANT

With more than five dozen books and over one hundred short stories to his credit, multiple Nebula and World Fantasy Award-winner Charles Grant is a pervasive presence in contemporary fantasy, a successful author whose ear tends toward mood and atmosphere and yet who reads human reaction like a country physician. He is a writer who knows the darker sides of love.

The clock in the belfry ends the morning's first hour with a single slow chime; the north wind ends the season with a single slow moan; and the trees in the backyard dance in stiff-armed, creaking steps to the wind, and the chime, and the clouds that slip the moon into a glove of starless black.

A nightbird on the peak of an uneven roof, waiting for prey with its eyes half closed.

The muffled crack of a small rock finally splitting in the cold.

A few lights in a few windows, mostly on the second floor; a car rushing down the Pike as if it knows it should be home; a leaf, a single leaf hanging on the wall that separates the Station from the graveyard flutters and cracks and falls in shreds to the frosted ground.

Timothy watched it, watched the pieces, and turned away from the gust that blew through the iron gates of Memorial Park. To be here now was foolish. To be here at any time was giving in to his loss when he ought to be home and sleeping, or working, or seeing his friends at the Chancellor Inn and flirting with the women and proving to the world that he had finally put it all behind him.

All of it.

His hands, chapped and fisted, pressed against his legs from within his overcoat pockets; his shoulders rose to help the scarf keep the wind from diving down the length of his spine. His feet began to ache from the cold and the standing and when he turned to walk away he did so with a sigh that was neither relief nor sorrow, just another sound for company to keep the other sounds away.

And once decided, he crossed Park Street in a hurry and headed north toward the dark hill that marked the village's northern boundary, following the houses on his right until he reached the next to last and stopped, panting out of breath, closing his eyes and opening them and seeing the place that had seen him being born, that had seen his marriage in the front room, that had seen him throughout his life, and protected him when he needed it, whenever Ellen wasn't around.

Nothing special, and more special than anything he'd ever owned—simple white clapboard and a peaked slate roof, canted chimney and solid porch, a frosted pane in the front door and windows that had watched him take his first steps as a child, take his first steps with his wife.

Nothing special.

A slow inhalation, and he swerved through the gap in the tall hedge that had never held a gate, lurched onto the small porch, pushed open the door with shoulder and hand, and slammed it shut behind him.

"Tim?"

"Here," he said, not quite loudly. Coat and scarf on the mirrored rack in the foyer, unworn gloves on the table that held a small silver bowl. "Just in, where are you?"

"The kitchen. You want some cocoa?"

Rubbing his hands, breathing the warm furnace air deeply, he took his time getting to the back of the house, squinting at the bright light as he sat at the table and scrubbed his cheeks with his palms.

Ellen, waist aproned and hair bunned, turned from the stove with a small sad smile. "You shouldn't be walking this time of night, you know. There'll be questions."

He shrugged, made a perfunctory swipe at his hair that was too thin to do much but lie there on his head in memory of its former brown, and accepted the cup she gave him with a wince at the heat that made his fingers tighten.

"I mean it," she told him, taking the seat opposite and holding her own cup as if it were fine china. "The police will start on you again, you know that."

He shrugged again. "Don't care. They can't arrest a guy for taking a walk, right?"

Her smile returned, warmer now, and wider. "After midnight? In the middle of the week? They'll think you're a pervert or something."

He laughed, briefly but true, and took a sip of the liquid because she was waiting. His tongue burned, his throat burned, but by the time it reached his stomach it felt fine, just fine.

The clock over the stove ticked another minute before they moved again, each blowing over the cocoa, watching the steam curl and vanish.

"Did you go in?"

"No. They always lock the gates."

"Oh. So you didn't try to climb the wall?"

"No."

"Oh."

He finished the drink quickly and politely refused another. Tired, he said, and wanted his sleep. Ellen understood and walked with him to the stairway, kissed his cheek, held his hand, patted his back as he started up. He looked down when he reached the turn at the darkened landing, watched her walk away, back to the kitchen, and wondered not for the first time how he'd managed to get so lucky to have a wife like that when even his closest friends were in hell in their marriages.

And it had to be luck. It wasn't because he worked at it; he didn't know how, not really. You just lived with each other, he thought as he undressed and slid into bed, you just lived with each other in a house you called your own and told her you loved her and either it works or it doesn't and there's no magic there at all.

He slept, lightly, barely feeling her join him several hours later, barely feeling the sun rise through the window on his left. He slept, and he didn't dream, and in silent prayer thanked the house for letting him have his own, for helping him carry on when carrying on sometimes seemed foolish.

When he awoke there was blue sky, and the furnace greeting him with a warm kiss.

And on his way to work at Station Motors he saw the squirrel at the curb.

"Jesus," he said, and turned his head away.

It must have been hit by a car the way it looked, and the early morning wind flopped its tail back and forth as if it were still alive and trying to get to its feet.

"Jesus," he said again, and hurried on, crossed the Pike and passed the library, ducked into the luncheonette and picked up a New York paper before moving on to the show-room.

Karl Judd was already there, three-piece brown suit and red cheeks, talking with a customer; Zaller was in his office, talking to a customer on the telephone, one hand scratching his scrawny neck while the other tapped a pencil on a blank sheet of pink paper. Timothy thought the place was too much like a funeral parlor and was tempted to start whistling just to see what they would do.

Tempted, but it passed, and he hung his coat up in his office, looked at the message slips on the blotter, and dropped into his chair where he closed his eyes and thought: if I never sell another car in my life, who would know except Ellen?

A knock on the doorframe.

He looked over and waved a hand. "C'mon in, Dan, pull up a chair and tell me how miserable you are."

Zaller shook his head and leaned against the jamb. "I was just talking to Hy Regal," he said.

Timothy covered his eyes, pulled at his nose, and grabbed a pen and began doodling on a purchase order he ripped off the pad. "Oh."

"Oh," the man said. "Right. You were supposed to call him last week, Tim. Twice you said you'd call." He shook his head; there was no sympathy left in him. "What happened?"

How many excuses did he have? None that would please his employer, and none, he knew, that would even please himself.

"I forgot."

Zaller stared at him. "You what?"

A spurt of anger, quickly settled. "Well, what do you want me to say, for Christ's sake—my grandmother died? The kids I don't have are in the hospital? I went to see my ailing father in an old folks' home in Denver?" He threw the pen down. "The hell with it. I forgot, that's all. No excuses, Dan. I forgot."

Zaller's face showed him nothing, but his left hand lightly slapped the jamb before he straightened, and straightened his tie. "Call him, Tim. In one hour, call him."

"I mean it, Tim. I can't carry you forever."

He lowered his head.

Zaller blew in exasperation. "Christ, Edding, it's your commission, you know, and you're not that hot that you can afford to snub a man like that."

No kidding, he thought, and watched the man amble across the showroom floor, touching a hood there, finger-dusting a fender there, standing at the entrance with hands in pockets and watching the street. He supposed that, given enough hard work and enough people who wanted cars priced as high as his salary, he too could be studiously casual, he too could treat the automobiles in the showroom as if they were nothing more than joy wagons for the young instead of machines that cost more than his house had when his father built it.

He supposed, but he doubted it, and he spent the next fifty minutes leafing through his empty appointment book, reading the understated brochures, and wishing that Zaller wouldn't keep looking at him like that—as if he were going to suddenly leap out of his leather chair and run screaming into the street, waving an ax and beheading young children.

Even Karl avoided him.

Then he called Hy Regal and made an appointment for the following morning, made no excuses, and was pleased that the man didn't demand a thing but his time.

That afternoon he sold a black-and-silver Rolls to a couple who had walked by the showroom several times before finding the courage to come in. Timothy knew the feeling: *they say it's an investment, but honey, are you sure this is what we really want?* He assured them it was, and he grinned as Dan Zaller gaped at the final papers.

"Edding, you're amazing," he said. "I can't figure you out."

"That's me, one of life's constant mysteries."

And on the way home, the sky darkening for snow and the wind snapping at his hair, he saw another squirrel beside the first one, freshly dead, still bleeding.

A look to the trees.

A look up and down the street.

A look at the tail being pushed by the wind, and when the body shifted, he swallowed hard and moved on, blinking, licking at his lips, tucking his chin to his chest and turning his head side to side.

At the walk he paused and looked over his shoulder at the wall of the park, frowned for a moment with indecision before taking the porch steps in a leap, throwing open the door, and calling Ellen's name. Loudly. Almost frantically. And sagging against the hall table when she didn't answer to her name.

Damn, he thought, and unbuttoned his coat as he walked into the kitchen, his nose up and ready to test for the scent of dinner. But the room was empty, and unlighted save for the glowing dial of the clock over the stove.

"Damn," he said, and went upstairs to change his clothes, lingering in the bathroom to watch his reflection in the dust-streaked mirror over the sink. It told him nothing, gave him no hints, and a fingertip touched it just to make sure it was real.

He ate a sandwich, drank cold milk, and sat in the living room until he couldn't see anymore.

Go to bed, he told himself.

Go to bed, his mother always told him; you're not going to learn anything by studying so late. Besides, the light in here is terrible, and you'll be wearing glasses for college. Go to bed, Timmy, I'll call you in the morning.

Go to bed, Ellen said, and remember your promise.

He shifted on the couch, stretched out his legs, made himself yawn. Without turning his head he glanced toward the black telephone on the table beside him. He could call, he supposed; there were any number of women who were already letting him know by their looks and by what they didn't say, that they'd be glad to have him call.

Well, maybe not any number of them. Two or three. Two, if he were pressed to be brutally honest.

He could call. He could go out. He could sit in the Inn or the Mariner Cove and talk about the weather, her life, her life, the state of the union; he could look into her eyes, at her lips, at her chest, at the way her hands cupped around the stem of a wine glass or the handle of a knife or the corner of a napkin as she touched it to her lips.

He rose.

He could.

But not yet.

Not until he knew.

And he pulled on his coat, shoved on a hat, and went

outside, down the steps, down the walk, across the street to
the high stone wall. He checked the street for approaching
headlights, for pedestrians, then crossed the narrow band of
grass and reached for a familiar handhold, a stone slightly
out from the plane that helped him reach the top, that served
as a step when he hauled himself up, that vanished into
shadow when he straddled the top and looked down.

Inside.

At the tombstones and mausoleums and crypts and copper plates, at the shadows of dead flowers and the shadows
of the trees and the shadows the moon cast from nothing but
the wind.

He sat there for nearly ten minutes before he jumped,
sprawling on the brittle grass, biting his lips against the pain
that filled his ankles and knees. Tasting blood. Feeling tears.
Then, with a groan, he rolled to his feet and followed a row
of oak trees to his right, almost to the low iron fence that
marked the cemetery's back section, the older graves, the
ancient ones, whose headstones were weather-smooth and
whose disintegrating coffins had caused the ground here and
there to form shallow bowls.

He hesitated, feeling the wind again, feeling the kiss of
the snow that hissed on his shoulders and rattled the leaves.
A shudder, and he stepped around a gnarled leafless tree to a
narrow path he followed for only ten paces. His hands, sting-
ing from the jump, bunched in his pockets. His head bowed.

And he waited for Ellen for almost a full hour.

Watching the square cut of her gravestone; watching the
black fill the words, and the dates, and the name in Gothic
script; watching a leaf try to climb it, fall back, and huddle;
watching a tuft of uncut grass bend away from him and trem-
ble.

He waited until his shoulders had epaulets of white.

He waited until he felt the freezing on his cheeks.

"There's got to be a reason, a good one, you know," he
said at last, his voice cracking in the cold. "I can't just go out
and do it. You think anyone, any of our friends, would believe I killed myself from grief?"

The leaf tried to climb the gravestone again.

His shoulders lifted to keep the wind from his spine, and
the epaulets shattered and drifted down his arms.

He pulled a hand from a pocket and stared at the back, at
the palm, and half-curled the fingers, suddenly clenching
them until his nails threatened to break the cold, stiff skin.

"But you promised me," she said sadly.

He turned his head and saw her standing on the path, muffler around her neck the way it used to be, when they were younger—up over her chin, nearly covering her mouth; and the red tam-o'-shanter now catching the snow, and the red boots whose tops were hidden under her coat.

Cheeks reddening, nose red-tipped, eyes bright in the moonlight, made glass by the cold to shine and reflect and let him see the hidden smile.

He turned away from the grave and walked toward her, head down and hand back in the pocket. She took his arm and led him back toward the entrance, and for a while, the short while it took before he began to be afraid, he remembered her as she was and allowed himself to sigh. In her time she was the most beautiful woman in the Station, not wealthy, not poor, pursued by the best and the worst of the unmarried males until she'd seen him in the showroom, standing beside a touring car with one hand in a jacket pocket. Posing, she'd said later; he was posing just for her, and it had been love at first sight.

"I know what you're thinking," she said as they walked through the locked gates.

"Just remembering, that's all."

"I know."

She always did. She knew when he'd made a sale before he even told her, knew when he'd lost his mother before the call even came; she knew about the woman in Harley, about the woman in Hartford, about the woman in the house three doors down who killed herself by lying on the tracks out in the valley and letting the express cut her in half.

On the sidewalk he paused and looked behind him. "I'm not going to do it."

"I know that too," she said.

An owl screamed.

"You're not mad?"

"Was I angry before?"

He shrugged; it had always been impossible to tell how she felt about anything. And when his escapades had been confessed, she'd only made him warm cocoa and watched him drink it, without a word.

"Well, I'm not angry now," she said, hugging his arm to her side as they stepped off the curb and started toward home. "I knew you wouldn't be able to keep your promise."

"Ellen—"

"A silly promise anyway, don't you think? Lovers don't kill themselves for love anymore. That's only in the movies."

"It would . . ." He turned at a sound, saw an automobile coming at them, too fast to stop. "It was the gesture I was thinking of, Ellen. I'm not stupid, you know."

"I know," she said. ":But sometimes you forget."

The car swept past them, the driver a black ghost with a green-lighted face.

"Now think of how you'd feel if he'd hit you," she said, guiding him up the curb and onto the pavement. "Think of the squirrels, Timmy. Think of the squirrels and the way they look on the street when they try to do something foolish."

Then she took him into the house, helped him off with his coat and hat, and told him to go into the kitchen—there was cocoa waiting, and she didn't want it to get cold.

He watched her go up the stairs, into the dark where the dust lay in inches and the windows were shattered and the green mold on the bed had crept over the sheet; he heard her walk down the hall where absent pictures left scars on the wallpaper that was left, where the floorboards were rotting, where the doors were off their hinges.

The house, in its time, had been more Ellen's than his.

And he knew neither one of them was letting go until they were good and ready.

"Ellen?"

"Hush," she called. Whispered.

"Ellen—"

"Come to bed, love." Whispering. The breath of the furnace, the sigh of a shadow. "Stop stalling and come to bed."

The hell with you, he shouted silently; I sold a goddamned Rolls Royce today without even half trying! Tomorrow I'll sell another. The hell with you! And the hell with this place!

He raised a hand, raised a fist, looked at it and grinned bitterly because he knew it was empty. Then he sighed and went into the kitchen, sat at the table, and picked up the cup.

A sip that scorched his tongue.

"I'm going to call someone tomorrow," he declared loudly. "I am, Ellen. I really am."

"I don't think so," she called back from the top of the stairs.

He put down the cup hard, smashing it, spilling the cocoa over his trousers and shoes. He felt the heat and closed his eyes.

I am, he thought; goddammit, I am.

No, Ellen told him.

He looked up and saw her, as she had been, as she was.

She held out a hand.

Plaster floated from the wall.

Now come to bed, Timmy, and think of the squirrels.

Nesting Instinct

by SCOTT BAKER

Scott Baker lives in Paris. His novels and stories of the fantastic, such as Dhampire *and "The Lurking Duck," are often grounded in the horrific, and his story "Still Life with Scorpion" won the World Fantasy Award in 1981.*

In the following story, Tracy goes to Paris, expecting a pleasant year living with her sister and studying at the Sorbonne. But Tracy's sister is gone and the Sorbonne is closed. Truly alone for the first time in her life, Tracy retreats into a strange round house.

The trickle of tear gas leaking in through the tightly shut windows caught in Tracy's throat, was making her cry—and yet for an instant, even though she knew that Liz might be out there with the other students the police were clubbing, all she could think about was how Father had warned her to watch out for the taxi drivers in Paris, that they always took advantage of Americans to take them the wrong way and run up their bill. The riots would give her driver the perfect excuse.

He leaned on the horn. All the drivers were stuck, honking and yelling as the students who'd evaded the police charge streamed across the street, leaping over car hoods, yelling to one another and back at the drivers.

Tracy sank down in her seat, tried to hide. She was here to be a student; she had the papers from the consulate in her purse. What if the soldiers thought she was one of them, dragged her out of the taxi and beat her up or threw her in jail?

One of the student saw her. He rapped on her window and shouted something, grinning at her, then pulled at the door handle, but the doors were locked and he couldn't get in. He was tall and scrawny, with long greasy hair, a scraggly beard, huge bloodshot eyes. Tracy shrank down in her seat, closed her eyes and pretended she wasn't there, that she was back home in Downers Grove, or driving into Chicago in Robbie's car with all her friends, anywhere but here.

The driver yelled something at the student. Tracy opened her eyes again in time to see him starting to get out of the car. The student slapped the car roof and ran off to rejoin the others. A moment later they all were gone, though she could still hear them somewhere a few blocks away. The driver was swearing to himself now, and even though Tracy had no idea what he was saying, it was obvious he hated being here as much as she did. Somehow that made her feel less helpless.

He turned around and asked Tracy something. He was fat, unshaven, oily, he sounded furious with her, but all she could do was shake her head no and say, "Jeu neu parla pa frawnsee," the way Liz had written it out for her phonetically in her last letter, almost two months ago. She pushed the piece of paper with Liz's friend's address on it at the driver again.

It wasn't fair of Liz to treat her like this. Liz should have been at the airport. Even the American papers she'd been reading on the plane over had been full of the student riots, what they were calling the May Revolution. Liz had to know how frightening it would be for Tracy; she knew how shy her sister was, that Tracy didn't speak any French and didn't feel safe alone even in Chicago. She needed Liz.

And even if Liz had had some good reason for not being at the airport, she should still have been waiting at her apartment. Not just have left a note taped to the door, where anybody could have read it, telling Tracy to go stay with some stranger, so she had to find her way there on her own through a city where people were rioting and burning cars. If their father ever found out he'd yank them both right back to the States.

In a way she was lucky that the whole thing had started just when she was due to leave, while he'd been off on a fishing trip in northern Michigan. By the time he got back it would all have probably died down and he might not ever know anything had happened at all. He didn't watch TV and never read anything but the local paper, and he didn't even believe much of what he read there; the only reason he read it at all was to make sure they printed his advertisements right.

It was night by the time the driver finally extricated them from the traffic jam and got her where Liz had sent her, a closed black metal gate in an ugly gray concrete wall out in some deserted part of the city, all sinister-looking warehouses and blank walls, a few storefronts with gray metal blinds locked down over them. The streetlight at the end of the block was too far away for its light to reach all the way to where she was and the street was too narrow for the half-moon she could glimpse overhead to illuminate anything.

She checked to make sure the number on the gate really matched the one Liz had written down, and that the gate was unlocked, then tried to pay the driver what the counter showed she owed, plus ten percent for his tip. But he just started yelling and gesturing at her all over again and wouldn't give her back her bags until she gave him another fifty francs.

Her eyes were still watering from the tear gas. She felt as though she was about to break down altogether as he drove away, but she wasn't going to let him see her cry. She pushed the gate open and dragged her suitcases in, then closed it again and looked around.

Her eyes had adjusted to the dark a bit better now. There was enough moonlight for her to see that everything inside the wall was totally different from anything the neighborhood could have ever led her to hope for. There was a three-story house, almost like back home, except it was round instead of square, with a conical roof rising to a central peak. There was even a tree, its branches whipping back and forth in the wind and brushing against the only lighted window she could see—all reds and greens, like a stained glass window—up on the top floor, where Liz's note had said her friend's apartment was.

Somehow it all helped—the round house, the tree, the stained glass window, all the unexpected differences hidden behind the ugly outer wall. Maybe she was going to find things here she would never have even guessed existed, in places she would never have thought to look. She felt herself beginning to regain a little of the excitement the riots had driven out of her.

When she tried what looked like a doorbell, the door sprang open with an angry mechanical buzzing noise. The hall inside was dark and stank of sewage, dank rot. She groped around until she found a light switch and a feeble naked bulb came on in the ceiling, accompanied by a ticking noise. She could see a spiral staircase at the far end of the hall, beyond the light.

The light went out again before she could drag all three suitcases inside, but when she tried the switch again the light and the ticking came back on. Some sort of clock mechanism that turned the electricity off when it wound down.

The hallway was damp, littered with trash; even the light bulb in the ceiling was clouded and rheumy, like the eye of an old man with cataracts. Halfway to the stairs she passed a closed door painted a cheap, shiny green, and stinking of years of excrement and vomit. The smell made her stomach lurch: she could never live anywhere she had to use a hall toilet like that. For an instant she just wanted to give up and turn back, even if she had to spend the night on the street, but when she made it past the door and the stench to where she could see the spiral staircase better she realized that, even old and filthy as it was, it was beautiful, curving upward in a tight spiral, with an art nouveau metal-and-wood banister all intertwining vines and carved flowers.

The lights went out a couple of times while Tracy was dragging the suitcases up one at a time, and the light switch on the top floor didn't work, but by running back down and then up ahead she managed to get everything up without getting caught in the dark.

The door marked Rouanne had a heavy knocker on it shaped like a greening brass dolphin with the enormous, protruding eyes of a goldfish. Tracy lifted it, hesitated an instant listening to the silence, and let it drop.

The sound of the knocker hitting the door was enormously loud in the deserted hallway. The lights went out again. She couldn't see any light under the door—she couldn't see any light under any of the doors—but she heard someone moving around inside.

A moment later a tiny dark-skinned woman wearing jeans and a tight navy blue sweater opened the door. She was skeletally thin and exhausted looking, with thick glossy black hair hanging in two long braids, like an American Indian woman's. She looked around thirty.

"Are you Isobel Viegas?" Tracy asked. Liz hadn't even

bothered to let her know if the woman spoke English.

"Yes. You must be Tracy." Her voice was flat and she sounded almost as exhausted as she looked, but though she had a strong accent she pronounced every word precisely and Tracy had no trouble understanding her. "I can tell by your hair. You've got the same hair as Liz."

Tracy opened her mouth, caught herself just before she started telling the woman that Liz's hair wasn't really red at all—Liz only dyed it to look like Tracy's and their mother's—when she realized how petty and mean that would sound, especially to a stranger. She hadn't meant it that way; she was just too tired to think straight. So she just said, "Yes, I'm Tracy."

Her eyes were still burning. She rubbed them with the back of her hand, feeling ashamed of herself. Liz's cry-baby little sister.

"I was supposed to stay with Liz, but Liz... Liz wasn't home. She left me a note, it said to come here and I could stay with you. That's all I know. I don't even know where she is."

"She's in Nice. With some friends. Come in. I'll help you with your suitcases." Her voice sounded kind. She brushed past Tracy before Tracy could protest and picked up the biggest suitcase, lifting it easily where Tracy could scarcely drag it, even though she was so much tinier and frailer looking. Tracy took the next biggest suitcase and followed her in through a tiny kitchen little wider than the door itself, with a sink, hot plate and tiny refrigerator on the left, some pots and pans on hooks and a few shelves on the right—as if somebody had taken a two-yard stretch of hall and decided to make a kitchen out of it—then out into a large room with a stained-glass window in the far wall.

"You look tired," Isobel said. "Sit down." She gestured Tracy to a threadbare green armchair in front of the window. "I'll bring the rest of your things in for you."

"Thank you. My taxi got caught in a riot and I..." But Isobel was already back out in the hall. Tracy sat down, looked around in dismay.

The room was an incredible mess. There were stretched but unframed acrylic landscapes on two walls, a drafting table and a tiny, uncomfortable-looking couch, both heaped precariously with stacks of black and green cardboard port-folios spilling watercolors and pen and ink drawings, chests of drawers gaping open with clothing falling out, and a shiny chromed display rack like in dress shops with some long, hippie-style dresses and a thick, shaggy, black hairy thing that could only be a bearskin coat, if it was real, hanging on it.

The stained-glass window looked as though it had started out as an ordinary window, the type with two sections that opened out, but the window glass had been replaced with the two halves of a stylized rose garden, incredibly detailed for stained glass, with tiny crimson and green panes scarcely bigger than Tracy's fingernails held in place by brass wires instead of leading.

Maybe it was her exhaustion or the tear gas or just the incredible disorder, but the whole room seemed out of focus, confused. *Wrong.* Then Tracy realized the reason everything looked so distorted was because the apartment really *was* a weird shape: all the clutter and artistic confusion had only served to mask the fact that, though the room looked square, none of the corners that should have been right angles really were.

The whole apartment was triangular, with the room she was sitting in at the wide end of the triangle and the little kitchen she'd come through on one side of the narrow part. It was because the house was round, she realized, so that when they'd divided it up into apartments they must have made them all wedge-shaped, like slices of pie.

Not even the ceiling was straight. It was less than six feet high by the outer wall where she was sitting, so that she couldn't have stood up straight with heels on, but as the room narrowed toward the kitchen it sloped sharply upward until just over the kitchen door it was at least fifteen feet high.

There was another doorway by the one to the kitchen. Through it Tracy could see the bathroom, with a huge antique white enameled metal bathtub on legs, a tiny sink with a little round mirror over it, and a toilet. Everything in the bathroom looked spotlessly clean. So if she had to stay here a while she at least wouldn't be forced to use that disgusting toilet downstairs.

Between the two doors a sturdy-looking wooden ladder had been attached to the wall with wrought iron brackets like huge black staples. It led up ten feet or so to a wide, oval-shaped hole in the wall behind which Tracy could make out a shadowy nook with a mattress in it. The nook was shaped like one end of an upside down boat, with its walls arching up to meet overhead, and narrowing to a point at the far end. The edges of the hole were crudely plastered, as though the nook had originally been some sort of waste space that somebody had broken through the wall to get to, not part of the apartment's original design. There was an extensible guard rail in front, the kind people with little children put at the top of their stairs, that must have been to keep Isobel from falling out of bed when she was asleep.

"That's where you'll be sleeping," Isobel said, startling Tracy, who hadn't noticed her come back in. Isobel's skin was stretched tight over the underlying bone, deeply creased, as though she hadn't been able to sleep for months and her face had hardened and shrunk around the lines of her anxiety, but Tracy suddenly saw that underneath the way her exhaustion had aged her she had the face of someone much younger, maybe only a few years older than Tracy herself. "I've got some more work to do on it, but it's pretty nice. I put clean sheets on for you."

There wasn't anywhere else to sleep in the apartment. "What about you?" Tracy asked.

"I'm going away tonight for a month. With Liz."

Tracy felt like screaming. She tried to keep her voice reasonable. "You said she was in Nice."

"She is. I'm meeting her there."

"Then why can't I just stay in Liz's apartment until she gets back? I mean, it's not that it isn't nice of you to let me stay here when you don't even know me, give me your own bed and all, but I came here because I wanted to be with Liz. Not just because I wanted a place to stay. She told me she wanted me to come."

"You can't stay in Liz's apartment because Marcelo is there."

"Who's Marcelo?"

"My cousin."

"I don't understand. Why doesn't he stay with you then, instead of at Liz's?"

"Because it's really his apartment, not hers."

Tracy hesitated, finally asked, "What you mean is, Liz is living with your cousin?"

"Liz didn't tell you?"

"No." Tracy tried to keep her voice down. "She didn't tell me. She didn't tell me anything. I was supposed to come over here and stay with her for the next year. She invited me, and I came because I thought she wanted me to live with her—"

"It's not really her apartment. It's Marcelo's apartment."

"That's why she wants me to stay here? Because she doesn't even have an apartment?"

"Yes. She should have told you. Maybe she was afraid you wouldn't come if she told you, and she wanted you to come."

"Why? If she really wanted me here she would have been here. I would have waited for her, not just left her a note and told her to go see somebody."

"She wanted to wait for you or take you along. But she had to go to Nice to make the arrangements for our trip, and you have to stay here to register for school. Anyway, Marcelo knows you're here. You can get your mail from him, and he'll help you with any problems you have until we get back."

"Where are you going?"

"Lisbon. In Portugal."

"Why?"

"My brother died there last year. That's where he's buried."

"Oh. I'm sorry." It still didn't make any sense. "But . . . I don't understand. Why do you have to go there, now?"

"Because he was a Jew. Like me. My family moved to Peru when the war started, but we come from Portugal originally. That's why Carlos was in Lisbon when he died, but they put him in a Christian grave with a cross on top. I've been having dreams ever since. He comes and tells me to take the cross off."

Isobel looked up, stared Tracy in the eye. For an instant there was something bright and hard, insectile, in her gaze, but her voice was soft, very calm. Too calm. "I know it sounds crazy. I told Carlos it was crazy when he came to me in my dreams. He is in a Christian cemetery, and if they find out he's a Jew they won't let him stay buried there. We don't have any money, I can't afford anywhere else. But he says that I have to take the cross off. Liz is going to help me. We're going to hitch there from Nice."

"I'm sorry," Tracy said again. She didn't know what else to say, what she was supposed to do now. Liz didn't even have an apartment, after Mother had been sending her money for it every month, so Tracy couldn't even ask for the money for an apartment of her own without getting Liz in trouble. And now Liz was going off to desecrate a grave in Portugal and probably get arrested for it.

"You're both going to be gone for the whole month?" she finally asked. "Liz too?"

"Yes. Maybe longer. We have to make sure they don't put a new cross up."

"What about the rent?"

"There isn't any rent. People own their own apartments here, it's not like the States, and the people who own this one are in Montreal. They haven't been back to France for twelve years. Since 1956. The apartment just gets passed along from friend to friend. Anyway, the whole building's been condemned, so they wouldn't have the right to charge anybody for living here even if they wanted to. There isn't anybody else left, just an Irish poet on the first floor who only comes back here a couple of months a year. There isn't even a real concierge, just a woman who comes by once a week to clean things up a little. But this was an artist's colony—Modigliani lived in this room for a while—so some people are fighting to get it classed as an historical monument. Nobody's going to tear it down.

"The only problem is, you have to use the phone in the café down the street. The phone company won't put in a phone, because the building is condemned. All you have to do is pay the water or electricity if you get a bill for Rouanne."

"Those are the people in Montreal?"

"Yes."

"And they don't mind if you just give their apartment away to somebody they've never met?"

"I've never met them either. It just goes from friend to friend. You'll be number seventeen. The rule is, you can use anything here but you can't keep it, and you have to leave something of your own when you go. And you can't leave the apartment empty, or else we'll lose it. If you move out you have to find someone to take your place."

She didn't want to keep any of it. "What happens when you get back?"

"Liz can help find you a place to live. But you don't need to worry, you can stay here as long as you need."

She didn't want to stay there, not alone in a condemned building while her oh-so-responsible older sister who was supposed to be looking after her was down in Portugal desecrating a Catholic graveyard, not afterward with somebody who seemed nice enough but was obviously totally out of her mind, but she didn't suppose she had any choice.

"I keep intending to put some lights there so I can read at night," Isobel said, and Tracy realized with a start that she was still staring up at the sleeping nook. "But it gets very bright in the day; there are some little windows in the ceiling you can't see now."

There was a cheap-looking stereo on one of the tables, a pile of thirty or forty albums on the floor. Tracy looked around again, at all the paintings, the moonlight illuminating the three just outside the window, shining through the stained glass. And this was a place where none of the violence she'd seen in the streets tonight could ever penetrate, where she'd be completely isolated from it. Safe. No one would even know that she was there unless she chose to tell them.

She had never spent any real time alone before. She had always had her family, friends, people who wanted to be with her, know what she was doing, where she'd been. Especially Robbie, who could never understand that, just because she liked him fine, it didn't mean that she wanted to sleep with him.

It would be nice to have May in Paris all to herself. To find out what she wanted to do on her own, alone, instead of what other people wanted her to be doing. She'd be bound to meet some people when school started, if she got too lonely. When Liz got back she could decide what she wanted to do after that.

A few hours later someone honked in the street outside, and Isobel left, carrying an old, scarred leather suitcase. Tracy felt a flash of panic when she heard the car drive away and realized she was all alone, all her friends were thousands of miles away and she had no one to turn to if anything went wrong.

She looked around the apartment for a while, nervously straightening things and checking out the sleeping nook. Its arched walls were covered with a dark blue Indian print with hundreds of fingernail-sized round plastic mirrors sewn into the cloth, and it had six tiny bull's-eye windows arranged like the points of a six-pointed star, three on each side of the angle where the arched sides met. With its fresh sheets and neatly made bed it was an island of order in the apartment's utter chaos.

She climbed back down again, tried to straighten up a little, but whenever she opened a drawer or cabinet to put something away it seemed like something else fell out, and there was no way she could do more than make a sort of little clearing for herself in the middle of the confusion unless she went through everything and reorganized it from the beginning. She gave up and sat down at the drafting table, took some of the paper and a felt-tip pen Isobel had left uncapped there and started to write Robbie a letter, all about the riots and the burning car and how she already missed him and all their friends, but not about Liz or where she was going to be living. After a few moments her panic subsided, and she put the letter aside for later, suddenly too tired to continue.

The narrow, cheap-looking, full length mirror nailed to the bathroom wall opposite the sink showed her that she looked as exhausted as she felt. The tub seemed clean, but Tracy scrubbed it thoroughly again just in case, put the soaps and shampoos Isobel had left behind away in the medicine cabinet and got out her own, then climbed into the huge old tub and lay there soaking in the hot water, just staring at the bright reflections the little twenty-five-watt bulb over the mirror above the sink made on the water and the way the light glinting from the shiny silver faucets shimmered off the ripples and soap bubbles. She could feel all of the tension and exhaustion draining out of her, until finally, without realizing what she was doing, she nodded off to sleep.

To dream that Robbie was there, that he'd just walked into the bathroom and sat down on the edge of the tub as if it were the most natural thing in the world. She was glad to see him, though she'd never let him see her all the way naked before, but it didn't matter because the light glimmering off the water had intensified until the whole bathtub was a pool of liquid fire cloaking her in radiance. It was a giant burning eye, her eye, she was looking out of it at him, and there was no more reason to be embarrassed about not having any clothes on than there would have been if she hadn't been there at all.

Robbie reached out and stroked her cheek. For an instant he wasn't Robbie at all, he was a dark-skinned, exotically handsome man she'd never seen before. She could feel his eyes on her and there was a crowd of people all around her, examining her critically, laughing at her nakedness. Then they were gone, Robbie was just Robbie again, and he was melting into the light with her, into the cool, comforting fire.

She felt immensely refreshed when she awakened, as though she'd had a whole night's sleep in the tub, though she could only have been asleep a few moments, because the water was still hot. She'd been dreaming about someone—not Robbie, she remembered dreaming about him at first, but someone else, a stranger. The kind of man she had always wanted to meet and never had, and yet in her dream she had felt closer to him than she had ever felt to Robbie or to anyone else. Almost like a brother, if she'd had a brother she loved the way she loved Liz, the way Isobel must have loved her brother. Yet when she tried to recapture his face, remember anything about him, it was all gone, and there was only the fading memory of how she'd felt, the certainty that she'd touched something precious, irreplaceable, only to lose it again.

She toweled herself off in front of the narrow mirror, dried her hair. The air was chilly and even though the dusty bulb over the sink was tiny and dim, no bigger than one of the little bulbs around electric make-up mirrors and not nearly so bright, there was still something paradoxically harsh about its light that made her look ugly, almost deformed, when she studied herself in the mirror. Yet she'd always known she was conventionally pretty, and even if she wasn't striking enough to ever be really beautiful, she'd still never needed to worry about being unattractive.

It had to be the cheap mirror, not the light. Some sort of warped plastic with flaws in it that distorted the way she really looked. Like those fun-house mirrors that made you look like a dwarf or as if you weighed two hundred pounds.

She felt better when she left the bathroom and put on one of the new cotton nightshirts her mother had bought her. The light switch was by the ladder. She turned the light off, then climbed up to the loft and crawled in between the clean, slightly rough sheets, so sleepy she almost forgot to pull the guard rail shut behind her.

The nook seemed warmer than the rest of the apartment, the faint odor of the foam rubber mattress, impregnated with memories of all the people who must have slept on it, somehow only part of that comforting warmth. Tracy lay there a moment, content and at peace, staring up at the arch of the ceiling with its Star-of-David constellation of tiny bull's-eye windows just above her, like portholes opening on the sky. Through the glass she could see the stars; and on her bed the faint gleams where the mirrors sewn into the fabric around her caught the starlight and threw it back.

She reached up and touched a finger to the cool glass of one of the tiny windows, traced a circle around its inside edge. Everything I need is right here, she realized, not even surprised, just before she fell asleep.

Tracy was awakened the next morning by crisp sunlight shining on her face, winking off the little plastic mirrors on the nook's walls. Propping herself up on her elbow, she looked down at the apartment. The sunlight streaming in through the stained glass threw pools of shifting color on the furniture and floor, and she could see that she must have done a better job of straightening up the night before than her exhaustion had allowed her to realize. Or perhaps the apartment's unusual shape had confused her. But now, looking down on it from the nook and seeing how it widened out below her to the stained-glass window's bright colors at the far end, she could see how the way the apartment was set up *made sense,* despite the clutter—like the house itself, which she'd assumed would be so ugly when she was outside the gate, but which had turned out to be totally different once she got inside.

She sensed the future opening out in front of her, unpredictable and exciting, full of rooms that didn't all have to be just rectangular boxes but could be any shape at all, full of things she couldn't imagine yet and wouldn't recognize for what they were until they happened.

As she was getting dressed she saw the unfinished letter to Robbie on the table. She reread the first few lines, then crumpled it up and threw it away. Everything she'd had to say about how terrifying Paris was with the riots and so forth seemed silly, childish. She'd write him another letter some other time, when she had something worth talking about.

Besides, Robbie had always gotten along too well with her parents for her to tell him anything about the riots that he might pass on to them. She'd better write him when she wrote her mother, tell them both about how peaceful everything really was and how much the papers were exaggerating what was going on. Coming from him it would be more convincing than if she just put it in the letter to her mother.

A bird was singing in the tree outside. She opened the window carefully—though the stained glass seemed sturdy enough—but the bird flew away before she could get a look

at it. With the window open she could see the tree was a
locust tree, with a weathered wooden bench beneath it. The
sun glinted off strings of multicolored plastic beads some
previous tenant had hung from the branches nearest the window.

She finished dressing and went out to explore the yard.
Off to the right she found an abandoned shed with the roof
falling in. In a neglected flower bed behind the house was a
concrete birdbath full of stagnant water and an overgrown
chunk of yellowish limestone with a grotesque imp's face
carved in it. Somehow the abandoned aspect of everything
made it all that much more picturesque, more private. Her
own secret garden.

She looked around the neighborhood and, from a little
corner grocery, bought herself enough food to fill up Isobel's
tiny refrigerator, then spent the rest of the day straightening
up the apartment, repositioning chairs and tables, moving
things out of cupboards and dressers to make room for her
own stuff, carefully stacking the portfolios and loose drawings away exactly as she found them. She glanced inadver-
tently at one or two of them, but tried to put the rest away
without looking at them, out of some obscure sense that if
she examined them without permission she'd be invading
Isobel's privacy.

The Sorbonne was closed when she went to register the
next morning, surrounded by the uniformed soldiers with
their Roman centurion helmets and plastic shields that had
been chasing the rioters the night before. Two girls she heard
speaking English told her the students had shut the school
down and were occupying the Theatre de l'Odéon, a few
blocks away. She went there to look, but one glance inside at
the chaos and all the people making incomprehensible
speeches was enough to tell her that there was no one there
she would have wanted to meet, nothing there for her.

She didn't really care if the Sorbonne was closed or not,
but if her parents learned she wasn't going to school they'd
yank her back to Downer's Grove and family dinners and
Saturday nights parking with Robbie because there wasn't
anything better to do. She had to find some other school
before her parents found out. Anything, just so that she
could convince them to let her stay in Paris until the Sorbonne started again.

Maybe Marcelo could help.

She disliked him as soon as he opened the door: emaciated, with long greasy black hair, skin-tight black jeans and some sort of pointy gray suede boots with buckles, the top buttons of his tight black silk shirt open to display a hairy chest and the fine gold chain he wore around his neck, heavy tasteless rings on his fingers. An ageing hippie gigolo, probably closer to forty than to Liz's twenty-two.

But when he realized who she was his smile transfigured his face and made him suddenly seem almost boyish, and when he invited her in, in his broken, heavily accented English, so much worse than Isobel's, his voice was warm, with only a trace of petulance to remind her of her first impression.

The apartment was small but neat. Marcelo apologized for not having been able to meet her when she'd arrived. He seemed so genuinely pleased to see her that, even though she still found him as physically repulsive as ever, she began to see a little of what must have made Liz like him.

When she explained her problem with the Sorbonne he told her about the Alliance française, which wasn't part of the university system and so hadn't been affected by the strike, then walked her over to it and helped her register. By the time he'd put her on the metro to take her home, she was enrolled for a one-month beginner's course, starting the next Monday. Yet she knew that no matter how helpful he'd been, she didn't really want to see him any more than she had to.

The gate was open—she must have forgotten to lock it—and the stench from the ground-floor bathroom hit her as soon as she opened the door to the house. It was far worse than the night before, almost as if something had died there and was rotting. Maybe something *had* died in there—a mouse or a rat or something—but more likely some bum had been using it, like the three winos she'd seen sharing a bottle in the metro. She checked to make sure the gate was securely locked behind her.

She held her breath as she locked the front door, then managed to keep from taking a new breath until she was halfway up the spiral staircase. The lights went out just as she was reaching the third floor, but there was a small skylight over the stairwell and enough light filtered in for her to find the door.

She could still catch a hint of the stench even on the top floor, but the door to her apartment sealed it out. In any case, the downstairs bathroom was a problem for the woman

Isobel had said came in to clean once a week, not for Tracy. And in a way the stench even helped Tracy keep her apartment that much more private: it was another barrier keeping people she didn't want to know from ever learning just how marvelous the house was upstairs, in the same way that the dull gray wall outside sheltered the house and garden from prying eyes.

As she locked the door to the hall she realized just how much the apartment was *hers*, in a way that nothing had ever been hers before—certainly not her room at home, with her mother going through her things whenever she cleaned it, her father's sneak inspections. She surprised herself hoping that something would happen to keep Liz and Isobel in Portugal longer so she wouldn't ever have to leave.

She spent her mornings putting the apartment in order. As she moved furniture around and went through everything in the various heaps and piles or hidden away in drawers and cabinets and closets, her original impression of the apartment as a sort of hippie magpie's nest cluttered with a random mixture of salvaged junk and art changed. Since new tenants could never throw out anything their predecessors had left behind, but only add to the accumulation, the seeming chaos was really a multitude of individual tastes and histories mingled together in overlapping layers, like the archaeological strata she'd seen scientists trying to disentangle in that documentary on excavations in the Holy Land she'd been shown in Sunday School when she was fourteen, but with each of the strata preserving something of one of the sixteen tenants who'd lived there before her.

Almost every piece of clothing or furniture, each kitchen utensil, had its own special feel to it, as though it were faintly impregnated with the memory of the person who had brought it into the apartment or of those who had used it in their own individual ways there afterward. Tracy found herself trying to picture the previous tenants, inventing names and faces, life stories, to go with the hints they had left behind. The armchair could only be Isobel's, probably bought in a flea market, and Isobel would have enjoyed sitting in it with the window thrown open, watching the wind whip the locust tree's branches around while the strings of plastic beads she had hung from them flashed in the sun. Yet Tracy was sure that it had been not Isobel but some previous tenant (a woman Tracy pictured as a tall Germanic blonde in her late thirties with a name like Dagmar, slender but severe-looking, always dressed in sober grays and greens) who had put the stained glass in the window. The man who'd left the bearskin coat behind had been there in winter, when the tree was bare and before the blonde woman had put in the stained glass; he would have kept the window closed, with curtains over it.

Like Tracy, they had all had to fit the things they inherited into their own individual constellations and labyrinths. They must have all discovered, as Tracy had, that there was only one place to put each thing in the apartment where it would be necessary and correct, and bring them closer to the order hidden within the apparent chaos.

After she'd finish working on the apartment she'd use what remained of the afternoon to do all the things tourists were supposed to do in Paris—shopping on the Right Bank, away from the Latin Quarter and its violence, visiting parks and museums and flea markets, sitting in cafés writing post cards back home about how beautiful Paris was—but above all doing them *alone,* and more out of some obscure sense of duty than because she wanted to be doing them.

The building was totally silent at night. When she got home she would run herself a bubble bath so hot she could barely stand to get into it, then lie there in the immense tub for hours, just watching the light play over the surface of the water, floating through dreams and fantasies and memories all tangled together, so that she was no longer just Tracy but someone as new and unexpected as the life she was finding here, so that she neither knew nor cared whether she was dreaming or awake, and Dagmar and the man in the bearskin coat seemed as real as Liz or her parents, as real as the apartment itself. Lying there in the hot water, totally relaxed and at peace, she would drift off to sleep, to reawaken only when she slipped down and got water in her nose or when the water grew so chill that the cold woke her. Then she would towel herself off hurriedly and crawl into bed in the shadowed darkness of the nook, where the hundreds of tiny plastic mirrors in the fabric on the walls caught the slivers of moonlight slanting in through the bull's-eye windows and broke them into faint, almost imperceptible stars, so that she slept in the center of her own private universe, with the constellations wheeling around her. And the next morning she would awaken gradually, with nothing to force her to get out of bed immediately, so that she could slip imperceptibly from her dreams into a waking that was as fresh and new, as much a solitary pleasure to be hugged to herself and cherished in secret, as her sleep.

At the end of the week she was moving a heavy portfolio from one cupboard to another, trying to make room, when one of the watercolors in it slipped out. She tried not to look at it as she picked it up, out of the same sense she had had, when she first put the portfolios away, that looking at it would be invading Isobel's privacy, when suddenly she realized that the portfolios and all the drawings and paintings in them were *hers,* just as everything else in the apartment was hers for so long as she stayed there, and it didn't make any difference whether or not Isobel was going to be coming back. She felt an unexpected sense of relief, as if she had finally put down some enormous weight that she'd been carrying without even knowing it was there, as she took out all the portfolios and paintings that she had so carefully stacked away in places they didn't belong, and began sorting through them.

She almost immediately found a portfolio full of sketches and drawings of Isobel, occasionally clothed but mostly in the nude. They were all by the same hand, and the signature on the ones which were signed was Carlos Viegas—Isobel's brother, she supposed, the one Isobel and Liz were trying to deliver from a too-Christian burial.

The drawings were in chronological order, starting when Isobel was thirteen or so and continuing up through what must have been just before Carlos's death. Almost all the drawings showed a very sweet-looking, fresh-faced and pretty young girl with none of the tension or exhaustion that had so dominated Isobel when Tracy had met her.

The last three drawings were totally different. Even the style had changed, so that if they hadn't been signed and dated she would never have believed they had been done by the same artist: the delicacy and grace were gone, replaced with an obsessive, leering precision.

All three drawings showed Isobel naked. In two of them she was depicted as ancient and shriveled, with the calculating eyes and mouth of a rapacious old woman, while in the third the same grotesque and leering crone was shown bloated and hideous, monstrously pregnant.

The drawings were sickening. No, not sickening, sick—literally sick, the work of someone insane. Tracy had never thought to ask what Isobel's brother had died of, but she was suddenly certain he had killed himself. There was so much insane hatred in those last drawings.

No wonder Isobel had looked so drawn, so worn.

Tracy tied the portfolio shut and put it away. She hesitated an instant, uncertain, then took out another. It held more drawings and sketches, but with Isobel's signature on them this time. The first one showed a fine-featured, startlingly handsome nude boy who resembled the Isobel in the pictures she'd just been looking at so much that Tracy knew he could only be her brother Carlos. She looked at the next picture—another drawing of Carlos, perhaps a few years younger.

She flipped back to the end, to see if there was a sketch showing Carlos as tortured and ugly as he must have looked when he'd done those hideous final drawings of Isobel, but the last drawing showed him sitting on the green chair with the stained-glass window half-open behind him, as handsome and insouciant as ever.

They must have spent their adolescence posing nude for each other. She felt that should have bothered her and yet, somehow, the grace and beauty of the drawings justified it, made it seem only natural.

She went back to the beginning, carefully studied the drawings one by one. Carlos reminded her of someone. Isobel? No. The resemblance was obvious, but that wasn't whom he reminded her of. And not Marcelo, either: neither Isobel nor Carlos looked at all like him.

Robbie? She frowned, irritated. What had made her think of Robbie? They didn't look at all alike. She couldn't even call up Robbie's face with much precision: he'd been athletic, good-looking in the same way as everyone else good-looking at their high school had been. Never striking like Carlos. She couldn't imagine anyone spending years drawing him over and over again.

She realized then that she'd been expecting to start missing Robbie and her friends, waiting for it, like right after she'd had her wisdom teeth pulled and she'd known that the anesthetic was wearing off, that the pain was going to be there even though she couldn't feel it yet. But there wasn't any pain. She didn't miss Robbie or her friends at all.

She couldn't imagine anyone caring enough to spend years drawing anyone she'd known back in high school.

In one of the cupboards she found a small glass-fronted case containing six beautiful iridescent blue-green scarab beetles mounted on black velvet, looking so much like jewels that for an instant she thought they were carved out of semi-precious stones. There were five other specimen cases in the same cupboard, full of other insects—more beetles, some butterflies, dragonflies, even one case full of three-inch tropical hornets, all mounted with the same meticulous care—but after glancing at them she put back all but the case with the scarabs in it.

She'd known the moment she saw the case that she needed it on her wall. She stored the acrylic mountainscape Isobel had had there away in a closet and put the scarabs up. Everything in the room seemed to rearrange itself around the specimen case, bringing the underlying order that much closer to manifesting itself—as though she were living in a Rorschach test like the ones she'd taken in school, and slowly learning to understand what its seemingly random blots and spirals told her about herself.

The morning of her first class she stuck her head out the window to see what the weather was like, only to discover a gray, football-shaped papier-mâché wasps' nest that she was certain hadn't been there before hanging from a drainpipe less than a yard from the window. Ugly black and yellow wasps, like overgrown yellow jackets, were crawling over the nest, and in and out of the opening in its bottom. Wasps terrified her—had always terrified her, ever since she was six and had kicked over a rusty tomato juice can in the backyard with a nest of yellow jackets in it. They'd come swarming out to attack her, and she'd been rushed to the hospital to be treated for more than forty stings.

Don't panic, she told herself. Forcing herself to move as slowly and deliberately as she could, so as not to anger them, she pulled the two halves of the window shut and latched it tight, locking the wasps outside, where they couldn't get at her to hurt her.

As she was closing the gate behind her on her way out she stopped and stared back up at the window, but the wasp's nest was invisible against the house's peeling gray paint.

By her third day at the school she had already met a man she was interested in.

She'd been sitting alone in the Alliance's cafeteria, trying to eat some weird sticky brown dessert that she'd thought at first was some sort of chocolate pudding, but which had turned out to be something else—though she had no idea what—when he sat down across from her. He was in his late twenties, slim and elegant looking, almost as strikingly handsome as Isobel's brother Carlos, but in a very French way. He was wearing a light green tweed sports coat with a belt and a tighter, more rakish, cut than you saw on anything in the States, yet somehow it looked right on him, not ridiculous the way it would have looked on anyone back home.

He smiled at her as he sat down and asked her something in French, which of course she didn't understand. When she told him that she didn't speak French yet, he asked her in English, speaking very slowly, as though testing each word, "Are you Liz's sister?"

"Yes."

"I recognized you because you have red hairs like her. And because you don't have the same face but you have the same air."

"The same air?" She liked his voice. It was soft and melodious, gentle without sounding weak or effeminate.

"The same way of looking. Like you are sisters."

She nodded. "How do you know Liz?"

"I am a friend of a friend of Liz. Marcelo Ruiz." Tracy nodded. "You are as student here?"

"Yes. I'm Tracy."

"My name is François. I am a professeur here."

They talked for a few minutes—she asked him what the brown stuff was and he told her it was chestnut puree, which was enough to make her sure she didn't like it—then he excused himself because he had a class to teach. After that he sometimes joined her at lunch or when she went to the Alliance's basement café across the street with people from her class... which she soon discovered gave her a certain prestige with the other American girls, not only because he was charming and good-looking and a teacher, but just because he was French. They were here because they were in love with the idea of Paris and the French, but all any of them were meeting was other foreigners like themselves— Arabs, Africans, Eastern Europeans, South Americans and South-East Asians, every sort of people except French people.

She spent that Saturday sitting on the bench under the locust tree doing what little homework she'd been assigned

—the Alliance catered mainly to foreigners just trying to pick up enough French to get by, either because they were in France to work or because they were spending a few months in Paris as tourists—and, when she'd finished with that, sketching.

Her courses were easy, and she'd been picking up French faster than she'd expected, so much so that she'd found herself spending as much time in class just daydreaming or filling the dead time with doodling and making little sketches of her teacher and classmates as she actually did improving her French—and her drawings, like her French, were much better than she would have expected. She'd always liked art back in school, even though she'd never been any good at it and had had to give it up because she kept getting terrible grades in art class. But somehow here, living in Paris in what could only be an artist's studio, with no one around to tell her that she didn't have any talent, things were different, and she could enjoy pretending she actually could draw.

Though maybe the problem had never really been that she didn't have any talent, maybe the problem had been that she'd never had anything interesting to draw. When she tried to sketch people she remembered from the States—Robbie and her friends back in Downer's Grove, or even Liz—the pictures came out as lifeless and insipid as ever, but when she tried to draw Isobel, other students from her class, even people she'd just glimpsed for an instant in the streets, she found that she could do much better.

Maybe it was only because they weren't Americans. There was something about Americans that made them all look the same, as though they were all wearing the same bland expressions over whatever underlying differences there might have been in their faces But there had to be something more involved: even the previous tenants she'd imagined to people the apartment—Carlos, of course, but also Dagmar, who'd put in the stained-glass window, and Jean-Luc, who'd had the bearskin coat, and Raoul and all the others—came alive when she drew them. Though that was probably because she had invented them—no, not invented them, but made them her own, taking their attributes, the clues that had told her who they had to be—the drawings and paintings, the stained-glass window, the scarabs in their display case—and rearranging them into meaningful constellations: a part of herself she'd projected on the outside world, a sort of mirror-image she was slowly constructing that would show her her true and secret self, like the apartment itself, part of the apartment, so that she was living *inside* the meaning, somehow, inside of who she was.

When evening came she told herself she should go out, *do* something, even if it was just see a movie, not just waste her time here in Paris. Maybe go to that party François had asked her to at one of his friends' apartment. Marcelo and some of Liz's French friends were going to be there. It would give her a chance to get to know them.

She had wanted to go, but something had made her say she didn't think she could, that she had a previous engagement she couldn't get out of with some friends of her family who were in Paris for a few days. François had given her his friend's address anyway, and told her to come after she was finished with them, the party would be going on most of the night and no one would mind if she showed up very late.

She should go. In a few weeks Isobel would be back, and she'd have to find someplace else to live, some other way to spend her time. Things would be a lot easier for her then if she'd already met people, started making friends. But she was scared to take the metro at night and didn't feel like fighting the crowds or risking getting caught in a riot—and François's friend lived near the Luxembourg Gardens, right where all the riots were going on.

No. It would be better to stay home. There'd be plenty of time to take advantage of the other things Paris had to offer when Isobel got back. Until then, her solitude was too precious to waste.

But she still felt nervous, jumpy for no good reason. She ran a bath to calm herself, found herself thinking, for some reason, about an article she'd read in *Time* or *Newsweek* about natural childbirth, whatever the method was where they had the women giving birth lie in the water to relax them, and then about a total-immersion baptism she'd once been conned into going to at somebody's house, with all the new converts leaping into the swimming pool and ruining their clothes while the preacher praised the Lord. She wondered what would happen if you combined the two, so the babies would be born already baptized.

Stretching out in the hot soapy water, she let the heat soak through her, relax her until she could just lie there, completely still, watching the light shimmer off the ripples

that radiated out from her with every shallow breath she
took, until at last the light merged into dream and she drifted
off again, as she had so many times before, to dream that
Carlos and Dagmar were there with her, holding her in their
arms and soothing her, protecting her from the wasps outside
the window.

The water was icy when she awakened. She must have
been asleep for hours. She felt confused, vaguely alarmed—
as though there was something she had to do, but she'd forgotten what it was; she could only remember that it was
important, that she had to do it.

She felt stiff as she got out of the tub, started drying herself. Even her body seemed strange and awkward, unfamil-
iar.

She glanced unthinkingly at the plastic full-length mirror
nailed opposite the sink. She'd gotten into the habit of using
the little round mirror over the sink, just letting her gaze
slide past the full-length mirror without ever really *looking* at
the distorted reflection it showed her, but this time something about the mirror caught her eye, and she stared at it in
shock.

Her image in the mirror now looked almost exactly like
the last pictures Carlos had drawn of Isobel. Her breasts and
flesh hung slack and flaccid on a stooped and twisted frame;
a stranger's rheumy eyes leered back at her out of some
withered crone's ancient face. Only her hair was the same,
still long and red—but now that red seemed false, like a
cheap wig that only accentuated her papery gray skin; how
hideous the rest of her had become.

And behind her now she could see Carlos, Dagmar, Jean-
Luc, all the others—some of them as clear and sharp as if
they were in the bathroom with her, others, like Isobel,
vague and blurred, more suggested than shown. Isobel
seemed to be asleep, but all of the others were staring out of
the mirror *at* her with the same cold, maniacal glee she could
read in her own reflection's eyes, feel bubbling up in herself,
rising to the surface of her mind from the depths where it had
been hiding...

She tore her eyes away from the mirror, squeezed them
shut, trying to blot it all out. But only her body was gone,
and she was trapped on the other side of the mirror, inside it,
staring hungrily out at her pitifully deformed physical self as
it squeezed its eyes shut in abject terror, its bloated belly

quivering and swelling as it ballooned outward with the eager new life within.

And then, somehow, she managed to make her body turn away, stumble out of the bathroom. She ran to the window and flung it open, stood there, panting, in the cold night air, trying to get her breath back. The night was starless, with only a faint hint of the city's diffuse glow to relieve its utter blackness.

She heard an enraged buzzing to her right, where the window had slammed into the outer wall, just below the wasps' nest. Panic-stricken, she grabbed the two halves of the window and pulled them closed. Before she could get the window latched a swarm of enraged wasps started beating themselves furiously against the colored panes, trying to get at her.

I've got to get out of here, she realized. I'm starting to see things. I've been spending too much time alone. I'll go to that party. I need to see François, talk to people. Then I'll be all right again.

But her hair-blower, her make-up, everything she needed to get ready was in the bathroom, and she couldn't go in there again.

That's crazy, she told herself, starting to get angry. I was still half-asleep; I must have had a nightmare. That's all.

But she still couldn't face all those reflections in that mirror again.

It was her apartment. Her mirror. She could do what she wanted with it.

I'll buy a new mirror, she told herself. A good one, where I can see myself as I really look. It'll be my contribution to the apartment.

There was a claw hammer in one of the kitchen drawers. She got it out, hefted it. Its weight was reassuring, like a weapon.

Before she had time to change her mind she squeezed her eyes shut again and groped her way back into the bathroom, over to the mirror. It was held in place by two nails through the top of the flimsy wooden frame. With her eyes still closed, she got the claw wedged in behind the frame, pried.

The mirror came away from the wall so easily she could probably have just yanked it off. It wobbled back and forth in her hands, like a big sheet of flimsy cardboard. She turned it around, away from her, finally dared open her eyes and look at it.

The back was rough brown fiberboard, with a gouge where the hammer's claw had bitten into it. There was nothing strange or frightening about it.

She felt ashamed of herself for her fear. Stupid. Just a hysterical woman, her father would have said. But as soon as she tried to carry the mirror out of the bathroom she felt the ordered meaning of the apartment around her shatter into senseless chaos, and through the fissures that had opened a flood of terrifying *wrongness* came pouring through. She took an involuntary step back, into the bathroom again, and the wrongness retreated, began to drain from the world again.

The mirror had to stay in the bathroom.

She stood there frozen, holding the mirror away from her, unable to make herself even try to take it out of the bathroom again, getting angrier and angrier as she told herself she was acting crazy: it was just a mirror; she could do what she wanted with it.

I'll nail it up backwards, she thought suddenly. Put its face to the wall.

She used the hammer to push the nails out, stuck them back in their holes from the other side. Holding the mirror in place against the wall, she hammered the first nail in—then suddenly, not giving herself time to think about what she was doing, pulled the second nail out of its hole in the frame and held it to the fiberboard instead, about three inches below the top, *right where her reflection's head had been,* and hammered it home as hard as she could.

The nail penetrated the fiberboard, hesitated an instant as the tough plastic mirror surface on the other side resisted it, stretched, then the nail punctured the plastic film and buried itself in the wall. The last of the wrongness drained away. She felt as though she'd just escaped something, freed herself from some enormous weight, and though she knew the whole thing was ridiculous she couldn't keep herself from grinning as she used the little round mirror over the sink to get ready. When she stepped back to get a better look at herself in the round mirror she glimpsed the other mirror's ugly brown back on the wall behind her. She needed a full-length mirror in the bathroom, but not that one. She'd put it in the closet tomorrow after all.

As she was leaving she glanced at the stained-glass window. The wasps were still there. They had stopped buzzing and hurling themselves against the panes of colored glass, but they were still crawling up and down, trying to get in.

She'd get some bug spray tomorrow, kill them all.

There was a man in a rumpled gray suit and no socks in her metro car, declaiming what sounded like poetry in a wild, crazed voice, spittle flying from his mouth. Everyone pretended not to see him and continued their conversations as if nothing unusual were going on, even when he came up and stared them in the face, shouted things at them. The car was crowded, and Tracy was back in the corner, where he couldn't get at her, but the elated confidence that had come over her as she'd hammered the mirror to the wall had deserted her: she could feel the insanity rolling off him, distorting everything around him, like a halo of heat waves making the air waver, and she didn't dare push past him when her stop came. She had to wait until he got off, which meant she had to change lines twice to end up at the St. Michel station, farther away from François's friend's apartment than she'd intended but still within walking distance.

The street outside the metro was full of students, hundreds of them standing around watching the blue-uniformed soldiers waiting in tense clusters by their buses with their clubs and guns and shields. CRS, for *Compagnies républicaines de sécurité,* François had told her. Everybody seemed excited, expectant, more like they were waiting for a football match to start than anything else.

She was just turning onto the rue St. Jacques when she heard the shouting begin behind her. She looked over her shoulder, saw tear gas bombs arching over the crowd and exploding, the students running her way, and then a line of CRS troopers was moving out across St. Jacques to block it off and she was caught up in the crowd, running away with the others as the CRS charged them. Sometimes the students would come to a halt, try to make a stand behind a makeshift barricade, but they always ended up getting routed, herded farther away.

By the time Tracy managed to get away from the others she was halfway across the Fifth Arrondissement, her sides aching and her eyes swollen and running from the gas. She didn't want to go to the party any longer, all she wanted to do was go home, but from where she was it looked as though it would be easier to get to the party than back to the apartment, and the only other alternative was to stay out in the street and risk getting gassed and beaten.

She circled around a few blocks to look as though she were coming from a different direction, planned what to do if the CRS stopped her—pull out her American passport and show it to them, tell them she was just an American tourist, she didn't even speak any French—but when she got near the address François had given her she saw that there were a dozen or more CRS on literally every corner, and she turned back.

It was 11:30 by the time she finally found a metro station, but it was already closed, though they were supposed to stay open past midnight. She didn't see any cabs, but her way home would take her away from anywhere there was likely to be trouble. She'd probably be better off just walking. Maybe she'd find a cab when she got farther away from the riots.

She didn't. It was almost three in the morning before she got back. She hadn't seen anybody on the street for the last hour, except for one bum snoring in a doorway.

It was only after she'd locked the gate behind her and could let herself relax that she finally realized just how hard she'd been working to keep herself from feeling terrified, so she could keep on going.

But she was home, safe. The whole thing with the mirror seemed silly, just some stupid trick of her overworked imagination. She'd turn the mirror back around tomorrow, until she could get a new one.

And it was silly to be so scared of the wasps. They wouldn't sting her, so long as she was careful and didn't fling the window open too violently or disturb their nest. That had been why she'd been stung so badly when she was a kid; she'd kicked the can with the yellow jackets' nest in it. They'd just been trying to defend their nest.

As she lay in the warm darkness of the nook, the stars shining through the bull's-eye windows over her head, she could sense the apartment all around her, sheltering and protecting her from the real violence outside.

She didn't see François at school Monday. On Tuesday she was sitting doodling on her napkin in the Alliance's café with Monika, an Italian girl from class, when she saw him come in, looking wonderful in a shiny gray leather jacket.

She waved to him, but he didn't seem to see her and went over to another table, started talking to two dark-haired, overly sophisticated-looking girls Tracy didn't know.

One girl asked François something in a teasing tone of voice. He looked around quickly, still without seeing Tracy, then took something black out of his coat, slipped the strap on one end over his right hand, and started slapping the palm of his other hand with it.

It was a short blunt club, a sort of teardrop shape with the heavy end wound with what looked like black electrical tape. A homemade blackjack.

François was grinning, clowning, acting out hitting some-one much taller than him—probably a CRS—over the head with the blackjack, and the girls were laughing with him. He gave one of them the club. She fitted it over her hand, testing its weight, then slapped the table with it.

Tracy could hear the noise it made all the way across the room. She felt disgusted, and worse than disgusted: be-trayed. He was as bad as the CRS and the rest of them.

François was too busy vaunting his political virility to even notice her walking past him as she left.

When she got back to the house there was a letter in her mailbox from Liz. She and Isobel were going to be in Portu-gal for two more months and Tracy was welcome to keep on using the apartment until they got back.

No explanations, no excuses, no apologies, but Tracy didn't care anymore. All that was important was that she was home, safe, and that she wasn't going to have to leave.

The smell of something dead and rotting in the downstairs bathroom was back again, stronger than ever, but it didn't bother her the way it had before. The smell was reassuring, its very disgustingness a shield that would hide and protect her against the world outside.

On impulse she pulled the bathroom door open, looked inside. There was a Turkish toilet there, just a hole in the tiled floor with two raised places for your feet on either side, but everything was clean, and the odor wasn't any worse than it had been in the hall.

She didn't leave the yard again for the rest of the week, just stayed home sketching and reading, or lying totally im-mobile in the nook's shadowed warmth for hours on end, listening over and over again to the records the previous ten-ants had left—almost all of the music strange stuff, including a half-dozen records of Tibetan temple music, with black-and-white photos on the cover of lamas blowing into huge conch-shell trumpets or playing instruments carved from

what looked like ivory, but which the liner notes said was
human bone. She could feel things moving inside her, like
great looming shapes rising slowly from the hidden depths of
some inner ocean, and she was content to let them come,
wait for them to show themselves.

On Sunday, she was reworking a Peruvian mountainscape
Carlos had sketched, letting the Tibetan temple music guide
her hand as she filled in the missing details, when her doorbell rang, startling her. She didn't want to answer the door,
but after a moment she decided she had to—it might be
Isobel and Liz, back early.

She turned the music down, opened the door. François
was standing there, holding a packet of letters. She was so
relieved that it wasn't Liz and Isobel, come to steal the
apartment from her, that it took her a moment to realize how
furious she was to see him there, intruding on her privacy.

"What do you want, François?"

"You did not go to school all of last week after Tuesday,
and your friends said they did not see you. I was afraid you
were sick. I asked Marcelo where you lived, and he said you
never came to get your mail. So Marcelo gave me the letters
and I came to see if you were all right."

"I'm okay. Everything's fine."

She took the envelopes he was holding out, waited for
him to go, but he just stood there, made no move to leave.

"I'm okay," she repeated. "Thanks for bringing me my
mail."

"I hope I am not disturbing you." He sounded unsure of
himself. "It was not only that you might be sick. I wanted to
see you."

She supposed she should have been flattered to have finally attracted his interest, but all it meant was that he wasn't
going to go away and leave her alone. "Come in. But I'm
busy. You can only stay a moment."

"Thank you."

She led the way into the apartment, moved the metal
yardstick that was leaning up against the armchair out of the
way. "Sit down. Would you like some water or orange juice?
I don't have anything else."

"Yes. Water would be good." He remained standing.
"Tracy—"

"What?"

"Monika showed this to me." He held out a paper napkin.
She recognized it as the one she'd been doodling on in the

Alliance's café. There was a recognizable likeness of François on it, looking almost as ridiculously idealized as the
drawings Isobel had always done of Carlos.

"It's not very good," she said, dismissing it.

"No—I mean, yes, this is quite good. I did not know you
could draw like that. When I saw it I knew how much I miss
you and I wanted to see you. What I want to ask you is, do
you mind if I keep this?"

In other words, he had been flattered by the way she saw
him and wanted to bask in it some more, feel like some sort
of romantic hero sweeping her off her feet. How could she
have ever failed to see how vain he was? "Of course you can
keep it. Sit down."

"Do you mind if I smoke?"

She minded, but it was easier to just let him smoke than
to try to stop him.

"Go ahead." She threw open the window.

He was looking around the room curiously. "This is very
strange. I never came here before. Isobel and I did not get
along. Really, I did not mind Isobel. It was Carlos who I
could not . . . could not support?"

"Stand."

"Yes. I could not stand him. He was living here with her
all the time. Before he killed himself. You know that he
killed himself?"

"That's why Isobel and Liz are down in Portugal. I'll get
you your water."

While she was getting the bottled water out of the refrigerator François stood up again, went to the window and
leaned out.

"It is so nice here. Like in the country, not like Paris at
all . . ."

He trailed off and she heard him moving around. Feeling
vaguely alarmed—he had no right to rummage around in her
things, spy on her—she looked up, saw him leaning out the
window with the yardstick gripped in both hands like a base-
ball bat.

"What are you doing?"

He didn't look back at her. "There is a nest of insects . . ."
He swiped at it, grunted with satisfaction, then pulled the
yardstick hurriedly back and closed the window.

He turned to her, very pleased with himself. St. George
clubbing the dragon to death and delivering the damsel in
distress. "You will not have to worry about them anymore."

His smug satisfaction irritated her anew. "I didn't have to worry about them at all. They never bothered me."

She reached past him, opened the window again, leaned out to look at the nest.

"Be careful! They are going to sting you!"

"No, they won't." She didn't know why, but she was sure.

Most of the wasps' nest was lying in the driveway below, with wasps buzzing angrily around it, but a fragment was still hanging from the drainpipe, like what was left of some gray fruit that had been devoured by birds while still on the tree.

In some of the ripped-open cylindrical cells she could see metamorphosing pupae that would never complete their transformations in adult wasps; in others, half-eaten caterpillars, still alive and twitching feebly in the sudden light, with the wasps' blind, maggotlike larvae crawling over them. She stared at them, sickened and fascinated.

François reached for the broom again. "They are disgusting. I will kill all of them for you."

"No. Leave them there."

"Leave them? Why?"

"They belong there." She saw he didn't understand. "I want them there."

"You like them? How can you like wasps?"

"Just leave them alone."

He finally realized that she meant what she was saying. "All right." He hesitated a moment, abruptly ill at ease again. "Well, so long as you are certain you are all right—"

"I already told you. I'm fine."

"I must leave now. Are you coming back to school this week?"

"I'm not sure. I've been pretty busy lately."

He gestured at the drawings on the table. "You are drawing all the time?"

"Yes."

"They are very good." He studied them a moment longer, suddenly frowned. "It is very clever, the way you make faces hidden in the mountain, but you must go out more." He looked so self-important, as though he were imparting the wisdom of the ages to her. He probably thought he was. "You are looking too thin. Just like Isobel. It is not good to pass too much of the time alone. Isobel was always here all alone or with Carlos, and this was not good for her. You must see more of Paris."

"I'm sure you're right, François," she said, dripping sincerity. "Maybe you can show me more of Paris soon, when I have a little more time?"

"I would like that." Equally sincere, giving her a long, meaningful, soulful look with his large brown eyes. Reassured and preening himself again.

"I'll walk you downstairs."

"All right."

The wasps' nest was lying on the driveway, the larvae and caterpillars all spilled out of it and writhing on the ground while the adults swarmed around above it in an angry cloud.

"You must not go too close!" He grabbed her by the wrist, tried to hold her back.

She shook him off, suddenly so furious with him for the smug, paternalistic way he kept treating her that she didn't really even care if the wasps stung her or not, and walked deliberately over to the nest. It would be worth getting stung just to shock him out of his self-satisfied superiority.

She bent down and picked up the nest, stood there holding it cradled gently in her hands while the wasps buzzed angrily around her but left her alone.

"You see?" She grinned back at François, delighting in the real fear she could see on his face, taunting him. "As long as you're not scared of them they won't sting you."

"Put it down! Please!"

She looked around, then carried the wasps' nest carefully over to the ruined shed, stretched up onto her tiptoes and put it on the sagging roof. François was still watching from the driveway.

"There," she said, still grinning contemptuously at him, enjoying her triumph. "You see? They didn't hurt me."

"You were very lucky, Tracy. I hope you will come back to school. It is not good to pass all your days alone here."

"Bye, François. Maybe I'll see you at school."

"Good-bye." He scurried off, more like some frightened little rodent than the elegantly cosmopolitan man of the world he was always trying so hard to convince her he was.

Standing there grinning at his retreating back, she suddenly realized what she'd just done—how strange it was, how insane. That was why he had been so frightened, not just because of the wasps, but because what she was doing was insane.

But I was right, so it wasn't insane, she told herself. I knew I didn't have any reason to be scared of the wasps, and I was right. They didn't sting me.

Tracy went back upstairs. The letters François had brought her were on the drafting table. There were four or five from Robbie, a dozen others from various friends in Downer's Grove she'd forgotten until their names recalled them to her.

She picked a letter at random, opened it, read a few lines: Betty Michaelis gushing on about how wonderful her life as a freshman at the University of Wisconsin was, all the exciting people she was meeting.

Tracy crumpled the letter up, threw it away. She couldn't imagine going back to those people, that life.

She went into the bathroom, studied her reflections in the full-length mirror.

There was only a faint gray-white discoloration, like a fleck of dirty paper in her reflected image's eye where the nail hole had been. She grinned at herself, at Carlos and Jean-Luc and all her other selves, showing her teeth, and they grinned back at her.

Isobel's image was filling in rapidly, getting sharper.

The next day the wasps were back outside her window, crawling over what remained of the nest on the drainpipe, rebuilding it. Some of them were cementing grayish fragments of what could only be the old nest into place, but she could already tell the rebuilt nest was going to be much bigger than before. She moved her table over by the window, where she could lean out to get a look at them without getting up, got out a fresh sheet of paper and started work on the mountainscape again, trying to work François's face, the nest's structure and forms, into the underlying contours of the rock.

By Tuesday morning, the nest outside her window was complete again and she was ready to go back to school. The day was already hot. She put on tight black jeans, a clinging T-shirt that emphasized her breasts. On her way out, she took a look at the broken nest on the shed. What cells remained were empty and deserted, the whole thing surrounded by a ring of dead larvae and pupae. The adults must have dragged them all out and killed them when they'd cannibalized the old nest.

Class that day was even easier than usual, though she hadn't spoken French or opened her textbook for a week. She found François in the café and sat down across from him, smiled half-mockingly at him.

"Hello, François." She put a throaty Scarlett O'Hara tone in her voice.

"Hello, Tracy." He seemed nervous, shifty; he wouldn't meet her eyes.

"You ran off so fast, I didn't get a chance to tell you how glad I was you came to see me."

He looked up sharply, started to say something angry, then came to a halt, finally blurted out, "Why did you do it?"

"You mean the wasps?"

"Of course I mean the wasps!"

She waited an instant, still smiling that mocking smile, then said, "Because I knew they wouldn't hurt me. They only sting you if you're scared of them or attack them."

"That's crazy." He downed his coffee, got up to go.

"If it's crazy, François, then why didn't they sting me?"

"I don't know why!"

"Anyway, that's not what you really wanted to ask, is it? What you really meant was, why did I want to do it?"

He nodded, said in a much quieter voice, "Why?"

"Because I wanted to see if you'd be worried for me."

"That's even crazier. Listen, I have to go. I have class now."

"Bye, François. Maybe I'll see you later. Or come by the apartment again."

She stayed in the café the rest of the afternoon, her new self-confidence making it easy to grab the center of attention for herself, so that her classmates were hanging on her every word, laughing with her when she wanted them to laugh.

Near the end of the afternoon François came in. He sat down alone at a table in the corner, ordered a coffee. She acted as though she hadn't seen him.

A few minutes later he pretended to notice that she was there, picked up his coffee and came over to join the group at her table.

She waited another week, until she could see in the mirror that she was ready and she was sure he would accept, before inviting him back to the apartment to spend the night.

When he rushed off the next morning, trying to get back to his own apartment in time to change and look fresh for his eight o'clock class, she could still sense something of him there in the nook, like a faint trace of some scent that was uniquely his, and when she looked at herself, at all her selves, in the mirror she could glimpse the beginning of a

new man-shaped cloudiness there, like a vague hint of con-
densation on the plastic surface.

Isobel's image was clearly visible. Her eyes were open
now, but she still looked like a sleepwalker, unaware of her
surroundings or of the others crowded around her. Tracy
could clearly sense her presence in the whole apartment now,
almost as strongly as she could sense Carlos and Dagmar and
Jean-Luc.

A few weeks later she came back from sketching Tibetan
Tonkas at the Musée Guimet to find Liz sitting at the top of
the stairs, wearing mirror sunglasses and smoking nervously.
She looked so much younger and more vulnerable than
Tracy remembered that for a moment Tracy didn't recognize
her.

"Hi, Tracy."

"Hi, Liz. You're back early. Where's Isobel?"

"Still down in Lisbon. She sneaks into the graveyard at
night and knocks the crosses off the graves—not just his
grave but other graves too, so they won't figure out which
one she's interested in. They've got guards posted now, trying to catch her. She's been able to avoid them so far, but
they're going to catch her pretty soon. I couldn't believe it,
it's like some sort of stupid Keystone Kops movie. She's
crazy."

"You just figured that out now?" Tracy unlocked the
door. "Come on in."

"She never used to be that crazy. The way she's going
now, she's probably going to end up killing herself like
Carlos." Liz studied Tracy. "You look different. Like you've
grown up a lot. And you've lost a lot of weight."

"I know. I've been on a diet."

"You look good. Maybe I should go on a diet too. I was
eating a lot of potatoes and grease down there, and it's going
to be hard to keep myself away from the pastries now that
I'm back here."

Liz moved a stack of watercolors Tracy had done off the
couch without looking at them, sat down. "Do you have anything to drink?"

"Some white wine open in the refrigerator and some orange juice. And water, of course."

"Give me a glass of white wine. And I need an ashtray."
She looked around the apartment critically. "You know,
you've got it looking like when Isobel first moved in here last

year. Except she had Carlos's paintings on that wall, not those beetles. I liked the paintings better. Not much, but better than the beetles."

Tracy handed her a saucer and the glass of wine.

"You're not drinking any yourself?"

"No. When did you get back?"

"Last night." She hesitated. "Look, I'm sorry . . . about not being here to meet you and everything, but Isobel needed me; she said she had to get away from here and she couldn't go alone. I thought you'd be all right—Marcelo could help you if you needed anything. Isobel said you were upset, but I couldn't talk about it in a letter. I tried a couple of times, but it didn't come out right. You're not mad at me any more, are you?"

"No. I was really angry for a while, but I'm starting to like it here now. How's Marcelo?"

"Okay, I guess." She stubbed out her cigarette, took a sip of her wine. "No, actually he's not okay. I let myself in with my key, and he was in bed with someone else. One of my friends, at least I thought she was my friend."

"So what happened?"

"She left. He apologized, said that he would never have slept with her there if he'd known I was coming back."

"What's that mean?"

"It means he would have slept with her somewhere else. So I'm moving out." She lit another cigarette, took a long drag on it. "I was planning to move out anyway, as soon as you got here. I've been saving the money Mother's been sending us all along so we could get a really nice place together, but that was part of why I didn't write, I didn't want to tell you about Marcelo in a letter. I wanted to see you first. Only this whole thing with Isobel just made it that much harder. Do you understand?"

"Sure."

"Good." Liz took another sip of her wine, glanced around nervously. "Can you open the window? It's too stuffy in here; it makes me feel claustrophobic. Like the walls are closing in on me. Let's get some fresh air."

Tracy walked over to the stained-glass window. Fleshy, almost transparent, pinkish-purple worms, the color of swollen veins beneath a baby's skin, were crawling languidly over the roses inside the glass. She opened the window, glanced at the wasps' nest outside just as a wasp landed on it, clutching

a paralyzed caterpillar much larger around than the wasp
itself.

"That is, if you still want to split an apartment," Liz said
behind her. "Marcelo told me you've been seeing François a
lot."

"He stays here sometimes, but that doesn't mean I want
to move in with him." Tracy turned back to Liz. "I came to
Paris to be with you. Look, why don't we stay here for a
while? Until Isobel gets back. We can always find someplace
else later."

Liz shook her head. She looked pink and fleshy, petulant.
"I don't like it here anymore. It's too creepy after all that
time with Isobel trying to appease her dead brother. Did she
tell you how Carlos killed himself?"

"No."

"It was in all the papers down there, with photos and all.
He was staying in a hotel there, and he just went and lay
down on the bathroom floor and opened up his stomach with
a kitchen knife. He didn't just cut a nice clean line across it,
either—you know, like the Japanese do when they commit
hara-kiri. He sliced a big oval a half inch deep all the way
around his stomach. They found him holding on to the oval,
like he'd started to peel it away so he could get at something
inside, but he died before he could finish. Anyway, Isobel
wanted us to stay in the room he did it in, but I said no, so
she stayed there and I ended up across the hall."

"He did that down in Portugal, not here," Tracy said.
"The only thing wrong with this apartment is I've been so
lonely here alone. Besides, you're better off with me than
with Marcelo. Just until we can find an apartment of our
own, someplace we really like. The longer we live here without paying rent, the more money we can save up to get a
place we'll really love."

The wasp dragged the caterpillar down across the gray
papier-mâché surface, then up in through the hole at the
bottom end of the nest. Inside, it would lay its eggs in the
caterpillar's paralyzed body, then wall the caterpillar away in
a cell where the maggotlike larvae that hatched in its living
body could feed on it as they grew slowly toward maturity
and metamorphosis. Some of the pupae would be almost
ready to complete their transformations and emerge from
their cells as full-grown adults, ready to begin reproducing
themselves in the bodies of their own paralyzed prey.

Tracy closed the window again. She turned to Liz, smiled

beseechingly at her. "Please, Liz. I've been so alone here. I need you here with me."

She could see herself reflected in Liz's sunglasses: a naive, defenseless young girl begging her sophisticated older sister for help, with Isobel and Carlos and all the others crowded in behind her, watching her performance. François was there with them, still faceless and blind, unaware, but taking on definition, beginning to come into sharper focus.

Liz hesitated, finally nodded. "All right. But just until we can find a place of our own."

Inside the stained-glass window, the soft, fleshy purple worms crawled over the roses, slowly eating them away from within.

Endless Night

by KARL EDWARD WAGNER

Karl Wagner is the lion of dark fantasy, equally admired for his works in heroic fantasy and for his eloquent, polished horror stories. One of the great unresolved issues of the twentieth century is: Who is to blame for systematic evil? Who is to blame for concentration camps, racism, Viet Nam? Almost as disturbing as the symptoms of evil is the realization that when we look for tidy cause-and-effect relationships between bad people and bad things, we find instead ordinary people doing their jobs. If art is the shining surface which allows us to glimpse impossible evil without turning our souls to stone, Karl Edward Wagner's story "Endless Night" offers us a reflected glimpse of the psychology of systematic evil.

> I runne to death, and death meets me as fast,
> And all my pleasures are like yesterday;
> —John Donne, *Holy Sonnet I*

The dream landscape always stretched out the same. It had become as familiar as the neighborhood yards of his childhood, as the condo-blighted streets of his middle years. Dreams had to have some basis in reality—or so his therapists had tried to reassure him. If this one did, it was of some unrecognized reality.

They stood upon the edge of the swamp, although somehow he understood that this had once been a river, and then a lake, as all became stagnant and began to sink. The bridge was a relic, stretched out before them to the island—on the far shore—beyond. It was a suspension bridge, from a period which he could not identify with certainty, but suspected was of the early 1930s judging by the Art Deco pylons. It seemed ludicrously narrow and wholly inappropriate for its task. As the waters had risen, or the land mass had sunk, its roadway, ridged and as gap-toothed as a railway trestle, had settled into the water's surface—so that midway across one must slosh through ankle-deep water, feeling beneath the scum for the solid segments of roadway. Spanish moss festooned the fraying cables; green lichens fringed the greener verdigris of bronze faces staring out from rotting concrete pylons. Inscriptions, no doubt explaining their importance, were blurred beyond legibility.

It was always a breathless relief to reach the upward-sloping paving of the far end, scramble toward the deserted shoreline beyond. His chest would be aching by then, as though the warm, damp air he tried to suck into his lungs were devoid of sustenance. There were ripples in the water, not caused by any current, and while he had never seen anything within the tepid depths, he knew it was essential not to linger in the crossing.

His companion or guide—he sometimes thought of her as his muse—always seemed to know the way, so he followed her. Usually she was blonde. Her bangs obscured her eyes, and he only had an impression of her face in profile—thin, with straight nose and sharp chin. He sensed that her cheekbones would be pronounced, her eyes large and watchful and widely spaced. She was barefoot. Sometimes she tugged up her skirt to hold its hem above the water, more often she was wearing only a long T-shirt over what he assumed was a swimsuit. He realized that he knew her, but he could never remember her name.

He supposed he looked like himself. The waters gave back no reflection.

It—the building—dominated the shoreline beyond. From the other side he often thought of it as an office building, possibly some sort of apartment complex. He was certain that he could see lights shining from its many-tiered windows. It appeared to have been constructed of some salmon-hued brick, or perhaps the color was another illusion of the declining sun. It was squat, as broad as its dozen-or-more storys of height, and so polyhedral as to seem almost round. Its architecture impressed him as featureless—stark walls and windows, Bauhaus utilitarian. Either its creator lacked any imagination or else had sacrificed external form to unguessable function.

The features of the shoreline never impressed themselves upon his memory. There was a rising of land, vague blotches of trees, undergrowth. The road dragged slowly upward toward the building. Trees overhung from either side, reaching toward one another, garlanded with hanging vines and moss —darkening skies a leaden ribbon overhead. The pavement was cracked and broken—calling to mind orphaned segments of a WPA-era two-lane highway, bypassed alongside stretches of the interstate, left to decompose into the wounded earth. Its surface was swept clean. Not disused; rather, seldom used.

Perhaps too frequently used.

If there were other structures near the building, he never noticed them. Perhaps there were none; perhaps they were simply inconsequential in comparison. Sometimes he thought of an immense office building raised out of the wilderness of an industrial park or a vast stadium born of the leveled wasteland of urban renewal, left alone and alien in a region where the *genius loci* ultimately reconquered. A barren space, encroached upon by that which was beyond, surrounded the building—sometimes grass-latticed pavement (parking lot?), sometimes a scorched and eroded barrier of weeds (ground zero?).

Desolation, not wholly dead.

Abandoned, not entirely forgotten.

The lights in the windows, which he was certain he had seen from across the water, never shone as they entered.

There was a wire fence, sometimes: barbed wire leaning from its summit, or maybe insulated balls of brown ceramic nestling high-voltage lines. No matter. All was rusted, corroded, sagging like the skeletal remains that rotted at its base. When there was a fence at all.

If there was a fence, gaps pierced the wire barrier like the rotted lace of a corpse's mantilla. Sometimes the gate lay in wreckage beneath its graffitied arch: Abandon Hope. Joy Through Work. War Is Peace. Ask Not.

My Honor Is Loyalty.

One of his dreams is a fantasy of Nazis.

He knows that they are Nazis because they are all wearing jack boots and black uniforms, SS insignia and swastika armbands, monocles and Luger pistols. And there are men in slouch-brim hats and leather overcoats, all wearing thick glasses—Gestapo, they have to be. White-clad surgeons with button-up-the-back surplices, each one resembling Lionel Atwill, suck glowing fluids into improbable hypodermics, send tentative spurts pulsing from their needles.

Monocles and thick-lensed spectacles and glass-hard blue eyes peer downward. Their faces are distorted and hideous—as if he, or they, someone, is viewing this perspective through a magnifying glass. The men in black uniforms are goose-stepping and Heil-Hitlering in geometric patterns behind the grinning misshapen faces of the doctors.

The stairway is of endless black marble, polished to a mirror-sheen, giving back no reflection. The SS officers, alike as a thousand black-uniformed puppets, are goose-stepping in orderly, powerful ranks down the polished stairway. Toward them, up the stairway, a thousand blonde and blue-eyed Valkyries, sequin-painted and brass-brassiered, flaxen locks bleached and bobbed and marcelled, are marching in rhythm—a Rockette chorus line of Lorelei.

> *Wir werden weiter marschieren,*
> *wenn alles in Sherben fällt,*
> *denn heute gehört uns Deutchland*
> *und morgen die ganze Welt!*

Needles plunge downward.

Inward.

Distancing.

Der Führer leans and peers inward. He wipes the needles with his tongue and snorts piggishly. *Our final revenge,* Hitler promises, in a language he seems to understand. The dancers merge upon the stairway, form a thousand black-and-white swastikas as they twist their flesh together into DNA coils.

Sieg Heil!

Someday.

A thousand bombs burn a thousand coupled moths into a thousand flames.

A thousand, less one.

Distance.

While he hated and feared all of his fantasies, he usually hated and feared this one most of all. When he peered through the windows of the building, he saw rows of smoke-stacks belching uncounted souls into the recoiling sky.

But often there was no fence. Only a main entrance.

A Grand Entrance. Glass and aluminum and tile. Uncorroded, but obscured by thin dust. A receptionist's desk. A lobby of precisely arranged furniture: art moderne or coldly functional—nonetheless serving no function in the sterile emptiness.

No one to greet him, to verify an appointment, to ask for plastic cards and indecipherable streams of numbers. He always thought of this as some sort of hospital, possibly abandoned in the panic of some unleashed plague virus.

He always avoided the lifts. (Shouldn't he think of them as elevators?) Instead he followed her through the deserted (were they ever occupied?) hallways and up the hollow stairwell that gave back no echo to their steps.

There is another fantasy that he cannot will away.

He is conscious of his body in this fantasy, but no more able to control his body than to control his fantasy.

He is small—a child, he believes, looking at the boyish arms and legs that are restrained to the rails of the hospital bed, and examining the muted tenderness in the faces of the white-clad supplicants who insert the needles and apply the electrodes to his flesh.

Electric current makes a nova of his brain. Thoughts and memories scatter like a deck of cards thrown against the sudden wind. Drugs hold his raped flesh half-alert against the torture. Smoke-stacks spew forth a thousand dreams. All must be arranged in a New Order.

A thousand cards dance in changing patterns across his vision. Each card has a face, false as a waxen mask. His body strains against the leather cuffs; his scream is taken by a soggy wad of tape on a wooden paddle.

The cards are telling him something, something very essential. He does not have time to read their message.

I'm not a fortune teller! he screams at the shifting patterns of cards. The wadded tape steals his protests.

The rape is over. They are wheeling him away.

The cards filter down from their enhanced freedom, falling like snowflakes in a dying dream.

And then he counts them all.

All are there. And in their former order.

Order must be maintained.

The Old Order is stronger.

But he knows—almost for certain—that he has never been a patient in any hospital. Ever.

His health is perfect. All too perfect.

She always led him through the maze within—upward, onward, forward. The Eternal Female/Feminine Spirit-Force. Goethe's personal expression of the ultimate truth of human existence—describing a power that transcended and revoked an informed commitment to damnation—translated awkwardly into pretentious nonsense in English. He remembered that he had never read Goethe, could not understand a word of German.

His therapists said it was a reaction to his adoption in infancy as a German war orphan by an American family. The assertive and anonymous woman represented his natural mother, whom he had never known. But his birth certificate proved that he had been born to unexceptional middle-class American parents in Cleveland, Ohio.

And his memories of them were as faded and unreal as time-leached color slides. Memories fade before light, and into night.

False memories. Reality a sudden celluloid illusion.

Lightning rips the night.

Doctor! It's alive!

Another fantasy evokes (or is invoked by, say his therapists) visions of *Macbeth,* of scary campfire stories, of old films scratched and eroded from too many showings. His (disremembered) parents (probably) only allowed him to partake of the first, but Shakespeare knew well the dark side of dreams.

Sometimes he is on a desolate stretch of moor, damp and furred with tangles of heather. (He supposes it is heather, remembering *Macbeth.*) Or perhaps he is on a high mountain, with barren rocks thrusting above dark forest. (He insists that he has never read *Faust,* but admits to having seen *Fantasia.*) Occasionally he stands naked within a circle of standing stone, huge beneath the empty sky. (He confesses to having read an article about Stonehenge.) And in this same Gothic context, he has another such fantasy, and he never speaks of its imperfectly remembered fragments to anyone—not to lovers, therapists, priests, or his other futile confidants.

It is, again (to generalize), a fantasy in which he is again the observor. Passive, certainly. Helpless, to be sure. But the restraints hold a promise of power to be feared, of potential to be unleashed.

Hooded figures surround him, center upon his awareness. Their cloaks are sometimes dark and featureless, sometimes fantastically embroidered and colored. He never sees their faces.

He never sees himself, although he senses he stands naked and vulnerable before them.

He is there. In their midst. *They* see him.

It is all that matters.

They reach/search/take/give/violate/empower.

There is no word in English.

His therapists tell him this is a homosexual rape fantasy.

There is no word in any language.

There is only the power.

The stairway climbed inexorably as she led him upward into the building. Returning—and they always returned, he knew now—the descent would be far more intolerable, for he would have his thoughts to carry with him.

A stairwell door: very commonplace usually (a Hilton or a Hyatt?), but sometimes of iron-bound oak, or maybe no more than a curtain. No admonition. No advice. On your own. He would have welcomed *Fire Exit Only* or *Please Knock*.

She always opened the door—some atavistic urge of masculine courtesy always surfaced, but he was never fast enough or certain enough—and she held it for him, waiting and demanding.

Beyond, there was always the same corridor, circling and enclosing the building. If there were any significance to the level upon which they emerged, it was unknown to him. She might know, but he never asked her. It terrified him that she might know.

There is innocence, if not guiltlessness, in randomness.

He decided to look upon the new reality beyond the darkened windows of the corridor. She was impatient, but she could not deny him this delay, this respite.

Outside the building he saw stretches of untilled farmland, curiously demarcated by wild hedgerows and stuttering walls of toppled stone. He moved to the next window and saw only a green expanse of pasture, its grassy limitlessness ridged by memories of ancient fields and villages.

He paused here, until she caught at his arm, pulled him away. The next window—only a glimpse—overlooked a city that he was given no time to recognize, had he been able to do so through knowledge of the fire that consumed it.

There were doors along the other side of the corridor. He pretended that some might open upon empty apartments, that others led to vacant offices. Sometimes there were curtained recesses that suggested confessionals, perhaps secluding some agent of a higher power—although he had certainly never been a Catholic, and such religion that he recalled only underscored the futility of redemption.

She drew aside a curtain, beckoned him to enter.

He moved past her, took his seat.

Not a confessional. He had known that. He always knew where she would lead him.

The building was only a façade, changing as his memory decayed and fragmented, recognizing only one reality in a dream-state that had consumed its dreamer.

A stadium. A coliseum. An arena.

Whatever its external form, it inescapably remained unchanged in its function.

This time the building's interior was a circular arena, dirt-floored and ringed by many tiers of wooden bleachers. The wooden benches were warped and weathered silver-gray. Any paint had long since peeled away, leaving splinters and rot. The building was only a shell, hollow as a whitened skull, encircled by derelict rows of twisted benches and sagging wooden scaffolding.

The seats were all empty. The seats had been empty, surely, for many years.

He sensed a lingering echo of "Take Me Out to the Ball Game" played on a steam calliope. Before his time. Casey at the bat. This was Muddville. Years after. Still no joy.

He desperately wished another reality, but he knew it would always end the same. The presentation might be random, might have some unknowable significance. What mattered was that he knew where he really was and why he was here.

Whether he wanted to be here was of no consequence.

She suggested, as always. *The woman at the bank who wouldn't approve the car loan. Send for her.*

She was only doing her job.

But you hated her in that moment. And you remember that hatred.

Involuntarily, he thought of her.

The numberless windows of the building's exterior pulsed with light.

A window opened.

Power, not light, sent through. And returned.

And the woman was in the arena. Huddled in the dirt, too confused to sense fear.

The unseen crowd murmured in anticipation.

He stared down at the woman, concentrating, channeling the power within his brain.

She screamed, as invisible flames consumed her being. Her scream was still an echo when her ashes drifted to the ground.

He looked for movement among the bleachers. Whatever watched from there remained hidden.

Another, she urged him.

He tried to think of those who had created him, this time to send for them. But the arena remained empty. Those he hated above all others were long beyond the vengeance of even his power.

Forget them. There are others.

But I don't hate them.

If not now, then soon you will. There is an entire world to hate.

And, he understood, too many nights to come.

> Some are Born to sweet delight,
> Some are Born to Endless Night.
> —William Blake,
> *Auguries of Innocence*

Trust Me

by JOSEPH LYONS

Joseph Lyons is a new writer and a student of Marta Randall. His first published story, "Trust Me" erodes our comfortable notions of the nature of horror and of reality. Because Lyons tells his tale with fablelike economy, of all stories in this volume his is the shortest.

At the first cry he looked up at the clock on the mantel and nodded. Almost four minutes late tonight.

At the second cry, the one that usually faded into a stifled moan, he rustled his newspaper and brought it closer to his face.

Thirty seconds later, with the first clear scream, he tightened all over, holding his breath, and slowly lowered his newspaper. Across the room his wife raised her head from her book.

"That child," she said, speaking into the air. When he said nothing: "The least a person might do is recognize when it's their turn."

He shook his newspaper. "She's old enough, goddammit, not to do this every night."

The next scream was louder. It rose and trailed off, erupting in muffled words.

He swore to himself and pushed himself heavily to his feet. The overstuffed chair sighed as he rose. "Next time . . . ," he said. "Just remember, it's your turn next time."

She waited until he had left the room and then dropped her eyes to her book.

The hallway was dark, because he insisted that no child nine years old still needed a night light. In the small bedroom the girl was already sitting up in bed, her fingers wound skin tight around the edges of the blanket clutched at her throat. He sat down on the bed and turned on her table lamp, and her eyes winced at the sudden spill of light between them. Deep shadows darkened the rest of the room.

"Don't tell me," he said, "let me guess. They came in that window, right?"

She nodded and swallowed, her eyes fixed on his.

"And then they saw you, and they came after you. They were all dark and crawly, slimy things—"

A soundless plea formed on her lips.

"—with long green fingers reaching for you. And they came up on the bed and slid along there, right toward you, little by little . . . right . . . toward . . . you . . ."

She choked back a scream and whispered faintly, "Don't. Stop."

He waited, watching her. "I don't know," he said. "Just what do you want? Damn it, what do you want me to do?" And when she only stared at him in silence, her face trembling, he said, "Okay, then, tell me: Where are they now?"

"They were so real, so real." She shook her head helplessly. "You don't believe me."

"That's right. I don't believe you." He glared at her until she looked down. "And I don't think you were asleep, either."

"But I was asleep. I had a dream. It was a nightmare."

He said, leaning slowly toward her, "No it wasn't." The bed creaked beneath him. "You didn't dream them at all. And you know why? Because they're real."

She searched his face, then twitched her gaze away, toward the dark corners behind him. A gust of wind flicked the tips of the curtains against his neck. He was saying: "Long green slimy things. With hands that reach out toward you . . ."

Her mouth opened before she could speak. "No," she said. "You never told me they were real."

"Well, I guess now you're old enough to know." He settled back, watching the blanket drop away from her clutching fingers, her thin white shoulders hunched forward, a vein throbbing on the side of her neck.

"Then do you see them too?"

He said nothing. He could almost feel her arms hugging

herself for comfort. His anger rose. "They're real, all right, believe me. And they came in the house to get you. Down the wall and across the floor to your bed—"

"Why me?" She shivered, her whispered voice almost soundless. Outside, the dry slither of wind among branches, of branch against window.

"How do I know?" he said. "Maybe they only come after kids." He saw the silent tears begin to stain her cheeks. "I never told you. All these times before, I figured it'd be better if you didn't know, if you thought it was a nightmare."

Her head moved helplessly to one side and then to the other, her gaze wandering off, over his shoulder, toward the steadily flickering curtain that was pushed by the wind. "How do you know they're real?"

"Because my father told me, that's how. Just like I'm telling you now." And he closed his eyes to hear again the high thin scream, endlessly prolonged, as it echoed down the corridors of his childhood.

In the doorway her mother nodded—once, twice, and the girl looked from her to the shadows that moved suddenly behind her father.

He felt the little fingers, like edges of the wind, playing with the hair on the back of his neck.

The Fetch

by ROBERT AICKMAN

A master of the English ghost story, Robert Aickman is the author of a number of collections of "strange stories" and his novel The Model *has just been published by Arbor House. He died in 1981, leaving a few unpublished stories. His work is characterized by significant and specific detail and the absolute refusal to allow that detail to resolve comfortably into a secure pattern. Here, a man unable to escape his heritage is destined to haunt his ancestral home while still alive.*

I

In all that matters, I was an only child. There was a brother once, but I never saw him, even though he lived several years. My father, a Scottish solicitor or law agent, and very much a Scot, applied himself early to becoming an English barrister, and, as happens to Scots, was made a Judge of the High Court, when barely in middle age.

In Court, he was stupendous. From the first, I was taken once every ten days by Cuddy, my nurse, to the public gallery in order to behold him and hearken to him for forty minutes or so. If I made the slightest stir or whimper, it was subtly but effectively repaid me; on those and all other occasions. Judges today are neither better nor worse than my father, but they are different.

At home, my father, only briefly visible, was a wraith with a will and power that no one available could resist. The will and power lingered undiminished when my father was not in the house, which, in the nature of things, was for most of the time. As well as the Court, and the chambers, there were the club and the dining club, the livery company and the military historical society, all of which my father attended with dedication and sacrifice. With equal regularity, he pursued the cult of self-defense, in several different branches and with little heed for the years. He was an elder of a Scottish church in a London suburb, at some distance from where we lived. He presided over several successive Royal Commissions, until one day he threw up his current presidency in a rage of principle, and was never invited again. After his death, I realized that a further center of his interest had been a club of a different kind, a very expensive and sophisticated one. I need not say how untrue it is that Scots are penny-scraping in all things.

I was terrified of my father. I feared almost everything, but there was nothing I feared more than to encounter my father or to pick up threads from his intermittent murmurings in the corridors and closets. We lived in a huge house at the center of Belgravia. No Judge could afford such an establishment now. In addition, there was the family home of Pollaporra—modest, comfortless, and very remote. Our ancestry was merely legal and commercial, though those words have vastly more power in Scotland than in England. In Scotland, accomplishments are preferred to graces. As a child, I was never taken to Pollaporra. I never went there at all until much later, on two occasions, as I shall unfold.

I was frightened also of Cuddy, properly Miss Hester MacFerrier; and not least when she rambled on, as Scottish women do, of the immense bags and catches ingathered at Pollaporra by our ancestors and their like-minded acquaintances. She often emphasized how cold the house was at all times and how far from a "made road." Only the elect could abide there, one gathered; but there were some who could never bear to leave, and who actually shed tears upon being compelled by advancing winter to do so. When the snow was on the ground, the house could not be visited at all; not even by the factor to the estate, who lived down by the sea loch, and whose name was Mason. Cuddy had her own methods for compelling the attention of any child to every detail she cared to impart. I cannot recall when I did not know about Mason. He was precisely the man for a Scottish nursemaid to uphold as an example.

My father was understood to dislike criminal cases, which, as an advanced legal theorist and technician, he regarded with contempt. He varied the taking of notes at these times by himself sketching in lightning caricature the figures in the dock to his left. The caricatures were ultimately framed, thirty or forty at a time; whereafter Haverstone, the odd-job man, spent upwards of a week hanging them at different places in our house, according to precise directions written out by my father, well in advance. Anybody who could read at all, could at any time read every word my father wrote, despite the millions of words he had to set down as a duty. Most of the other pictures in our house were engravings after Landseer and Millais and Paton. Generations of Scottish aunts and uncles had also contributed art works of their own, painstaking and gloomy.

I was afraid of Haverstone, because of his disfigurements and his huge size. I used to tiptoe away whenever I heard his breathing. I never cared or dared to ask how he had come to be so marked. Perhaps my idea of his bulk was a familiar illusion of childhood. We shall scarcely know; in that Haverstone, one day after my seventh birthday, fell from the iron railway bridge at Southall into the main road beneath and was destroyed by a lorry. Cuddy regarded Haverstone with contempt and never failed to claim that my father employed him only out of pity. I never knew what he was doing on the railway bridge, but later I became aware of the huge mental hospital nearby and drew obvious conclusions.

My mother I adored and revered. For better or for worse, one knows the words of Stendhal: "My mother was a charming woman, and I was in love with my mother . . . I wanted to cover my mother with kisses and wished there weren't any clothes. . . . She too loved me passionately. She kissed me, and returned those kisses sometimes with such passion that she had to leave me." Thus it was with me; and, as was with Stendhal, so was the sequel.

My mother was very dark, darker than me, and very exotic. I must suppose that only the frenzy of Scottish lust brought my father to marrying her. At such times, some Scots lose hold on all other considerations; in a way never

noticed by me among Englishmen. By now, my father's fit
was long over. At least he did not intrude upon us, as Stendhal's father did. I am sure that jealousy was very prominent
in my father, but perhaps he scorned to show it. He simply
kept away from his wife entirely. At least as far as I could
see. And I saw most things, though facing far from all of
them, and acknowledging none of them.

Day after day, night after night, I lay for hours at a time in
my mother's big bed, with my head between her breasts, and
my tongue gently extended, as in infancy. The room was perfumed, the bed was perfumed, her night dress was perfumed,
she was perfumed. To a child, it set the idea of Heaven. Who
wants any other? My mother's body, as well as being so dark,
was softer all over than anyone else's, and sweeter than anything merely physical and fleeting, different and higher altogether. Her rich dark hair, perfumed of itself, fell all about
me, as in the East.

There was no social life in our home, no visiting acquaintances, no family connections, no chatter. My father had detached himself from his own folk by his marriage. My mother
loved no one but me. I am sure of that. I was in a position to
know. The only callers were her hairdresser, her dressmaker,
her maker of shoes and boots, her parfumier, her fabricator
of lingerie, and perhaps one or two others of the kind. While
she was shorn, scented, and fitted, I sat silently in the corner
on a little gray hassock. None of the callers seemed to object. They knew the world: what it was like; and would soon
enough be like for me. They contained themselves.

I was there whatever my mother did; without exception.

Cuddy dragged me off at intervals for fresh air, but not
for very long. I could see for myself that Cuddy, almost familiar with my father, was afraid of my mother. I never knew
why, and am far from certain now, but was glad of the fact. It
was the key circumstance that transformed the potential of
utter wretchedness for me into utter temporary bliss.

My mother taught me all I know that matters; smiling and
laughing and holding me and rewarding me, so that always I
was precocity incarnate; alike in all concepts, dignity, and
languages. Unfortunately, my mother was often ill, commonly for days, sometimes for weeks; and who was there to
care, apart from me, who could do nothing—even if there
was something others could have done? My lessons ceased
for a spell, but as soon as possible, or sooner, were bravely
resumed.

Later, I strayed through other places of education, defending myself as best I could—and not unsuccessfully either—and, of what I needed, learning what I could. It was not my father who despatched me. He regarded me without interest or expectation. To him I was an enduring reminder of a season's weakness. The ultimate care of me lay with Trustees, as often in Scotland; though only once did I see them as individuals, and hardly even then, because the afternoon was overcast, and all the lights were weak, for some reason that I forget.

Before all that formal education, I encountered the woman on the stairs. This brief and almost illusory episode was the first of the two turning points in my life and I suspect the more important.

I had been playing on the landing outside the door of my mother's room. I do not know how long she had been ill that time. I feared to count the days, and never did so. I am not sure that it was longer than on various previous occasions. I was alarmed, as always; but not especially alarmed.

My mother had been instrumental in my being given a railway, a conjuring outfit, and a chemical set: those being the things that small boys were supposed to like. My father should have given me soldiers, forts, and guns; possibly a miniature, but accurate, cricket bat: but he never once gave me anything, or spoke at all in our house if he could avoid it—except, on unpredictable occasions, to himself, memorably, as I have hinted.

I mastered the simple illusions, and liked the outfit, but had no one to awe. Even my mother preferred to hug me than for me to draw the ace of spades or a tiny white rabbit from her soft mouth. The chemical effects, chlorine gas and liquid air, I never mastered at that time, nor wished to. The railway I loved (no other word), though it was very miniature: neither 1 gauge (in those days) nor 0 gauge, but something smaller than 00. The single train, in the Royal Bavarian livery of before the First World War, clinked round a true circle; but en route it traversed a tunnel with two cows painted on top and one painted sheep, and passed through two separate stations, where both passengers and staff were painted on the tin walls, and all the signs were in Gothic.

That day, I had stopped playing, owing to the beating of my heart; but I had managed to pack everything into the boxes. I needed no bidding to do that, and never had done. I was about to lug the heap upstairs, which by then I could perfectly well do. I heard the huge clock in the hall strike half past three. The clock had come from Pollaporra, and reached to the ceiling. I looked at my watch, as I heard it. I was always doing that. It was very late autumn, just before Christmas, but not yet officially winter. There is nothing in this world I know better than exactly what day of the year it was. It was forever written in the air before me.

My ears were made keen by always listening. Often, wherever I was, even at the top of the house, I waited motionless for the enormous clock to strike, lest the boom take me by surprise. But the ascending woman was upon me before I had heard a footfall. I admit that all the carpets were thickest Brussels and Wilton. I often heard footfalls, nonetheless, especially my father's strangely uneven tread. I do not think I heard the woman make a sound from first to last. But last was very close to first.

She had come up the stairs, beyond doubt, even though I had neither heard nor seen anything; because by the time I did observe her, she was still two or three steps from the top of the flight. It was a wide staircase, but she was ascending in a very curious way, far further from the rail than was necessary and far nearer to the wall, and with her head and face actually turned to the wall.

At that point, I did hear something. I heard someone shut the front door below; which could not be seen from where I stood. I was surprised that I had not heard the door being opened, and the words of enquiry and caution. I remember my surprise. All these sounds were unusual in our house at that time.

I felt the cold air that the woman had brought in with her from the December streets and squares, and a certain cold smell; but she never once turned toward me. She could easily have been quite unaware of me; but I was watching her every motion. She had black hair, thin and lank. She was dressed in a dirty red and blue plaid of some kind, tightly wound. I was of course used to pictures of people in plaids. The woman's shoes were cracked and very unsuited to the slush outside. She moved with short steps, and across the carpet she left a thin trail of damp, though I knew that it was not raining. It was one of those things that I always knew. Everything about the woman was of a kind that children particularly fear and dislike. Women, when frightening, are to children enormously more frightening than any man or men.

I think I was too frightened even to shrink back. As the

woman tottered past, I stood there with my boxes beside me. My idea of her motion was that she had some difficulty with it, but was sustained by extreme need. Perhaps that is a fancy that only came to me later.

I never had any doubt about where the woman was going but, even so, I was unable to move or to speak or to do anything at all.

As she traversed the few yards of the landing, she extended her right arm and grimy hand out from her plaid, the hand and arm nearer to me, still without in any degree turning her head. In no time at all, and apparently without looking, she had opened the door of my sweet mother's room, had passed within, and had shut the door behind her.

I suppose it is unnecessary for me to say that when my mother was ill, her door was never locked; but perhaps it is not unnecessary. I myself never entered at such times. My mother could not bear me to see her when she was ill.

There was no one sympathetic to whom I could run crying and screaming. In such matters, children are much influenced by the facilities available. For me, there was only my mother, and, in fact, I think I might actually have gone in after the woman, though not boldly. However, before I was able to move at all, I heard Cuddy's familiar clump ascending the stair behind me as I gazed at the shut door.

"What are you doing now?" asked Cuddy.

"Who was that?" I asked.

"Who was who?" Cuddy asked me back. "Or what?"

"The woman who's gone in there."

"Whist! It's time *you* were in bed with Christmas so near."

"It *wasn't* Father Christmas," I cried.

"I daresay not," said Cuddy. "Because it wasn't anybody."

"It was, Cuddy. It *was*. Go in and look."

It seems to me that Cuddy paused at that for a moment, though it may only have been my own heart that paused.

It made no difference.

"It's bed for you, man," said Cuddy. "You're overexcited, and we all know where that ends."

Needless to say, it was impossible for me to sleep, either in the dark or in the light: the choice being always left to me, which was perhaps unusual in those days. I heard the hours and the half hours all through the night, and at one or two o'clock my father's irregular step, always as if he were dodging something or someone imperfectly seen, and his periodical mutterings and jabberings as he plodded.

All was deeply upsetting to a child, but I must acknowledge that by then I was reasonably accustomed to most of it. One explanation was that I had no comparisons available. As far as I knew, all people behaved as did those in my home. It is my adult opinion that many more, in fact, do so behave than is commonly supposed, or at least acknowledged.

Still, that night must have proved exceptional for me; because when Cuddy came to call me in the morning, she found that I was ill too. Children, like adults, have diseases that it is absurd to categorize. Most diseases, perhaps all, are mainly a collapse or part-collapse of the personality. I daresay a name for that particular malady of mine might in those days have been brain fever. I am not sure that brain fever is any longer permitted to be possible. I am sure that my particular malady went on for weeks, and that when I was once more deemed able to make sense out of things, I learned that my mother was dead, and, indeed, long buried. No one would tell me where. I further gathered that there was no memorial.

About four weeks after that, or so it now seems to me, but perhaps it was longer, I was told that my father was proposing to remarry, though he required the consent of the Trustees. A judge was but a man as far as the Trustees were concerned, a man within the scope of their own settlement and appointment. Thus it was that I acquired my stepmother, née Miss Agnes Emily Fraser, but at the moment a widow, Mrs. Johnny Robertson of Baulk. To her the Trustees had no objection, it seemed.

I still have no idea of why my father married Agnes Robertson, or why he remarried at all. I do not think it can have been the motive that prompted his earlier marriage. From all that, since his death, I have learned of his ways, the notion would seem absurd. It was true that the lady had wealth. In the end, the Trustees admitted as much; and that much of it was in Burmah Oil. I doubt whether this was the answer either. I do not think that more money could have helped my father very much. I am not sure that by then anything could have helped him. This is confirmed by what happened to him, conventional in some ways though it was.

Moreover, the marriage seemed to me to make no difference to his daily way of life: the bench, the chambers, the club, the dining club, the livery company, the military historical society, the self-defense classes, the kirk; or, I am sure, to those other indulgences. On most nights, he continued to ponder and by fits and starts to cry out. I still tiptoed swiftly away and, if possible, hid myself when I heard his step. I seldom set eyes upon my stepmother, though of course I am not saying that I never did. I took it for granted that her attitude to me was at least one thing that she shared with my father. That seemed natural. I found it hard to see what else she had any opportunity of sharing. It had, of course, always been Cuddy to whom I was mainly obliged for information about my father's habits and movements, in so far as she knew them. Cuddy was much less informative about my stepmother.

One new aspect of my own life was that my lessons had stopped. I believe that for more than a year I had nothing to do but keep out of the way and play, as far as was possible. Now there seemed to be no callers at all, and assuredly not parfumiers and designers of lingerie. No doubt my stepmother's circle was entirely in Scotland, and probably to the north of the Forth and Clyde Canal. She would not have found it easy to create an entirely new circle in Belgravia. I suppose there were two reasons why I suffered less than I might have done from the unsatisfactory aspects of my situation. The first was that I could hardly suffer more than I was suffering from my sweet mother's death. The second reason was my suspicion that any other life I might be embarked upon would be even more unsatisfactory.

In the end, the Trustees intervened, as I have said; but, before that, Cuddy had something to impart, at long last, about my stepmother. She told me that my stepmother was drinking.

It debarred her, Cuddy informed me in a burst of gossip, from appearing in public very often. That was exactly how Cuddy expressed it; with a twinkle or a glint or whatever may be the Scottish word for such extra intimations. I gathered that my stepmother seldom even dressed herself, or permitted herself to be dressed by Cuddy. One thing I was not told and do not positively know is whether or not the poor lady was drinking as hard as this before her second marriage. It is fair to her to say that the late Johnny Robertson was usually described as a scamp or rogue. Certainly my stepmother's current condition was something that would have had to be concealed by everyone as far as possible at

that time in Belgravia, and with her husband a High Court
Judge.

In any case, after the Trustees had taken me away and
sent me to an eminent school, I began to hear tales. At first,
I knocked about those who hurled and spat them at me. I
discovered a new strength in the process; just as the ground-
ing (to use the favored word) provided by my mother en-
abled me to do better than most in class, not so much by
knowing more as by using greater imagination and ingenuity,
qualities that tell even in rivalry among schoolboys. The jibes
and jeers ceased, and then I began cautiously to inquire after
the facts. The school was of the kind attended by many who
really know such things. I learned that my father too had
long been drinking; and was a byword for it in the counties
and the clubs. No doubt in the goals also, despite my father's
dislike of criminal jurisdiction.

One morning, Jesperson, who was the son of a Labour
ex-minister and quite a friend of mine, brought me *The
Times* so that I could see the news before others did. I read
that my father had had to be removed from his Court and
sent for treatment. *The Times* seemed to think that if the
treatment were not successful, he might feel it proper to retire. There was a summary of the cases over which he had
presided from such an unusually early age (some of them had
been attended by me, however fleetingly); and a reference to
his almost universal popularity in mainly male society.

I was by then in a position at school to take out any cha-
grin I might feel upon as many other boys as I wished, but I
was too introspective for any such easy release, and instead
began for the first time to read the *Divine Comedy*.

There was nothing particularly unusual in what had happened to my father so far, but the treatment seems, as far as
one can tell, to have been the conclusive ordeal, so that he
died a year later in a mental hospital, like poor Haverstone,
though not in the same one. My father returned in spirit to
his sodden, picturesque wilderness, and is buried in the kirkyard four or five miles by a very rough road from Pollaporra.
It was the first instruction in his will, and the Trustees
heeded, as a matter of urgency, to the last detail.

I could not myself attend the funeral, as I was laid low by
a school epidemic, though by then in my last term, and older
than any of my confreres. My stepmother also missed the
funeral, though she had returned to Scotland as soon as she
could. She had resolved to remain there, and, for all I know,

she is there still, with health and sobriety renewed. Several times I have looked her up in directories and failed to find her, despite reference to all three of her known surnames; but I reflect that she may well have married yet again.

My father had left her a moiety of his free estate, in equal part with various organizations he wished to benefit, and which I have already listed. She possessed, as I have said, means of her own. My father left me nothing at all, but he lacked power, Judge though he was, and a Scots solicitor also, to modify the family settlement. Therefore, I, as only surviving child, inherited a life-interest in Pollaporra, though not in the house in Belgravia, and a moderate, though not remarkable, income for life. Had my brother survived, he would have inherited equally. Thinking about him, I wondered whether demon drink, albeit so mighty among Scotsmen, had not rather been a symptom of my father's malady than the cause of it. Thinking of that, I naturally then thought about my own inwardness and prospects. Eugene O'Neill says that we become like our parents of the same sex, even when we consciously resolve not to. I wept for my mother, so beloved, so incomparable.

II

Immediately, the question arose of my going to a university. The idea had of course been discussed before with the Trustees, but I myself had rejected it. While my father had been alive, my plan had been simply to leave the country as soon as I could. Thanks to my mother, I had made a good start with two European languages, and I had since advanced a little by reading literature written in them: *Die Räuber* and *Gerusalemme Liberata*. The other boys no longer attacked or bullied me when they found me doing such things; and the school library contained a few basic texts, mostly unopened, both in the trade sense and the literal sense.

Now I changed my mind. The Trustees were clamant for Edinburgh, as could be expected; but I scored an important victory in actually going to Oxford. Boys from that school did not proceed to Edinburgh University, or did not then. It had never been practicable to send me to Fettes or Loretto. My friend, Jesperson, was at Oxford already. Oxford was still regarded by many as a dream, even though mainly in secret and in silence.

I read modern languages and modern history, and I graduated reasonably, though not excitingly. I surprised myself by making a number of friends. This brought important benefits, in the short term and the long.

I now had no home other than Pollaporra, which, as will be recalled, could not always be visited during the winter, in any case. I spent most of my vacations with new friends; staying in their homes for astonishingly generous periods of time, or traveling with them, or reading with them. With the Second World War so plainly imminent and so probably apocalyptic, everyone traveled as much as he could. I met girls, and was continually amazed at myself. My closest involvement was with a pretty girl who lived in town; who wrote poetry that was published; and who was almost cripple. That surprised me most of all. I had learned something about myself, though I was unsure what it was. The girl lived, regardless, at the top of the house, which taught me something further. Her name was Celia. I fear that I brought little happiness to her or to any of the others, do what I would. I soon realized that I was a haunted man.

As for the main longer term benefit, it was simple enough, and a matter of seemingly pure chance. My friend, Jack Oliver, spoke to his uncle, and as soon as I went down, modestly though not gloriously endorsed, I found myself en route to becoming a merchant banker. I owe Jack a debt that nothing can repay. That too is somehow a property of life. Nothing interlocks or properly relates. Life gives, quite casually, with one hand, and takes away rather more with the other hand, equally unforeseeably. There is little anyone can do about either transaction. Jack Oliver was and is the kindest man I have known, and a splendid offhand tennis player. He has a subtle wit, based on meiosis. From time to time, he has needed it. I have never climbed or otherwise risen to the top of the banking tree, but the tree is tall, and I lived as a child in a house with many stairs.

It was Perry Jesperson who came with me on my first visit to Pollaporra. He had borrowed one of his father's cars.

Even on the one-inch map, the topography was odd. It had struck me as odd many years before. I had always thought myself good with maps, as solitary children so often are; but now that I had been able to travel frequently, I had come to see that one cannot in every case divine from a map a feature of some kind that seems central when one actually arrives and inspects. In that way, I had made a fool of myself on several occasions, though sometimes to my own knowledge only. When it comes to Scotland, I need hardly say that many one-inch maps are sometimes needed for a journey from one place to another, and that some of the maps depict little but heaving contours and huge hydroelectric installations.

Pollaporra stood isolated amid wild altitudes for miles around. Its loneliness was confirmed by its being marked at all. I knew very well that it was no Inveraray or even Balmoral. It stood about three and a half miles from the sea loch, where Mason lived. That of course was as the crow flies, if crows there were. I had miled out the distance inaccurately with thumb and forefinger when I had still been a child. I had done it on many occasions. The topographical oddity was that the nearest depicted community was eight miles away in the opposite direction, whereas in such an area one would expect it to be on the sea, and to derive its hard living therefrom. It was difficult to think of any living at all for the place shown, which was stuck down in a hollow of the mountains, and was named Arrafergus. An uncolored track was shown between Pollaporra and Arrafergus; the rough road of which I had heard so much, and along which my father's corpse had passed a few years before. One could see the little cross marking the kirk and kirkyard where he lay. It was placed almost halfway between the two names, which seemed oddest of all. For much of the year, no congregation could assemble from either house or village. A footpath was shown between Pollaporra and the sea loch, but one could hardly believe in more than a technical right of way, perhaps initiated by smugglers and rebels.

I had commented upon all this to Jesperson before we left. He had said: "I expect it was an effect of the clearances."

"Or of the massacres," I had replied, not wishing to become involved in politics with Jesperson, even conversationally.

The roads were already becoming pretty objectionable, but Jesperson saw it all as progress, and we took it in turns to drive. On the third morning, we were advancing up the long road, yellow on the map, from dead center of Scotland to little Arrafergus. By English standards, it should not have been shown in yellow. Even Jesperson could hardly achieve more than a third of his normal speed. We had seen no other human being for a very long time, and even animals were absent, exactly as I had expected. Why was Arrafergus placed where it was, and how could it survive? Long ago, the soaking mist had compelled us to put up the hood of the roadster. I admit that it was April.

In the early afternoon, the road came to an end. We were in a deep cleft of the rock-strewn hills, and it would have been impossible for it to go further. There was a burn roaring, rather than gurgling, over the dark stones. There was no community, no place, not even a roadsign saying where we were or prohibiting further progress, not a shieling, not a crow. I speculated about what the funeral cortège could have done next.

"Do you want to get out and look for the foundations?" inquired Jesperson. "There's probably the odd stone to be found. The landlords razed everything, but I'm told there are usually traces."

"Not for the moment," I said. "Where do you suppose is the track to Pollaporra?"

"Up there," said Jesperson immediately, and pointed over my head.

How had I missed it? Despite the drizzle, I could now see it quite plainly. Nor must I, or anyone, exaggerate. The track was exceedingly steep and far from well metaled, but, apart from the angle of incline, hardly worse to look at than the yellow road. Obviously, it must be difficult to keep the maps up to date, and in certain areas hardly worthwhile at present prices.

"Are we game?" I asked Jesperson. "It's not your car, and I don't want to press."

"We've got to spend the night somewhere," said Jesperson, who had not even stopped the engine.

After that, all went surprisingly well. Cars were tougher and more flexible in those days. We ascended the mountain without once stopping, and there were no further major gradients until we came within sight of Pollaporra itself. I had feared that the track would die out altogether or become a desert of wiry weeds, such as spring up vengefully on modern roads, if for a moment neglected.

The little kirk was wrapped in rain which was now much heavier. There were a few early flowers amid and around the crumbling kirkyard walls. By June there would be more.

Jesperson drew up and this time stopped the engine reverently.

"It's all yours," he said, glancing at me sideways.

I stepped out. The huge new monument dominated the scene.

I scrambled across the fallen stones.

My father's full name was there, and his dates of birth and death. And then, in much smaller lettering, A JUST MAN A BRAVE MAN AND A GOOD. That was it: the commemorated was no one's beloved husband or beloved father; nor were any of his honors specified; nor was confident hope expressed for him, or, by implication, for anyone, he having been so admirable.

Around were memorials, large and small, to others among my unknown ancestors and collaterals; all far gone in chipping, flaking, and greening, or all that I studied. Among us we seemed to cram the entire consecrated area. Perhaps the residue from other families had no mementos. I was aware of the worms and maggots massed beneath my feet, crawling over one another, as in a natural history exhibit. At any moment, the crepe rubber soles of my shoes might crack and rot. Moreover, did the Church of Scotland ritually consecrate any place? I did not know. I turned round and realized that in the distance I could see Pollàporra also.

The house, though no more than a gray stone, slate-roofed rectangle, neither high nor particularly long, dominated the scene from then on, probably because it was the only work of man visible, apart from the bad road. Also it seemed to stand much higher than I had expected.

Jesperson wisely refused to set his father's car at the final ascent. We went up on foot. From the ridge we could make out the sea loch, green and phantasmal in the driving drizzle.

Cuddy was living in the house now; virtually pensioned off by the Trustees, and retained as caretaker: also as housekeeper, should the need arise, as it now did, almost certainly for the first time.

"Cuddy," I cried out in my best English university style, and with hand outstretched, as we entered. I was desirable to seem entirely confident.

"Brodick," she replied, not familiar perhaps, but independent.

"This is Mr. Jesperson."

"It's too late for the shooting and too early for the fishing," said Cuddy. I think those were her words. I never quite remember the seasons.

"Mr. Leith has come to take possession," said Perry Jesperson.

"It's his for his life," said Cuddy, as if indicating the duration of evening playtime.

"How *are* things?" I asked in my English university way. I was trying to ignore the chill, inner and outer, which the place cast.

"Wind and watertight as far as this house is concerned. You can inspect it at once. You'll not find one slate misplaced. For the rest you must ask Mr. Mason."

"I shall do so tomorrow," I replied. "You must set me on the way to him."

"It is a straight road," said Cuddy. "You'll not go wrong."

Of course it was not a road at all, but a scramble over rocks and stones, all three miles: slow, slippery, and tiring. I could see why Mason spent little of his time visiting. Nonetheless, the way was perfectly straight to the sea; though only from the top could one discern that. Jesperson had volunteered to look for some sport. Cuddy had been discouraging, but the house was as crammed with gear as the kirkyard with ancestral bones.

Mason lived in a small, single-story house almost exactly at the end of the path, and at the edge of the sea. The local letter-box was in his gray wall, with a single collection at 6:30 A.M. each day, apart from Saturdays, Sundays, and Public Holidays. There were a few other small houses, too small for the map but apparently occupied, and even a shop, with brooms in the window. The shop was now closed, and there was no indication of opening hours. A reasonably good, though narrow, road traversed the place, and in both directions disappeared along the edge of the loch. It ran between the path from Pollaporra and Mason's house. There was no detectable traffic, but there was a metal bus-stop sign, and a timetable in a frame. I looked at it. If Jesperson's father's car were to break down, as seemed quite likely, we should need alternative transport. I saw that the bus appeared at 7 A.M. on the first Wednesday in each month between April and September. We had missed the April bus. I persisted and saw that the bus returned as early as 4:30 P.M. on the same day, and then went on to Tullochar at the head of the loch. Despite the length of the inlet, the waves were striking the narrow, stony beach sharply and rapidly. A few small and broken boats were lying about, and some meshes of sodden net, with shapeless cork floats. There was even a smell of dead crustaceans.

I realized that all these modest investigations were being observed by Mason himself. He had opened the faded brown door of his house and was standing there.

"Brodick Leith," he said, in the Scottish manner.

"Mr. Mason," I replied. "I am very glad to meet you. I have heard about you all my life."

"Ay," said Mason, "you would have. Come indoors. We'll have a drop together and then I'll show you the books. I keep them to the day and hour. There's not as much to do as once there was."

"That was in my father's time?"

"In the Judge's time. Mr. Justice Leith. Sir Roderic Leith, if you prefer. A strong man and a mysterious."

"I agree with what you say."

"Come inside," said Mason. "Come inside. I live as an unmarried man."

Mason opened a new bottle, and before I left, we had made our way through all of it and had started on the remains of the previous one. Though I drank appreciably less than half, it was still, I think, more spirit than I had drunk on any previous occasion. The books were kept in lucid and impersonal handwriting, almost as good as my father's, and were flawless, in so far as I could understand them; my career in banking having not yet begun. Mason left me to go through them with the bottle at my elbow, while he went into the next room to cook us steaks, with his own hands. I could see for myself that the amounts brought out as surplus or profit at the end of each account were not large. I had never supposed they would be, but the costs and responsibilities of land ownership were brought home to me, none the less. Until then, I had been a baby in the matter, as in many others. Most people are babies until they confront property ownership.

"I know you attended my father's funeral, Mr. Mason," I said. "How was it? Tell me about it." The steak was proving to be the least prepared that I had ever attempted to munch. No doubt the cooking arrangements were very simple. I had not been invited to inspect them.

"Ay," said Mason, "and the funeral was the least of it." He took a heavier swig than before and stopped chewing altogether, while he thought.

"How many were there?" I had always been curious about that.

"Just me, and Cuddy MacFerrier, and the Shepstones."

The Shepstones were relatives. I had of course never set eyes upon even one of them. I had never seen a likeness. Millais had never painted a single Shepstone, and if one or more of them had appeared upon a criminal charge, my father would hardly have been the Judge.

"How many Shepstones?" I asked, still essaying to devour.

"Just the three of them," replied Mason, as if half-entranced. I am making little attempt to reproduce the Scottishness of his speech, or anyone else's. I am far from being Sir Walter or George Douglas.

"That is all there are?"

"Just the three. That's all," said Mason. "Drink up, man."

"A minister was there, of course?"

"Ay, the minister turned out for it. The son was sick, or so he said."

"I am the son," I said, smiling. "And I *was* sick. I promise you that."

"No need to promise anything," said Mason, still motionless. "Drink up, I tell you."

"And no one else at all?" I persisted.

"Maybe the old carlin," said Mason. "Maybe her."

For me that was a very particular Scottish word. I had in fact sprung half to my feet, as Mason spoke it.

"Dinna fash yoursel'. She's gone awa' for the noo," said Mason.

He began once more to eat.

"I saw her once myself," I said, sitting right down again. "I saw her when my darling mother died."

"Ay, you would," said Mason. "Especially if maybe you were about the house at the time. Who let her in?"

"I don't know," I replied. "Perhaps she doesn't have to be let in?"

"Och, she does that," said Mason. "She always has to be let in."

"It was at the grave that you saw her?"

"No, not there, though it is my fancy that she was present. I saw her through that window as she came up from the sea."

I know that Mason pointed, and I know that I did not find it the moment to look.

"Through the glass panes or out on the wee rocks you can view the spot," said Mason. "It's always the same." Now he was looking at nothing and chewing vigorously.

"I saw no face," I said.

"If you'd seen that, you wouldn't be here now," said Mason. He was calm, as far as I could see.

"How often have you seen her yourself?"

"Four or five times in all. At the different deaths."

"Including at my mother's death?"

"Yes, then too," said Mason, still gazing upon the sawn-up sections of meat. "At the family deaths she is seen, and at the deaths of those, whoever they be, that enter the family."

I thought of my brother whom I had never known. I wasn't even aware that there had been any other family deaths during Mason's likely lifetime.

"She belongs to those called Leith, by one right or another," said Mason, "and to no one at all else."

As he spoke, and having regard to the way he had put it, I felt that I saw why so apparently alert a man seemed to have such difficulty in remembering that I was presumably a Leith myself. I took his consideration kindly.

"I didn't see anyone when the Judge died," I remarked.

"Perhaps in a dream," said Mason. "I believe you were sick at the time."

That was not quite right of course, but it was true that I had by no means been in the house.

We dropped the subject, and turned once more to feu duties, rents, and discriminatory taxes; even to the recent changes in the character of the tides and in the behavior of the gannets.

I have no idea how I scrambled back to dismal Pollaporra, and in twilight first, soon in darkness. Perhaps the liquor aided instead of impeded, as liquor so often in practice does, despite the doctors and proctors.

III

After the war, Jack Oliver was there to welcome me back to the office off Cornhill. He was now a colonel. His uncle had been killed in what was known as an incident, when the whole family house had been destroyed, including the Devises and De Wints. The business was now substantially his.

I found myself advanced very considerably from the position I had occupied in 1939. From this it is not to be supposed, as so many like to suppose, that no particular aptitude is required for success in merchant banking. On the contrary, very precise qualities both of mind and of temperament are needed. About myself, the conclusion I soon reached was that I was as truly a Scottish businessman as my ancestors in the kirkyard, whether I liked it or not, as O'Neill says. I should have been foolish had I *not* liked it. I might have preferred to be a weaver of dreams, but perhaps my mother had died too soon for that to be possible. I must add, however, that the business was by no means the same as when I had entered it before the war. No business was the same. The staff was smaller, the atmosphere tenser. The gains were illusory, the prospects shadowy. One worked much less hard, but one believed in nothing. There was little to work for, less to believe in.

It was in the office, though, that I met Shulie. She seemed very lost. I was attracted by her at once.

"Are you looking for someone?" I asked.

"I have just seen Mr. Oliver." She had a lovely voice and a charming accent. I knew that Jack was seeking a new secretary. His present one had failed to report for weeks, or to answer her supposed home telephone number.

"I hope that all went well."

Shulie shook her head and smiled a little.

"I'm sorry about that."

"Mr. Oliver had chosen a girl who went in just before me. It always happens."

"I'm sure you'll have better luck soon."

She shook her head a second time. "I am not English."

"That has advantages as well as disadvantages," I replied firmly.

It struck me that she might be a refugee, with behind her a terrible story. She was small, slender, and dark, though not as dark as my mother. I could not decide whether or not she looked particularly Jewish. I daresay it is always a rather foolish question.

"No advantages when you are in England," she said. "Can you please tell me how to get out of this place?"

"I'll come with you," I said. "It's difficult to explain."

That was perfectly true. It matters that it was true, because while we were winding through the corridors, and I was holding swingdoors, I was successful in persuading Shulie to have lunch with me. Time was gained for me also by the fact that Shulie had a slight limp, which slowed her down quite perceptibly. I am sure she was weary too, and I even believe that she was seriously underfed, whatever the exact reason. I perceived Shulie as a waif from the start; though also from the start I saw that it was far from the whole truth about her. I never learned the whole truth about her. Perhaps one never does learn, but Shulie refused, in so many words, to speak about it.

It was February, and outside I could have done with my overcoat. Jack Oliver still went everywhere in a British warm. He had several of them. There was snow on the ground and on the ledges. We had been under snow for weeks. Though do I imagine the snow? I do not imagine the cold. Shulie, when the blast struck her, drew into herself, as girls do. She was certainly not dressed for it; but few girls then were. The girlish image was still paramount. I myself actually caught a cold that day, as I often did. I was laid up for a time in my small flat off Orchard Street, and with no one in any position to look after me very much. Later, Shulie explained to me that one need never catch cold. All that is necessary is a firm resolution against it: faith in oneself, I suppose.

On most days, Jack and I, together or apart, went either to quite costly places or to certain pubs. That was the way of life approved, expected, even enforced; and, within the limits of the time, rewarded. I, however, had kept my options more open than that. I took Shulie to a nearby teashop, though a somewhat superior teashop. We were early, but it was filling fast. Still, we had a table to ourselves for a time.

"What's your name?"

"Shulie."

Her lips were like dark rose petals, as one imagines them, or sometimes dreams of them.

I have mentioned how lamentably sure I am that I failed to make Celia happy; nor any other girl. During the war, I had lived, off and on, with a woman married to another officer, who was never there when I was. I shall not relate how for me it all began. There was a case for, and a case against, but it had been another relationship inconducive to the ultimate happiness of either party.

When I realized that I was not merely attracted by Shulie, but deeply in love with her, and dependent for any future I might have upon marrying her, I applied myself to avoiding past errors. Possibly in past circumstances, they had not really been errors; but now they might be the difference between life and death. I decided that, apart from my mother, I had never previously and properly loved anyone; and that with no one else but my mother had I been sufficiently honest to give things a chance. When the time came, I acted at once.

Within half an hour of Shulie tentatively accepting my proposal of marriage, I related to her what Mason had told me, and what I had myself seen. I said that I was a haunted man. I even said that she could reverse her tentative decision, if she thought fit.

"So the woman has to be let in?" said Shulie.

"That's what Mason told me."

"A woman who is married does not let any other woman in, except when her husband is not there."

"But suppose you were ill?"

"Then you would be at home looking after me. It would not be a time when you would let in another woman."

It was obvious that she was not taking the matter seriously. I had been honest, but I was still anxious.

"Have you ever heard a story like it before?"

"Yes," said Shulie. "But it is the message that matters more than the messenger."

After we married, Shulie simply moved into my small flat. At first we intended, or certainly I intended, almost immediately to start looking for somewhere much larger. We, or certainly I, had a family in mind. With Shulie, I wanted that very much, even though I was a haunted man, whose rights were doubtful.

But it was amazing how well we seemed to go on living exactly where we were. Shulie had few possessions to bring in, and even when they were increased, we still seemed to have plenty of room. It struck me that Shulie's slight infirmity might contribute to her lack of interest in the normal ambition of any woman: a larger home. Certainly, the trouble seemed at times to fatigue her, even though the manifestations were very inconspicuous. For example, Jack Oliver, at a much later date, denied that he had ever noticed anything at all. The firm had provided me with a nice car and parking was then easier than it is now. Shulie had to do little walking of the kind that really exhausts a woman; pushing through crowds, and round shops at busy hours.

As a matter of fact, Shulie seldom left the flat, unless in my company. Shulie was writing a book. She ordered almost all goods on the telephone, and proved to be skillful and firm. She surprised me continually in matters like that. Marriage had already changed her considerably. She was plumper, as well as more confident. She accompanied me to the Festival Hall, and to picnics in Kew Gardens. The picnics were made elegant and exciting by her presence, and by her choice of what we ate and drank, and by the way she looked at the flowers, and by the way people and flowers looked at her. Otherwise, she wrote, or mused upon what she was about to write. She reclined in different sets of silk pyjamas on a bright blue daybed I'd bought for her, and rested her square, stiff-covered exercise book upon her updrawn knees. She refused to read to me what she had written, or let me read it for myself. "You will know one day," she said.

I must admit that I had to do a certain amount of explaining to Jack Oliver. He would naturally have preferred me to marry a woman who kept open house and was equally good with all men alike. Fortunately, business in Britain does not yet depend so much upon those things as does business in America. I was able to tell Jack that setting a wife to attract business to her husband was always a chancy transaction for the husband. For better or for worse, Jack, having lately battled his way through a very complex divorce, accepted my view. The divorce had ended in a most unpleasant situation for Jack financially, as well as in some public ridicule. He was in no position even to hint that I had married a girl whom he had rejected for a job. His own wife had been the daughter of a baronet who was also a vice-admiral and a former Member of Parliament. Her name was Clarissa. Her mother, the admiral's wife, was an M.F.H.

After my own mother's death, I should never have thought possible the happiness that Shulie released in me. There was much that remained unspoken to the end, but that may have been advantageous. Perhaps it is always so. Perhaps only madmen need to know everything and thus to destroy everything. When I lay in Shulie's arms, or simply regarded her as she wrote her secret book, I wished to know nothing more, because more would diminish. This state of being used to be known as connubial bliss. Few, I believe, experience it. It is certainly not a matter of deserts.

Shulie, however, proved to be incapable of conception. Possibly it was a consequence of earlier sufferings and endurances. Elaborate treatments might have been tried, but Shulie shrank from them, and understandably. She accepted the situation very quietly. She did not seem to cease loving me.

We continued to dwell in the flat off Orchard Street.

I asked Shulie when her book would be finished. She replied that the more she wrote, the more there was to be written. Whenever I approached her, she closed her exercise book and lifted herself up to kiss me. If I persisted at all, she did more than kiss me.

I wanted nothing else in life than to be with Shulie, and alone with her. Everything we did in the outside world was incorporated into our love. I was happy once more, and now I was happy all the time, even in the office near Cornhill. I bought a bicycle to make the journey, but the City men laughed, and nicknamed me, and ragged me, so that Jack Oliver and the others suggested that I give it up. Jack bought the bicycle himself, to use at his place in the country, where, not necessarily on the bicycle, he was courting the divorced daughter of the local High Sheriff, a girl far beyond his present means. She was even a member of a ladies' polo team, though the youngest. When one is happy oneself, everyone seems happy.

Our flat was on the top floor in a small block. The block had been built in more spacious days than the present, and there were two lifts. They were parallel shafts. Above the waistline, the lifts had windows on three sides; the gate being on the fourth. They were large lifts, each "Licensed to carry 12 people"; far more than commonly accumulated at any one time. The users worked the lifts themselves, though, when I had first taken the flat, the lifts in Selfridges round the corner had still been worked by the famous pretty girls in breeches, among whom an annual competition was held. The two lifts in the flats were brightly lit and always very clean. Shulie loved going up and down in them; much as she loved real traffic blocks, with boys ranging along the stationary cars selling ice cream and evening newspapers. None the less, I do not think she used the lifts very much when I was not there. Traveling in them was, in fact, one tiny facet of our love. When Shulie was alone, I believe she commonly used the stairs, despite her trouble. The stairs were well lighted and well swept also. Marauders were seldom met.

Tenants used sometimes to wave to one another through the glass, as the two lifts swept past one another, one upwards, one downwards. It was important to prevent this becoming a mere tiresome obligation. One morning I was alone in the descending lift. I was on my way to work: Bond Street Underground station to Bank Underground station. There had been a wonderful early morning with Shulie, and I was full of joy; thinking about nothing but that. The other lift swept upward past me. In it were four people who lived in the flats, three women and one man; all known to me by sight, though no more than that. As a fifth, there was the woman whom I had seen when my mother died.

Despite the speed with which the lifts had passed, I was sure it was she. The back was turned to me, but her sparse hair, her dirty plaid, her stature, and somehow her stance, were for ever unmistakable. I remember thinking immediately that the others in the lift must all be seeing the woman's face.

Melted ice flowed through me from the top of my head to the soles of my feet. There was a device for stopping the lift: "To be used only in Emergency." And of course I wanted to reverse the lift also. I was so cold and so shaky that I succeeded merely in jamming the lift, and neatly between floors, like a joke in "Puck" or "Rainbow," or a play by Sartre.

I hammered and raved, but most of the tenants had either gone to work or were making preparations for coffee mornings. The other lift did not pass again. As many as ten minutes tore by before anyone took notice of me, and then it was only because our neighbor, Mrs. Delmer, wanted to descend from the top, and needed the lift she always used, being, as she had several times told us, frightened of the other one. The caretaker emerged slowly from his cubicle and shouted to me that there was nothing he could do. He would have to send for the lift company's maintenance men. He was not supposed to be on duty at the hour anyway, he said. We all knew that. Mrs. Delmer made a detour as she clambered down the staircase, in order to tap on the glass roof of my lift and give me a piece of her mind, though in refined phrases. In the end, I simply sank upon the floor and tried to close myself to all thoughts or feeling, though with no success.

I must acknowledge that the maintenance men came far sooner than one could have expected. They dropped from above, and crawled from below, even emerging from a trap in the lift floor, full of cheerful conversation, both particular and general. The lift was brought slowly down to the gate on the floor immediately below. For some reason, the gate would not open, even to the maintenance men; and we had to sink, slowly still, to the ground floor. The first thing I saw there was a liquid trail in from the street up to the gate of the other lift. Not being his hour, the caretaker had still to mop it up, even though it reeked of seabed mortality.

Shulie and I lived on the eighth floor. I ran all the way up. The horrible trail crossed our landing from the lift gate to under our front door.

I do not know how long I had been holding the key in my hand. As one does at such times, I fumbled and fumbled at the lock. When the door was open, I saw the trail wound through the tiny hall or lobby and entered the living room. When the woman came to my mother, there had been a faint trail only, but at that time I had not learned from Mason about the woman coming from the sea. Fuller knowledge was yielding new evidence.

I did not find Shulie harmed, or ill, or dead. She was not there at all.

Everything was done, but I never saw her again.

IV

The trail of water soon dried out, leaving no mark of any kind, despite the rankness.

The four people whom I had seen in the lift, who lived in the flats, denied that they had ever seen a fifth. I neither believed or disbelieved.

Shulie's book was infinitely upsetting. It was hardly fiction at all, as I had supposed it to be, but a personal diary, in the closest detail, of everything we had done together, of everything we had been, of everything she had felt. It was at once comprehensive and chaste. At one time, I even thought of seeking a publisher for it, but was deterred, in an illogical way, by the uncertainty about what had happened to Shulie. I was aware that it had been perfectly possible for her to leave the building by the staircase, while I had been caged between floors in the lift. The staircase went down a shaft of its own.

The book contained nothing of what had hapened to Shulie before she met me.

Shulie's last words were: "So joyful! Am I dreaming, or even dead? It seems that there is no external way of deciding either thing." Presumably, she had then been interrupted. Doubtless, she had then risen to open the door.

I had been married to Shulie for three years and forty-one days.

* * *

I wrote to the Trustees suggesting that they put Pollaporra on the market, but their law agent replied that it was outside their powers. All I had done was upset both Cuddy and Mason.

I sold the lease of the flat off Orchard Street, and bought the lease of another one, off Gloucester Place.

I settled down to living with no one for no one. I took every opportunity of traveling for the firm, no matter where, not only abroad, but even to Peterhead, Bolton, or Camborne. Previously, I had not wished or cared to leave Shulie for a single night.

I pursued new delights, such as they were, and as they came along. I joined a bridge club, a chess club, a mah-jongg society, and mixed fencing group. Later, I joined a very avant-garde dance club, and went there occasionally.

I was introduced by one of the people in my firm to a very High Anglican church in his own neighborhood, and went there quite often. Sometimes I read one of the lessons. I was one of the few who could still do that in Latin.

Another partner was interested in masonics, but I thought that would be inconsistent. I did join a livery company: it is expected in the City.

I was pressed to go in for regular massage, but resisted that too.

I was making more paper money than I would ever have thought possible. Paper money? Not even that. Phantom wealth, almost entirely: taxes took virtually the whole of it. I did not even employ a housekeeper. I did not wish for the attentions of any woman who was not Shulie. All the same, I wrote to Celia, who replied at once, making clear, among very many other things, that she was still unmarried. She had time to write so long and so prompt a letter. She had hope enough to think it worthwhile.

It is amazing how full a life a man can lead without for one moment being alive at all, except sometimes when sleeping. As Clifford Bax says, life is best treated as simply a game. Soon enough one will be bowled middle stump, be put out of action in the scrum, or ruled offside and sent off. As Bax also says, it is necessary to have an alternative. But who really has?

None the less, blood will out, and I married again. Sometime before, Shulie's death had been "presumed." Mercifully, it was the Trustees who attended to that.

I married Clarissa. I am married to her now.

The court had bestowed upon Clarissa a goodly slice of Jack's property and prospects, and Jack was recognized by all as having made a complete fool of himself, not only in the area of cash; but Clarissa never really left at all. Even though Jack was now deeply entangled with Suzanne, herself a young divorcée, Clarissa was always one of Jack's house party, eager to hear everything, ready to advise, perhaps even to comfort, though I myself never came upon her doing that. She might now be sleeping in the room that had once been set aside for the visits of her sister, Naomi, but of course she knew the whole house far more intimately than Jack did, or than any normal male knows any house. She continued being invaluable to Jack; especially when he was giving so much of his time to Suzanne. One could not know Jack at all well, let alone as well as I knew him, without continuing to encounter Clarissa all the time.

The word for Clarissa might be deft—the first word, that is. She can manage a man or a woman, a slow child or a slow pensioner, as effortlessly as she can manage everything in a house, at a party, in a shop, on a ship. She has the small but right touch for every single situation—the perfect touch. Most of all, she has the small and perfect touch for every situation, huge or tiny, in her own life. Few indeed have *that* gift. No doubt Clarissa owes much to her versatile papa. On one occasion also, I witnessed Clarissa's mother looking after a difficult meet. It was something to note and remember.

Clarissa has that true beauty which is not so much in the features and body, but around them: nothing less than a mystical emanation. When I made my proposal to Clarissa, I naturally thought very devoutly of Shulie. Shulie's beauty was of the order one longs from the first to embrace, to be absorbed by. Of course, my mother's dark beauty had been like that also. Clarissa one hardly wished or dared to touch, lest the vision fade. A man who felt otherwise than that about Clarissa would be a man who could not see the vision at all. I imagine that state of things will bear closely upon what happens to Clarissa. There is little that is mystical about Clarissa's detectable behavior, though there must be *some* relationship between her soul and the way she looks. It is a question that arises so often when women as beautiful as Clarissa materialize in one's rose garden. I myself have never seen another woman as beautiful absolutely as Clarissa, or certainly never spoken to one.

Clarissa has eyes so deep as to make one wonder about

the whole idea of depth, and what it means. She has a voice almost as lovely as her face. She has a slow and languorous walk: beautiful too, but related, I fear, to an incident during her early teens, when she broke both legs in the hunting field. Sometimes it leads to trouble when Clarissa is driving a car. Not often. Clarissa prefers to wear trousers, though she looks perfectly normal in even a short skirt, indeed divinely beautiful, as always.

I fear that too much of my life with Clarissa has been given to quarreling. No one is to blame, of course.

There was a certain stress even at the proposal scene, which took place on a Saturday afternoon in Jack's house, when the others were out shooting duck. Pollaporra and its legend have always discouraged me from field sports, and all the struggling about had discouraged Clarissa, who sat before the fire, looking gnomic.

But she said Yes at once, and nodded, and smiled.

Devoted still, whether wisely or foolishly, to honesty, I told her what Mason had told me, and what I had myself seen on two occasions, and that I was a haunted man.

Clarissa looked very hostile. "I don't believe in things like that," she said sharply.

"I thought I ought to tell you."

"Why? Did you want to upset me?"

"Of course not. I love you. I don't want you to accept me on false pretenses."

"It's got nothing to do with my accepting you. I just don't want to know about such things. They don't exist."

"But they do, Clarissa. They are part of me."

From one point of view, obviously I should not have persisted. I had long recognized that many people would have said that I was obsessed. But the whole business seemed to me the explanation of my being. Clarissa must not take me to be merely a banker, a youngish widower, a friend of her first husband's, a faint simulacrum of the Admiral.

Clarissa actually picked up a book of sweepstake tickets and threw it at me as I sat on the rug at her feet.

"There," she said.

It was a quite thick and heavy book, but I was not exactly injured by it, though it had come unexpectedly and had grazed my eye.

Clarissa then leaned forward and gave me a slow and searching kiss. It was the first time we had kissed so seriously.

"There," she said again.

She then picked the sweepstake tickets off the floor and threw them in the fire. They were less than fully burnt ten minutes later, when Clarissa and I were more intimately involved, and looking at our watches to decide when the others were likely to return.

The honeymoon, at Clarissa's petition, was in North Africa, now riddled with politics, which I did not care for. For centuries, there has been very little in North Africa for an outsider to see, and the conformity demanded by an alien society seemed not the best background for learning to know another person. Perhaps we should have tried Egypt, but Clarissa specifically demanded something more rugged. With Shulie there had been no honeymoon.

Before marrying me, Clarissa had been dividing her life between her flat and Jack's country house. Her spacious flat, very near my childhood home, was in its own way as beautiful as she was, and emitted a like glow. It would have been absurd for me not to move into it. The settlement from Jack had contributed significantly to all around me, but by now I was able to keep up, or nearly so. Money is like sex. The more that everyone around is talking of little else, the less it really accounts for, let alone assists.

Not that sex has ever been other than a problem with Clarissa. I have good reason to believe that others have found the same, though Jack never gave me one word of warning. In any case, his Suzanne is another of the same kind, if I am any judge; though less beautiful, and, I should say, less kind also. Men chase the same woman again and again; or rather the same illusion; or rather the same lost part of themselves.

Within myself, I had of course returned to the hope of children. Some will say that I was a fool not to have had that matter out with Clarissa before marrying her, and no doubt a number of related matters also. They speak without knowing Clarissa. No advance terms can be set. None at all. I doubt whether it is possible with any woman whom one finds really desirable. Nor can the proposal scene be converted into a businesslike discussion of future policy and prospects. That is not the atmosphere, and few would marry if it were.

With Shulie, the whole thing had been love. With Clarissa, it was power; and she was so accustomed to the power being hers that she could no longer bother to exercise it, except indirectly. This was and is true even though Clarissa is exceedingly good-hearted in many other ways. I had myself experienced something of the kind in reverse with poor Celia, though obviously in a much lesser degree.

Clarissa has long been impervious to argument or importunity or persuasion of any kind. She is perfectly equipped with counterpoise and equipoise. She makes discussion seem absurd. Almost always it is. Before long, I was asking myself whether Clarissa's strange and radiant beauty was compatible with desire, either on her part or on mine.

There was also the small matter of Clarissa's black maid, Aline; who has played her little part in the immediate situation. On my visits to the flat before our marriage, I had become very much aware of Aline, miniature and slender, always in tight sweater and pale trousers. Clarissa had told me that Aline could do everything in the place that required to be done; but in my hearing Aline spoke little for herself. I was told that often she drove Clarissa's beautiful foreign car, a present from Jack less than a year before the divorce. I was also told, as a matter of interest, that Jack had never met Aline. I therefore never spoke of her to him. I was telling him much less now, in any case. I certainly did not tell him what I had not previously been told myself: that when I was away for the firm, which continued to be frequently, Aline took my place in Clarissa's vast and swanlike double bed. I discovered this in a thoroughly low way, which I do not propose to relate. Clarissa simply remarked to me that, as I knew, she could never sleep well if alone in the room. I abstained from rejoining that what Clarissa really wanted was a nanny—one of those special nannies who, like dolls, are always there to be dominated by their charges. It would have been one possible rejoinder.

Nannies were on my mind. It had been just then that the Trustees wrote to me about Cuddy. They told me that Cuddy had "intimated a wish" to leave her employment at Pollaporra. She wanted to join her younger sister, who, I was aware, had a business on the main road, weaving and plaiting for the tourists, not far from Dingwall. I could well believe that the business had become more prosperous than when I had heard about it as a child. It was a business of the sort that at the moment did. The Trustees went on to imply that it was my task, and not theirs, to find a successor to Cuddy. They reminded me that I was under an obligation to maintain a property in which I had merely a life interest.

It was a very hot day. Clarissa always brought the sun.
She had been reading the letter over my shoulder. I was
always aware of her special nimbus encircling my head and
torso when she did this. Moreover, she was wearing nothing
but her nightdress.

"Let's go and have a look," she said.

"Are you sure you want to?" I asked, remembering her
response to my story.

"Of course I'm sure. I'll transform the place, now I've got
it to myself."

"That'll be the day," I said, smiling up at her.

"You won't know it when I've finished with it. Then we
can sell it."

"We can't," I said. "Remember it's not mine to sell."

"You must get advice. Jack might be able to help."

"You don't know what Pollaporra's like. Everything is
bound to be totally run down."

"With your Cuddy in charge all these years, and with
nothing else to do with herself? At least, you say not."

I had seen on my previous visit that this argument might
be sound, as far as it went.

"You can't possibly take on all the work."

"We'll have Aline with us. I had intended that."

By now, I had seen for myself also that Aline was indeed
most competent and industrious. It would have been impossible to argue further: Clarissa was my wife and had a right
both to accompany me and to take someone with her to help
with the chores. If I were to predecease her, she would have
a life interest in the property. Moreover, Clarissa alone could
manage very well for us when she applied herself. I had
learned that too. There were no sensible, practical objections
whatever.

"Aline will be a help with the driving as well," added
Clarissa.

There again, I had seen for myself how excellent a driver
little Aline could be. She belongs to just the sort of quiet
person who in practice drives most effectively on the roads of
today.

"So write at once and say we're arriving," said Clarissa.

"I'm not sure there's anyone to write to," I replied.
"That's the point."

I had, of course, a set of keys. For whatever reason, I did
not incline to giving Mason advance notice of my second
coming, and in such altered circumstances.

"I'm not sure how Aline will get on with the High-landers," I remarked. There are, of course, all those stories in Scotland about the intrusion of huge black men, and sometimes, I fancy, of black females. They figure in folklore everywhere.

"She'll wind each of them three times round each of her fingers," replied Clarissa. "But you told me there *were* no Highlanders at Pollaporra."

Clarissa, when triumphing, looked like Juno, or Diana, or even Minerva.

Aline entered to the tinkling of a little bell. It is a pretty little bell, which I bought for Clarissa in Sfax; her earlier little bell having dropped its clapper. When Aline entered in her quiet way, Clarissa kissed her, as she does every morning upon first sighting Aline.

"We're all three going into the wilderness together," said Clarissa. "Probably on Friday."

Friday was the day after tomorrow. I really could not leave the business for possibly a week at such short notice. There was some tension because of that, but it could not be helped.

When we did reach Pollaporra, the weather was hotter than ever, though there had been several thunderstorms in London. Aline was in her element. Clarissa had stocked up the large car with food in immense quantity. When we passed through an outlying area of Glasgow, she distributed two pounds of sweets to children playing in the roads of a council estate. The sweets were melting in their papers as she threw them. The tiny fingers locked together.

When we reached the small kirkyard, Clarissa, who was driving us along the rough road from Arrafergus, categorically refused to stop.

"We're here to drive the bogies out," she said, "not to let them in."

Clarissa also refused to leave the car at the bottom of the final slope, as Perry Jesperson had done. My friend Jesperson was now a Labour M.P. like his father, and already a Joint Parliamentary secretary, and much else, vaguely lucrative and responsible. Clarissa took the car up the very steep incline as if it had been a lift at the seaside.

She stood looking at and beyond the low gray house. "Is that the sea?" she asked, pointing.

"It's the sea loch," I replied. "A long inlet, like a fjord."

"It's a lovely place," said Clarissa.

I was surprised, but, I suppose, pleased.

"I thought we might cut the house up into lodges for the shooting and fishing," said Clarissa. "But now I don't want to."

"The Trustees would never have agreed," I pointed out. "They have no power to agree."

"Doesn't matter. I want to come here often. Let's take a photograph."

So, before we started to unpack the car, Clarissa took one of Aline and me; and, at her suggestion, I took one of Aline and her. Aline did not rise to the shoulders of either of us.

Within the house, the slight clamminess of my previous visit, had been replaced by a curiously tense airlessness. I had used my key to admit us, but I had not been certain as to whether or not Cuddy was already gone, and Clarissa and I went from room to room shouting for her, Clarissa more loudly than I. Aline remained among the waders and antlers of the entrance hall, far from home, and thinking her own thoughts. There was no reply anywhere. I went to the door of what I knew to be Cuddy's own room, and quietly tapped. When there was no reply there either, I gently tried the handle. I thought the door might be locked, but it was not. Inside was a small unoccupied bedroom. The fittings were very spare. There were a number of small framed statements on the walls, such as "I bow before Thee," and "Naught but Surrender,"and "Who knows All," without a mark of interrogation. Clarissa was still calling from room to room. I did not care to call back, but went after her on half-tiptoe.

I thought we could conclude we were alone. Cuddy must have departed some time ago.

Dust was settling everywhere, even in that remote spot. The sunlight made it look like encroaching fur. Clarissa seemed undeterred and undaunted.

"It's a lost world and I'm queen," she said.

It is true that old gray waders, and wicker fish baskets with many of the withies broken, and expensive guns for stalking lined up in racks, are unequaled for suggesting loss, past, present, and to come. Even the pictures were all of death and yesterday; stags exaggeratedly virile before the crack shot, feathers abnormally bright before the battue, men and ancestors in bonnets before, behind, and around the ornamentally piled carcasses, with the lion of Scotland flag stuck in the summit. When we reached the hall, I noticed that Aline was shuddering in the sunlight. I myself had never been in the house before without Cuddy. In practice, she had been responsible for everything that happened there. Now I was responsible—and for as long as I remained alive.

"We'll paint everything white and we'll put in a swimming pool," cried Clarissa joyously. "Aline can have the room in the tower."

"I didn't know there was a tower," I said.

"*Almost* a tower," said Clarissa.

"Is there anything in the room?" I asked.

"Only those things on heads. They're all over the walls and floor."

At that, Aline actually gave a little cry. Perhaps she was thinking of things on walls and floors in Africa.

"It's all right," said Clarissa, going over to her. "We'll throw them all away. I promise. I never ask you to do anything I don't do myself, or wouldn't do."

But, whatever might be wrong, Aline was uncomforted. "Look!" she cried, and pointed out through one of the hall windows, all of them obstructed by stuffed birds in glass domes, huge and dusty.

"What have you seen this time?" asked Clarissa, as if speaking to a loved though exhausting child.

At that moment, it came to me that Clarissa regularly treated Aline as my mother had treated me.

Aline's hand fell slowly to her side, and her head began to droop.

"It's only the car," said Clarissa. "*Our* car. You've been driving it yourself."

I had stepped swiftly but quietly behind the two of them. I admit that I too could see nothing but the car, and, of course, the whole of Scotland.

I seldom spoke directly to Aline, but now was the moment.

"What was it?" I asked, as sympathetically as I could manage. "What did you see?"

But Aline had begun to weep, as by now I had observed that she often did. She wept without noise or any special movement. The tears just flowed like thawing snow; as they do in nature, though less often on Change.

"It was nothing," said Clarissa. "Aline often sees nothing, don't you, Aline?" She produced her own handkerchief, and began to dry Aline's face, and to hug her tightly.

The handkerchief was from an enormous casket of objects given us as a wedding present by Clarissa's grandmother (on the mother's side), who was an invalid, living in Dominica. Clarissa's grandfather had been shot dead years before by thieves he had interrupted.

"Now," said Clarissa after a few moments of tender reassurance. "Smile, please. That's better. We're going to be happy here, one and all. Remember. Happy."

I suppose I was reasonably eager, but I found it difficult to see how she was going to manage it. It was not, as I must in justice to her make clear, that normally I was unhappy with Clarissa. She was too beautiful and original for that to be the word at any time. The immediate trouble was just Pollaporra itself: the most burdensome and most futile of houses, so futile as to be sinister, even apart from its associations, where I was concerned. I could not imagine any effective brightening; not even by means of maquillage and disguise: a pool, a discothéque, a sauna, a blackjack suite. To me Pollaporra was a millstone I could never throw away. I could not believe that modern tenants would ever stop there for long, or in the end show us a profit. For all the keep-nets and carcass-sleighs in every room, I doubted whether the accessible sport was good enough to be marketed at all in contemporary terms. Nor had I started out with Clarissa in order that we should settle down in the place ourselves. When I can get away from work, I want somewhere recuperative. About Pollaporra, I asked the question all married couples ask when detached from duties and tasks: what should we do all day? There was nothing.

"I have never felt so free and blithe," said Clarissa later that evening, exaggerating characteristically but charmingly. She was playing the major part in preparing a quite elaborate dinner for us out of tins and packets. In the flat, Aline had normally eaten in her own pretty sitting room, but here she would be eating with us. Clarissa would be tying a lace napkin round her neck, and heaping her place with first choices, and handing her date after date on a spike. Employees are supposed to be happier when treated in that way, though few people think it is true, and few employees.

"We'll flatten the roof and have li-los," said Clarissa, while Aline munched with both eyes on her plate, and I confined myself to wary nibblings round the fringe of Rognons Turbigo, canned but reinvigorated. The plates at Pollaporra depicted famous Scots, such as Sawney Bean and Robert Knox, who employed Burke and Hare, the body snatchers. Mr. Justice Leith, who despised the criminal law, had never been above such likenesses, as we know; nor had he been the only sporting jurist in the family—very far from it.

"I think to do that we'd have to rebuild the house," I remarked.

"Do try not to make difficulties the whole time. Let yourself go, Brodick."

It is seldom a good idea, according to my experience, and especially not in Scotland, but of course I could see what Clarissa meant. There was no reason why we should not make of the trip as much of a holiday as was possible. It would be a perfectly sensible thing to do. If Clarissa was capable of fun at Pollaporra, I was the last person with a right to stand in her way.

"We might build a gazebo," I said, though I could feel my heart sinking as I spoke.

Aline, with her mouth full of prunes (that day), turned her head toward me. She did not know what a gazebo was.

"A sort of summer house," explained Clarissa. "With cushions and views. It would be lovely. So many things to look at."

I had never known Clarissa so simple-minded before—in the nicest sense, of course. I realized that this might be a Clarissa more real than the other one. I might have to consider where I myself stood about that. On the other hand, Pollaporra instead of bringing out at long last the real woman, might be acting upon her by contraries, and have engaged the perversity in her, and to no ultimately constructive end. I had certainly heard of that too, and in my time seen it in action among friends.

"I don't want to look," said Aline, expelling prune stones into spoons.

"You will by tomorrow. You'll feel quite different. We're going to drive all the banshees far, far away."

I am sure that Aline did not know what a banshee was either, but Clarissa's general meaning was clear, and the word has an African, self-speaking sound in itself, when one comes to think about it. Words for things like that are frightening in themselves the world over.

Only Clarissa, who believed in nothing she could not see or imagine, was utterly undisturbed. I am sure that must have played its part in the row we had in our room that night.

There were small single rooms, of course, several of them. There were also low dormitories for body servants and sporting auxiliaries. All the rooms for two people had Scottish double beds. Clarissa and I had to labor away in silence making such a bed with sheets she had brought with us. Blankets we should have had to find in drawers and to take on trust, but on such a night they were unnecessary. Aline, when not with Clarissa, always slept in a striped bag, which that night must have been far too hot. Everything, everywhere, was far too hot. That contributed too, as it always does. Look at Latin America!

I admit that throughout the evening I had failed to respond very affirmatively to Clarissa's sequence of suggestions for livening up the property and also (she claimed) increasing its market value; which, indeed, cannot, as things were and are, be high. I could see for myself how I was leading her first into despondency, then into irritation. I can see that only too well now. I was dismayed by what was happening, but there was so little I could conscientiously offer in the way of encouragement. All I wished to do with Pollaporra was patch up some arrangement to meet my minimum obligations as a life tenant, and then, if possible, never set eyes upon the place again. One reason why I was cast down was the difficulty of achieving even a program as basic as that. I daresay that Clarissa's wild ideas would actually be simpler to accomplish, and conceivably cheaper also in the end. But there is something more than reason that casts me down at Pollaporra. Shall I say that the house brings into consciousness the conflict between my hereditament and my identity? Scotland herself is a land I do well to avoid. Many of us have large areas of danger which others find merely delightful.

There was no open row until Clarissa and I went upstairs. One reason was that after doing the washing-up, Aline had come into the sitting room, without a word, to join us. I was not surprised that she had no wish to be alone; nor that she proved reluctant to play a game named Contango, of which Clarissa was very fond, and which went back to her days with Jack, even though Jack had always won, sometimes while glancing through business papers simultaneously, as I had observed for myself. Both Clarissa and Aline were wearing tartan trousers, though not the same tartan. I had always been told by Cuddy that there was no Leith tartan. I have never sought further to know whether or not that is true.

As soon as we were in bed, Clarissa lay on her front, impressing the pillow with moisture from her brow, and quietly set about me; ranging far beyond the possibilities and deficiencies of Pollaporra. Any man—any modern man—would have some idea of what was said. Do the details matter? I offered no argument. At Pollaporra, I spoke as little as I could. What can argument achieve anywhere? It might have been a moment for me to establish at least temporary dominance by one means or another but Pollaporra prevented, even if I am the man to do it at any time. I tried to remember Shulie, but of course the circumstances left her entirely unreal to me, together with everything else.

And, in the morning, things were no better. I do not know how much either of us had managed to sleep. For better or worse, we had fallen silent in the heat long ago. In the end, I heard the sea birds screaming and yelling at the dawn.

Clarissa put on a few garments while I lay silent on the bed and then told me that as there was nothing she could do in the house she was departing at once.

"I should leave Aline behind, but I need her."

"I quite understand," I said. "I advised you against coming in the first place. I shall go over to see Mason and try to arrange with him for a caretaker. It won't take more than a day or two."

"You'll first need to change the place completely. You are both weak and pigheaded."

"They sometimes see things differently in Scotland. I shall come down as soon as I can." I might have to hire a car to some station, because I did not think Mason owned one, or anyone else in his small community. That was a trifle; comparatively.

"No hurry. I shall use the time deciding what to do for the best." She was combing her mass of hair, lovely as Ceres's sheaf. The comb, given her by the Aga Khan, was made of ebony. The air smelled of hot salt.

I suppose I should have begged her pardon for Pollaporra and myself, and gone back to London with her, or to anywhere else. I did not really think of it. Pollaporra had to be settled, if at all possible. I might never be back there.

In a few moments, Clarissa and I were together in the hall, the one high room, and I saw Aline silently standing by the outer door, as if she had stood all night; and the door was slightly open. Aline was in different trousers, and so was Clarissa.

"I can't be bothered to pack up the food. You're welcome to all of it."

"Don't go without breakfast," I said. "The lumpy roads will make you sick."

"Breakfast would make me sick," said Clarissa.

Clarissa carried very few clothes about. All she had with her was in the aircraft holdall she clutched. I do not know about Aline. She must have had something. I cannot remember.

"I don't know when we'll meet again," said Clarissa.

"In two or three days," I said. "Four at the most." Since I had decided to remain, I had to seem calm.

"I may go and stay with Naomi. I want to think things out."

She was wearing the lightest of blouses, little more than a mist. She was exquisite beyond description. Suddenly, I noticed that tears were again streaming silently down Aline's face.

"Or I may go somewhere else," said Clarissa, and walked out, with her slight but distinctive wobble.

Instead of immediately following her, as she always did, Aline actually took two steps in my direction. She looked up at me, like a rococo cherub. Since I could not kiss Clarissa, I lightly kissed Aline's wet lips, and she kissed me.

I turned my back in order not to see the car actually depart, though nothing could prevent my hearing it. What had the row been really about? I could surmise and guess, but I did not know. I much doubted whether Clarissa knew. One could only be certain that she would explain herself, as it were to a third party, in a totally different way from me. We might just as well belong to different zoological species, as in the Ray Bradbury story. The row was probably a matter only of Clarissa being a woman and I a man. Most or all rows between the sexes have no more precise origin; and, indirectly, many other rows also.

I think I stood for some time with my back to the open door and my face to the picture of an old gillie in a tam, with dead animals almost to his knees. It had been given us by the Shepstones. It was named "Coronach" in Ruskinian letters, grimly misapplied. Ultimately, I turned and through the open door saw what Aline may have seen. The auld carlin was advancing across the drive with a view to entering.

Drive, I have to call it. It was a large area of discolored nothingness upon which cars stood, and before them horses, but little grew, despite the lack of weeding. Needless to say, the woman was not approaching straightforwardly. Previously, I had seen her only when she had been confined to the limits of a staircase, albeit a wide one, a landing, and, later, a lift. If now she had been coming straight at me, I might have had a split second to see her face. I realized that, quite clearly, upon the instant.

I bounded forward. I slammed the door. The big key was difficult to turn in the big lock, so I shot the four rusty bolts first. Absurdly, there was a "chain" also and, after I had coped with the stiff lock, I "put it on."

Then I tore round the house shooting other bolts, making sure that all other locks were secure, shutting every possible window and aperture, on that already very hot early morning.

It is amazing how much food Clarissa laid in. She was, or is, always open-handed. I am sure that I have made that clear. Nor of course does one need so much food—or at least want so much—in this intense heat. Nor as yet has the well run dry. Cuddy refused to show me the well, saying the key was lost. I have still not seen either thing.

There is little else to do but write this clear explanation of everything that has happened to me since the misfortune of birth. He that has fared better, and without deceiving himself, let him utter his jackass cry.

Not that I have surrendered. There lies the point. Pollaporra is not on the telephone, nor ever could be, pending the "withering away of the State"; but before long someone may take note that I am not there. The marines may descend from choppers yet. Clarissa may well have second thoughts. Women commonly do, when left to themselves. She loves Pollaporra and may well devise a means of wresting my life-interest away from me, and welcome. I don't know where Aline would enter into that hypothesis. Possibly I made a mistake in not writing to Mason that I was coming. But I doubt whether in such personal matters his time-scale is shorter than months.

Off and on, I see the woman at one window or another; though not peeking through, which, as will have been gathered, is far from her policy. At least twice, however, it has been at a window upstairs; on both occasions when I was about to undress for some reason, not necessarily slumber, of which I have little. At these times, her slimy-sleek head, always faceless, will tip-tap sharply against the thick glazing bars. The indelicacy, as Jack might put it (I wonder how Cuddy would put it?), set me upon a course of hard thinking.

So long as I keep myself barred up, she can achieve nothing. Mason seemed quite certain of that, and I accept it. But what does the woman aim to do to me? When she appeared to me before, my poor mother soon passed away. When she appeared to me a second time, my dear, dear Shulie vanished from my life. It is not to be taken for granted that either of these precise fates is intended for me. I am not even ill or infirm. There may be a certain room for maneuver, though I can foresee no details.

More often, I see the woman at corners of what used to be the lawn and garden, though never in my time. It lies at the back of the house, and far below lies the loch. Sometimes too, the creature perches on the ornaments and broken walls, like a sprite. Such levitations are said to be not uncommon in the remoter parts of Scotland. Once I thought I glimpsed her high up in a tree, like dirty rags in a gale. Not that so far there has been any gale, or even any wind. The total silent stillness is one of the worst things. If I die of heat and deoxygenation, it will be one solution.

Yes, it is a battle with strong and unknown forces that I have on my hands. "But what can ail all of them to bury the old carlin in the night time?" as Sir Walter ventures to inquire; in *The Antiquary,* if I remember rightly.

Visitors

by JACK DANN

Jack Dann has edited some of the most important fantasy and science fiction anthologies of the last dozen years and is the author of a significant body of fiction, including the heart-wrenching time trap fantasy "Camps." There is an anguish in his work that is barely hinted at by the word angst. *Yet his vision is clear and his sense of irony acute. Here is an unsettling story of life and death, of affirmation.*

After Mr. Benjamin died, he came back to Charlie's room for a visit.

He was a tall man, taken down to the bone by cancer. His face had a grayish cast; and his thick white hair, of which he had been so obviously proud, had thinned. But he was still handsome even as he stood before Charlie's bed. He was sharp-featured, although his mouth was full, which softened the effect of his piercing, pale blue eyes; he wore silk pajamas and a turquoise robe, and was as poised and stiff as an ancient emperor.

"They closed all the doors again," Charlie said to Mr. Benjamin—they always closed the doors to the patients' rooms when they had to wheel a corpse through the hallway.

"I guess they did," Mr. Benjamin said, and he sat down in the cushioned chair beside Charlie's bed. He usually came for a visit before bedtime; it was part of his nightly ritual.

But here he was, and it was midafternoon.

Sunlight flooded through a tripartite window into the large high-ceilinged room, magnifying the swirling dust motes that filled the room like snow in a crystal Christmas-scene paperweight. The slate-grey ceiling above was barrel-vaulted, and although cracked and broken and discolored, the plaster was worked into intricate patterns of entwined tendrils. A marble fireplace was closed off with a sheet of metal, and there was an ancient mahogany grandfather clock ticking in the corner. The hospital had once been a manor, built in the 1800s by the wealthiest man in the state; its style was Irish Gothic, and every room contained the doric columns and scrolled foliage that were a trademark of the house.

"I wonder who died?" Charlie asked.

Mr. Benjamin smiled sadly and stretched his long legs out under Charlie's bed.

Charlie was fifteen and had had an erection before Mr. Benjamin came into the room, for he was thinking about the nurses, imagining how they would look undressed. Although Charlie's best friend had been laid, Charlie was still a virgin; but he looked older than he was and had even convinced his best friend that he, too, had popped the cork. He had been feeling a bit better these last few days. He had not even been able to think about sex before; there was only pain and drugs, and even with the drugs he could feel the pain. All the drugs did were let him investigate its shape; Charlie had discovered that pain had shape and color; it was like an animal that lived and moved inside him.

"How are you feeling today?" Mr. Benjamin asked.

"Pretty good," Charlie said, although the pain was returning and he was due for another shot. "How about you?"

Mr. Benjamin laughed. Then he asked, "Where's Rosie?" Rosie was Charlie's private nurse. Charlie's father was well-to-do and had insisted on round-the-clock private nurses for his son. But Charlie didn't want private nurses or a private room; in fact, he would have preferred a regular double room and a roommate, which would have been much less expensive; and if Charlie had another setback, his roommate would be able to call for a nurse for him. Charlie had been deathly ill: he had developed peritonitis from a simple appendectomy, and his stomach was still hugely distended. Drainage tubes were sunk deeply into his incisions, and they smelled putrid. He had lost over thirty pounds.

Charlie seemed to be slipping in and out of a dream; it was just the Demerol working through his system.

"Rosie's off today," he said after a long pause. He had

been dreaming of whiteness, but he could hear clearly through the dream. He came fully awake and said, "I love her, but it's such a relief not to have her banging everything around and dropping things to make sure I don't fall asleep. The regular nurses have been in a lot, and I got two backrubs." He grinned at Mr. Benjamin. It was a game he played with Mr. Benjamin: who could win the most points in wooing the nurses. One night, when Charlie had been well enough to walk across the hall and visit Mr. Benjamin, he found him in bed with two nurses. Mr. Benjamin had a grin on his face, as if he had just won the game forevermore. The nurses, of course, were just playing along.

Mr. Benjamin leaned back in the chair. It was a bright, sunny day, and the light hurt Charlie's eyes when he stared out the window for too long. Perhaps it was an effect of the Demerol, but Mr. Benjamin just seemed...not quite defined, as if his long fingers and strong face were made out of the same dust motes that filled the air and the room.

"Is your wife coming over today?" Charlie asked. "It's Wednesday." Charlie was in on Mr. Benjamin's secret: two women came to visit him religiously—his mistress, a beautiful young woman with long red hair, on Tuesdays and Thursdays; and his wife, who wasn't beautiful, but who must have been once, and who was about the same age as Mr. Benjamin, every Monday, Wednesday, Friday, and Sunday. His friends came to see him on Saturday, but not his women.

"No, not today," Mr. Benjamin said.

"That's too bad."

And just then one of the nurses came into the room. She was one of the old hands, and she said hello to Charlie, fluffed up his pillow, took his temperature, and gave him a shot all the while she talked, but it was small talk. The nurse ignored Mr. Benjamin, as she tore away the bandages that covered the drainage tubes in Charlie's stomach. Then she pulled out the tubes, which didn't hurt Charlie, and cleaned them. After she had reinserted the tubes—two into the right side of his abdomen, one on the left—and replaced the bandages, she hung another clear plastic bag of saline solution on the metal pole beside the bed and adjusted the rate of fluid that dripped into the vein in Charlie's right wrist.

"Who died?" Charlie asked her, wishing one of the pretty nurses' aides had been sent in or had at least accompanied her.

She sat down on the bed and rubbed Charlie's legs. He

had lost so much weight that they were the size his arms had once been. This nurse was one of Charlie's favorites, even though she was old—she could have been fifty or sixty-five, it was difficult to tell. She had a wide, fleshy face, a small nose, and perfect, capped teeth. "You'll have to know anyway," she said without looking up at him. "It was Mr. Benjamin. I know how close you felt to him, and I'm so very sorry, but as you know he was in a lot of pain. This is the best thing for the poor man; you've got to try to believe that. He's in a happier place now."

Charlie was going to tell her she was crazy, that he was right here and had a mistress and a wife and an architect job to go back to, and that it was all bullshit about a happier place, but he just nodded and turned toward Mr. Benjamin. She made a fuss over Charlie, who was ignoring her, and finally left. "Are you sure you'll be okay?" she asked.

Charlie nodded. His mouth felt dry; the Demerol would soon kick-in. "Yeah, I'll be fine." Then, turning back to Mr. Benjamin, he asked, "Are you really dead?"

Mr. Benjamin nodded. "I suppose I am."

"You don't look dead."

"I don't feel dead. My goddamn legs are still aching and itching like hell."

Charlie's face felt numb. "Why are you in here if you're dead."

"How the hell should I know. There are worse places I can think of. I just got out of bed and walked in here, same way as I always do."

"Are you going to stay?"

"For a while. Do you mind?"

Charlie just shook his head and took comfort, as he always did, in Mr. Benjamin's presence. But then the man in the next room started screaming again, praying to God to relieve him of his pain, begging and whining and whimpering and waking up the other patients.

It was difficult to rest with all that commotion going on.

The Demerol came upon him like a high tide of anesthesia. It soaked into him, and everything in the hospital room turned white, as if the molding and wall panels and ceiling scrollwork and inlaid marble chimneypiece were carved out of purest snow. He dreamed of winter and castles and books he had read when he was a child. He was inside a cloud, his thoughts drifting, linking laterally, as he dreamed of chalk

and snow and barium, of whitewash and bleach, of silver and
frost and whipped cream, of angels and sand, of girls as
white as his Demerol highs, chalky and naked with long
white hair and pale lips, long and thin and small breasted,
open and wet and cold, cold as snow, cold as his icicle erection, cold as his thought of glacially slow coitus.

He woke up shivering in a dark room, sweat drying on his
goose-bumped skin. Gray shadows crawled across the room,
a result of traffic on the street below.

Mr. Benjamin was still sitting beside the bed.

"Have you been here all this time?" Charlie asked. It was
late. The nurses had turned out the lights in his room, and
the hallway was quiet. If he listened carefully and held his
breath, he could hear the snoring and moaning of other patients between the tickings of the clock. His mouth was
parched, and he reached for the water tumbler. It sat on his
1950s-style night table, which also contained the remote control unit that turned the television on and off and also allowed him to buzz the nurse's station. He poured some ice
water into a paper cup. "You look more...real," Charlie
said.

"What do you mean?" Mr. Benjamin asked.

"I dunno, you looked kinda weak before."

"Well, I'm feeling better now. My legs stopped itching,
and they only ache a little bit now. I can stand it, at least.
How about you?"

"I feel like crap again," Charlie said. "I thought I was
getting better." The pain in his stomach was intense and
stabbing; it hadn't been this bad in a long time. "And I know
that old fat Mrs. Campbell isn't going to give me another
shot until I start screaming and moaning like the guy across
the hall."

Charlie's night nurse thought he was becoming too dependent on painkillers.

"He's getting worse," Benjamin said.

"Who?" Charlie asked.

"The guy across the hall, Mr. Ladd. Rosie told me he's
had most of his stomach removed."

"I just wish he would stop crying and begging for the pain
to go away. I can't stand it. He makes such a racket. There's
something pitiful about it. And he's not the only one who's in
pain around here."

"Well, who knows, maybe he can cut a deal," Mr. Benjamin said.

"You're not dead," Charlie said.

Mr. Benjamin shrugged.

"I thought you said you had all kinds of contracts to build new buildings and stuff. You said you wanted to work until you dropped dead, that you wanted to travel and all. And what about Miss Anthony . . . and your wife?"

"It's all gone," Mr. Benjamin said.

"Doesn't it bother you?"

"I don't know," he said, surprised. "I don't really feel anything much about it. Maybe a little sad. But I guess not even that."

"Tell me what it's like to be dead."

"I don't know. The same as being alive, I would suppose, except my legs feel better."

"You're not dead," Charlie said.

"I'll take your word for it, Charlie."

Charlie became worse during the night. He used the speaker in the night table to call Mrs. Campbell for a shot, but she told him he wasn't due for another hour. He tried to argue with her, he kept calling her, but she ignored him. He listened to the clock on the wall and turned this way and that, trying to find a comfortable position. Goddamn her, Charlie thought, and he tried to count himself to sleep. If he could fall asleep for just a little while, it would then be time for his shot.

Goddamn, it hurts . . .

And Mr. Ladd across the hall started screaming and whining and trying to make a deal with God again. Charlie gritted his teeth and tried to pretend that the room was turning white and that he was numb and frozen, made of blue ice. Ice: the absence of pain.

"Mr. Benjamin, are you still there?" Charlie asked.

But there was no answer.

Finally, it was time for his shot, and Charlie slept, drifting through cold spaces defined by the slow ticking of the clock.

Although it was four in the morning and everyone was asleep, the nurses and orderlies ritually closed the doors, as they always did, when they wheeled a corpse down the hallway.

Charlie was awake and feeling fine when Mr. Benjamin brought Mr. Ladd into the room; the pain was isolated and the metallic taste of the drugs was strong in his mouth. Mr.

Ladd appeared nervous. He was in his sixties and bald. He was thin, emaciated-looking, and his skin was blemished with age marks.

"Our friend here hasn't quite gotten used to being dead," Mr. Benjamin said to Charlie. "I found him wandering around the hallway. You mind if he stays a while?"

"I dunno," Charlie said, although he didn't want the old man in his room. "What's he going to do here?"

"Same thing you're doing. Same thing I'm doing."

Mr. Ladd didn't even acknowledge Charlie. He looked around the room, his head making quick, jerky motions; then he walked across the room, sat down on the stained cushion of the windowseat, and looked down into the street.

"At least your pain's gone," Mr. Benjamin called to him, but the old man just stared out the window, as if he hadn't heard him. "How about you?" Mr. Benjamin asked Charlie.

"I'm okay, I guess," but then someone else came into the room. A middle-aged woman in a blue bathrobe. She exchanged greetings with Mr. Benjamin and walked over to the window. "You know her?" Charlie asked.

"Yeah, I sat with her some yesterday and tonight she was real bad. But I guess you can't win. I left Mr. Ladd to be with her. Now they're both here." Mr. Benjamin smiled. "I feel like a goddamned Florence Nightingale."

But Charlie had fallen asleep.

He awoke to bright sunlight. His condition had deteriorated further, for now he had an oxygen tube breathing icy air into one nostril, while in the other was a tube that passed down his esophagus and into his stomach. His private nurse Rosie was in the room, moving about, looking starched and efficient and upset. His mother sat beside the bed, leaning toward him, staring at him intently, as if she could think him well. Her small, delicate face seemed old to him, and her dyed jet-black hair looked as coarse and artificial as a cheap wig. But both his mother and Rosie seemed insubstantial, as if *they* were becoming ghosts. His mother blocked out most of the light coming through the windows, but some of it seemed to pass through her, as if she were a cloud shaped like a woman that was floating across the sun. Her voice, which was usually high and piercing, was like a whisper; and her touch felt dry, like leaves brushing against his skin. He suddenly felt sorry for his mother. She loved him, he supposed, but he felt so removed from her. He probably felt like

Mr. Benjamin did when he died. Just a little sad.

Charlie just wished that everyone would leave. He looked toward the light and saw Mr. Benjamin, Mr. Ladd, and the woman who had walked into his room last night standing near the window. He called for Mr. Benjamin; neither Rosie nor his mother seemed to understand what he was saying.

"Mr. Benjamin?"

His mother said something to Rosie, who also said something to Charlie, but Charlie couldn't understand either of them. Their voices sounded far away; it was like listening to static on the radio and only being able to make out a word here or there. It was as if Rosie and his mother were becoming ghosts, and the visitors, who were already dead, were gaining substance and reality.

"Yes?" Mr. Benjamin said as he walked over to the bed and stood beside Charlie's mother. "I'm afraid you've had a bit of a setback."

"What are they still doing here?" Charlie asked, meaning Mr. Ladd and the woman who had come into his room last night.

"Same thing I am," said Mr. Benjamin.

"Okay, what are *you* doing here?"

"Making sure you won't be alone."

Charlie closed his eyes.

Perhaps his mother sensed the presence of the visitors, too, for she suddenly began to cry.

Charlie's mother stayed for the rest of the day. She talked about Charlie's father, as if nothing was going wrong with their marriage, as if she could simply ignore the other dark-haired woman who had come into her husband's life. Charlie knew about Laura, the other woman; but he had learned a lot about such things from watching Mr. Benjamin's wife and mistress come and go every week. He supposed it was just the way adults behaved. He couldn't stand to see his mother hurt, yet he couldn't get angry with his father. He felt somehow neutral about the whole thing.

She sat and talked to Charlie as she drank cup after cup of black coffee. She would nod off to sleep for a few minutes at a time and then awaken with a jolt. At five she took her dinner on a plastic tray beside Charlie's bed. Charlie couldn't eat; he was being fed intravenously. He slept fitfully, cried out in pain, received a shot, and lived in whiteness for a while. When he was on the Demerol, his mother and Rosie would all but disappear, yet he would be able to see Mr. Benjamin and the visitors. But Mr. Benjamin wouldn't talk much to him when his mother or hospital personnel were in the room.

Finally, Rosie's shift was over. Rosie tried to talk Charlie's mother into leaving with her, but it was no use. She insisted on staying. Mrs. Campbell, the night nurse, talked with Charlie's mother for a while and then left the room, as she always did. Charlie would need a shot soon.

His mother held his hand and kept leaning over him, brushing her face against his, kissing him. She talked, but Charlie could barely hear or feel her.

Charlie came awake with a jolt; it was as if he had fallen out of the bed. He was sweaty and could taste something bitter in his mouth. The drugs were still working, but the pain was returning, gaining strength. It was an animal tearing at his stomach. Only a shot and the numbing chill of white sleep would calm it down . . . for a time.

"Hello," said a young woman standing by the bed beside Mr. Benjamin. She had straight, shoulder-length dark brown hair, a heart-shaped face, blue eyes set a bit too widely apart, a small, upturned nose, and full, but colorless lips. She looked tiny, perhaps five feet one, if that, and seemed very shy.

"Hello," Charlie replied, surprised. He felt awkward and looked over to Mr. Benjamin, who smiled. It was dark again. He turned toward the spot where his mother had been sitting, but he couldn't tell if she was still there. He could only hear the clock and the sound of leaves rustling that he imagined might be his mother's voice. The room was dimly lit, and there seemed to be a shadow, a slight flutter of movement, around the chair. Except for the visitors, the hospital seemed empty and devoid of doctors, nurses, orderlies, aides, and candy stripers. Charlie felt numb and cold. The air in the room was visible . . . was white as cirrus clouds and seemed to radiate its own wan light.

"This is Katherine," Mr. Benjamin said. "She's new here, and a bit disoriented, I think." Katherine seemed to be concentrating on the foot of the bed and avoiding eye contact with Charlie. But Charlie noticed that she didn't seem as real, as corporal, somehow, as Mr. Benjamin. Perhaps she wasn't dead long enough. That would take some time. "I'll step aside and give you a chance to win this time," Mr. Benjamin continued.

Charlie blushed. Mr. Benjamin walked to the other side of the room to be with the other visitors.

"How did you die?" Charlie asked Katherine.

She just shook her head, a slight, quick motion.

"Do you feel all right?" he asked. "Are you scared or anything?"

"I just feel alone," she said in almost a whisper.

"Well, you got Mr. Benjamin," Charlie said.

She smiled sadly. "Yeah, I guess." She sat down on the bed. Her robe was slightly opened and Charlie could see a hint of her cleavage. "Are you dying?" she asked.

That took him by surprise, although as soon as she said it, he realized that it shouldn't have. "I dunno. I've just been sick."

"Do you want to live?"

"Yeah, I guess so. Wouldn't you?"

"It feels kinda the same," she said, "only..."

"Only what?"

"I don't know, it's hard to explain. Just alone, like I said. You seem out of focus, sort of," she said. She touched his hand tentatively, and Charlie could feel only a slight pressure and a cool sensation. Charlie held her hand. It was an impulsive move, but she didn't resist. Her hand felt somehow papery, and Charlie had the feeling that he could press his fingers right through her flesh with but little resistance. She leaned toward him, resting against him. It felt like the cool touch of fresh sheets. She seemed weightless. "Thank you," she whispered.

He curled up against her, put his arm around her waist and rested his hand on her leg. He remembered taking long baths and letting his arms float in the water. Although the water would buoy them up, it also felt as if he were straining against gravity. That's what it felt like to touch Katherine.

Charlie wanted this to last; it was perfect. He felt the pain in his stomach, but it was far away. Someone else was groaning under its weight.

They watched visitors file into the room. Each one looking disoriented and out of focus. Each one walking across to the other side, to the window, to be with the others, who began to seem as tangible and fleshy as Charlie.

Charlie tried to ignore them. He pulled the sheets over himself... and Katherine. He pressed himself as closely as he could to her, and she allowed him to kiss and fondle her.

As everything turned white, numbed by another shot given to him by a ghost, his nurse, Charlie dreamed that he was making love to Katherine.

It was cool and quiet, a wet dream of death.

At dawn Mr. Benjamin called Charlie to leave. The room was empty; the last of the other visitors had just left without a footfall. Mr. Benjamin looked preternaturally real, as if every line of his face, every feature had been etched into perfect stone. Katherine rose from the bed and stood beside Mr. Benjamin, her robe tightly pulled around her. She, too, looked real and solid, more alive than any of the shadows flitting through the halls and skulking about his room: the nurses and aides and orderlies. Charlie found it difficult to breathe; it was as if he had to suck every breath from a straw.

"Why are you leaving?" Charlie asked, his voice raspy; but his words were glottals and gutturals, sighs and croakings.

"It's time. Are you coming?"

"I can't. I'm sick."

"Just get up. Leave what's in the bed," Mr. Benjamin said impatiently, as if dying was not a terribly important or difficult thing to do.

Katherine reached for his hand, and her flesh was firm and real and strong. "I can see you very clearly now," she said. "Come on."

But someone moved in the chair beside Charlie. A shadow, more of a negative space. Charlie tried to make it out. Into a soft focus came the outlines of a woman, his mother. But she was a wraith. Yet he could make her out, could make out her voice, which sounded as distant as a train lowing through the other side of town. She was talking about his younger brother Stephen and the sunflowers behind the house that had grown over six feet tall. The sunflowers always made Charlie feel sad, for they signaled the end of summer and the beginning of school. He could feel the warm, sweaty touch of her hand on his face, touching his forehead, which was the way his mother had always checked his temperature.

"I love you, Charlie," she said, her voice papery. "Everything's going to be all right for all of us. And you're going to get well soon. I promise..."

Katherine's hand slipped away, and then Charlie felt the

warm, almost hot touch of his mother's hand upon his own.
She clutched his fingers as if she knew she might be losing
him, and in the distance, Charlie could hear that train sound:
now the sound of his mother crying. And he remembered the
rich and wonderful smells that permeated her tiny kitchen
when she was making soup; he could see everything in that
room: the radio on the red painted shelves, the china bric-a-
brac, the red and black electric cat clock on the wall that had
a plastic tail and eyes that moved back and forth; and he
remembered his grandmother, who always brought him a gift
when she visited; and he could almost hear the voices of his
friends, as if they were all passing between classes; he remembered kissing Laurie, his first girlfriend, and how he had
tried unsuccessfully to feel her up behind her house near the
river; and even with his eyes closed he could clearly see his
little brother, who always followed him around like a duck,
and his gray haired, distant father who was always "working"; he remembered the time he and his brother hid near
the top of the red-carpeted stairs and watched the adults
milling around and drinking and laughing and kissing each
other at a New Year's Eve party, and how his father had
awakened him and his brother at four o'clock in the morning
on New Year's Day so they could eat eggs and toast and home
fries with him and Mom in the kitchen; he remembered going to Atlantic City for two weeks in the summer,
the boardwalk hot and crowded and gritty with sand, the
girls in bikinis and clogs, their skin tanned and hair sun-
bleached; he remembered that his mother always tanned
quickly, and she looked so young that everyone thought she
was his girlfriend when they went shopping along the boardwalk; and suddenly that time came alive, and he could smell
salt water taffy and taste cotton candy and snow cones that
would immediately start to melt in the blazing, life-giving
sun.

Charlie could feel himself lifting, floating; yet another
part of him was heavy, fleshy.

He thought of Katherine, of her coolness, the touch of
her pale lips and icy breasts, and then his mother came into
focus: age-lines, black hair, shadows under frightened hazel
eyes—his eyes.

And her touch was as strong as Katherine's.

He floated between them . . . caught.

Soon, he would have to choose.

Gentlemen

by JOHN SKIPP
and CRAIG SPECTOR

*John Skipp and Craig Spector are young innovaters in the
horror field. Most of their work is done in collaboration, including their novels* The Light at the End *and* The Cleanup.

*In the 1960s, the women's movement swept through Ameri-
can culture, cleansing it of centuries-old patterns of accepted
behavior between men and women which no new etiquette has
yet replaced. "Gentlemen" is a terrifying portrayal of the state
of contemporary masculinity, terrifying because of the brutal-
ity within the relationships depicted, but ultimately uplifting
because "Gentlemen" goes beyond the familiar "oh isn't it terrible how badly we men treat women" horror story, into cul-
turally uncharted territory.*

TO BE A MAN.

The words are carved on the sweat-smeared oak of the
bar's surface. They're the only four that never seem to
change. Like the troll at the taps, the regulars that surround
him, the TVs and the black velvet painting of the Hooter
Girl that hangs in sad-eyed judgment over all.

TO BE A MAN.

As if that were all there is.

I always hated Bud. He loves it. We drink it. One after
another, we pour them down, while Ralph Kramden bellows
about trips to the moon.

And the guys all laugh. You're goddamn right.

They know about being a man.

And now, at last, so do I.

I remember the night that my edification began. Every
nuance. Every shade. The phone started ringing at 12:45,
precisely. It was LeeAnn, of course. She'd just crashed and
burned with another asshole relationship, and she needed to
talk. And drink. Right now. I knew all this by the first ring.
No one else ever called this late. No one.

"Damn," I muttered. "Not again."

There were a lot of good reasons for not answering. It was
a shit-soaked night outside, cold rain falling in thick sheets.
The steam head had finally kicked in, and I was down to my
jeans. I was halfway into a lumpy joint of some absurdly
good Jamaican. *Star Trek* would be on in fifteen minutes.
Seeing LeeAnn would make me miserable, and I'd just wind
up sourly wanking off when I got home. Yep, a lot of good
reasons. I took another toke and settled back in my chair.

The phone rang again. I choked. The smoke exploded in my
lungs. I began to cough violently, great red-meat wrenching
hacks. The phone rang again. I roared back at it, defiant, my
eyes tearing and my throat desperately lubing itself with bile.

The phone rang again, and I got out of the chair. What was
the point? The phone would ring forever. The night was already completely ruined; LeeAnn's face had control of my
mind. I snubbed the joint and placed the butt in my pocket, for
later. The phone rang once more before I caught it. I coughed a
little bit more at the receiver as I brought it to the side of my
head. What did it matter? I already knew what the first words
would be. First, my name. No *howdy, stranger,* no *long time no
see.*

Just:

"David?"

Then:

"David, I need you..."

Like clockwork. I gave brief, fleeting audience to the idea
of just hanging up, of pitching the receiver into the cradle
without so much as a whimper. But then her voice, so characteristically vulnerable, spoke the final two words in the equa-
tion:

"David, *please...*"

I was slaughtered.

"Where are you?" I asked. Coughing had made me
roughly twenty times more stoned in a matter of seconds; the

air seemed thicker, my head felt muddier, and the crackle over the phone line raked like needles in my ears.

She let out a laugh I recognized: the resigned and barely-in-control one. I coughed. She laughed. I spoke.

"I still don't know where you are."

"I'm at this place called . . ." She paused; I could almost hear her neck craning, " . . . dammit, I can't tell. It's at Forty-eighth and Eighth. The beer is cheap. The guys are all jerks. It's my kind of place. Can you come?"

"Shouldn't the question be, 'How fast can you get here?'"

"Jesus, I really *am* predictable."

"You're not the only one," I assured her wearily. "Give me some time, okay? I don't have any clothes on."

"Hubba hubba."

"Don't tease me, LeeAnn. I'm not a well man."

"Aw, poor baby."

I closed my eyes, and LeeAnn was behind them: leaning against a bar with brass rails, china-doll lips pouting, green-eyed gaze languidly drifting as her T-shirt slowly hiked its way past her breasts and over her ash-blonde head. *Never happen*, my rational mind reminded me flatly. It sounded barely-in-control, too.

LeeAnn must have heard it. The teasing stopped. "Please hurry," she said. "I need you."

"I'm on my way. Stay there."

The phone went dead. LeeAnn never said good-bye any-more; it was too commital. I set down the receiver and caught a glimpse of myself in the bureau mirror. Gaunt, sensitive features. Aquiline nose. Deep-set eyes. Quietly receding hairline. An interesting face: not handsome, certainly not repulsive. I smiled. Loads of character. The face of a poet, even . . .

Who was I kidding? I thought. *It's the face of a fool.* The reflection nodded in sad affirmation. I looked at the piles of dirty clothes on the floor and grabbed up a dirty sweatshirt. Dress for success, I always say. Or *said*, rather.

Whatever.

At any rate, I was suited up and out the door before manly Captain Kirk had pronged the first of this evening's deep-space bimbos, way out where no man had gone before. The last three words from her lips echoed through me like a curse.

I need you.

Sure.

* * *

The cab ride was long and wet, cold rain pounding on the windows like a billion tiny fists. The whole way up, I brooded about LeeAnn. The whole way up, I hit alternately on the dwindling vial of blow in my jacket pocket and one of the two jumbo oilcans of Foster's lager that I'd scored just for the trip. The irony of getting wasted as a prelude to meeting a friend for drinks was not lost on me, but what could I say? LeeAnn made me crazy: the same kind of crazy that would inspire me to tromp out into a maelstrom on a moment's notice and woefully underdressed, from my army-surplus field jacket down to a pair of battered Reeboks with a dime-sized hole in the right sole. She unnerved me that thoroughly. I snorted and watched the passing streets slip by: each one, rain-slicked and on the verge of flooding; each one, dark and bleak and utterly depressing.

Any of them, an escape route: infinitely preferable to where I was going.

If I'd been stronger, maybe, I'd have taken one. Sure. Of course, the same line of inarguable reasoning could be applied to any other quarter of my world, from my unpublished short stories to my unfinished novel to my utterly unrequited love life, with exactly the same results. The gross total of which, combined with fifty cents, would buy me a packet of Gem safety blades.

The better to slit my miserable fucking throat with.

The thought deflated as quickly as it came. Of course I would never really do that. Neither, of course, would I tell the cabbie to turn around and take me home, or just grab LeeAnn by the hair and force her to my heap big masculine will, or do *anything* but what I always, always did. Which was to go to her: whenever, wherever her next whirlwind sortie ended. In tears, in disaster; in rain, sleet, or snow, good ol' Dave would be there, day or night, with the right words and the right drugs and a shoulder to cry on. Good ol' Dave was never more than a phone call away. I hated myself for being such a stooge to this endlessly cyclical farce, for being so hapless in the face of my own flaccid desire.

The cab sploshed indifferently onto Tenth Avenue, heading uptown. The beer sploshed in my roiling guts, heading south. And the memories came boiling up . . .

We went back a little ways, LeeAnn and I. Long enough to count. Worked for the same messenger service: humping the bullshit of the business world by day, pounding at the walls of our dreams at night. She was in the office, I was on

the streets. She was sharp and funny and smarter than anyone else in the whole fleabag organization; I was the only
one in the entire company who would talk to her without
staring incessantly at her tits. No easy task, let me tell you.
But I did it, because I valued her trust almost as much as I
hungered for her touch.

So there we were, sharing in the adventure of being young
and piss-poor in New York, trying desperately to make it in
our respective careers: clone of Kerouac meets fledgling
Bourke-White. Came to spend a lot of time together: scru-
tinizing my first drafts and her black-and-whites over a dinner of ravioli and Riunite; wandering the streets and parks in
search of inspiration and free entertainment. We grew very
tight. Very close.

With one rather glaring exemption.

You see, for all that deep meaningful contact, it never
quite gelled for LeeAnn and me. It was ridiculous, yes. I
mean, I'd heard the most heartfelt feelings she'd ever cared
to offer without blushing or batting an eye; I would have
taken a bullet or thrown myself gleefully into traffic to save
the tiniest hair on her head.

Sure. I could do all that. But somehow I couldn't bridge
the safe, comfy distance between friend and lover. I just
couldn't bring myself to tell her how I felt, to grab her and
give her the kind of kiss that would make her reciprocate my
passion, my love.

In retrospect, I realize that I was waiting for *her* to do it. I
cringe to think of it now, but it's true. Part of my heart sincerely
believed that she would wake up one day with the realization
that no one would ever love her like I did. No one else could be
so tender, so compassionate, so understanding. No one else
would bear with her through her tragedies and madness, de-
vote themselves so selflessly and completely to her needs.

She would wake up one day, I told myself, kicking herself
for her foolishness. And she would throw herself, weeping,
into my arms. And I would tell her that it was okay, it was
over now. And we would be swept away into a love that not
even death could destroy.

One day, I knew, she would realize just how much she was
saying when she said the words *Dave, I need you.*

That was the bullshit *I* believed. I preferred it to the cold
hard truth.

As for LeeAnn, well . . .

LeeAnn preferred a different kind of guy.

A guy like Rodney, for example. I grimaced as his sneering pug loomed up like the answer in a magic eight-ball toy. Rod the bod, punk hunk *par excellence*. Took her on a three-month, nightmare tour of the Lower East Side, every nook and alley and rathole club that charged four bucks a beer. Rod, the artiste. Rod, the super-intense. He was inspiring her, giving her photography a whole new edge. Sure. Asshole inspired her, all right: eventually o.d.'ed on crack and went nuts in her apartment, damned near inspiring her to death before heading off to be shot by the police.

I upended the first can, draining the dregs, and popped the second in a ceremonial toast. *Rot in hell, Rodney.*

If they'll have you . . .

After that it was Willis, the far side of the pendulum. I think she met him at a Soho gallery opening. Willis of the shining white mane, who was strong and stable and financially secure and about old enough to be her father. Willis wined and dined her like a princess; my god, he even proposed to her. And she actually accepted, to my unending shock and horror, though I think it was more political than emotional. He had connections. He could *help* her. That is, until she found that her Svengali absolutely forbade her to work after the wedding. Not a woman's place, you understand. LeeAnn shouldn't worry her pretty little head with thoughts of careers. LeeAnn should worry about tending to Willis's earthly needs.

Or how 'bout Roger, her latest disaster. Yeah, Roger was great. Handsome and fortyish and too hip to hurt; cut him and he'd probably bleed Ralph Lauren aftershave. Now *they* were an item, and *soooo* good for each other. He was doing a book on Central America, was going to take her along as his photographer. Maybe her big break. I remember her coming out of the office at checkout time, pulling me aside to tell me the great news . . .

The great news ended rather abruptly at the Midtown Women's Services clinic, at precisely the same microsecond that the urine test came back positive. That was six weeks ago, give or take a millenium.

Well, he did pay for exactly half of the costs, which was awfully decent of him. But he wasn't there for her on the day it happened, with a smile or a hug or a hand to hold. I was. And he wasn't there in the guilt-wracked weeks after, or ever again.

I was.

Yeah, Roger was slime, and Roger went the way of the

wind. But even he wasn't the worst. First, there was Martin.

There was *always* Martin. . . .

The cab cut up Tenth Avenue like a shark through dark waters. Forty-second Street floated by; I blinked back fractured patterns of garish light and color that winked like beacons to hungerlust and loneliness, previews of coming attractions that would never hit town. The moron-parade marched on in my brain: an onslaught of compelling, charismatic bastards who, for all their disparate differences, had held one thing in common. Which I had not.

LeeAnn.

Lithe, lissome bane of my existence. An otherwise intelligent woman who wouldn't take two ounces of the same shit on the job that she ate buckets of in her personal life. And who, for some equally unfathomable reason, liked her men either old and sensitive or young and macho. Old, macho men were chauvinistic pig-dog bastards.

Young, sensitive men were wimps . . .

I winced, biting back the thoughts, denying any possible truth. The cab turned onto Forty-eighth and crossed Ninth Avenue as the last of the Foster's slid down my throat. I felt bilious, and I needed to take a leak. My mind was burnt crispy. My nerves were live wires.

But as the cab slid up to the corner, I resolved that this time, *this* time it would be different. Tonight would mark the end of her love affair with the scum of the earth. I felt a queasy determination that I underscored with a toot of cocaine courage, an alkaloid surge of ersatz bravado. *It's my turn, dammit!* I told myself. If it could be done, it would be done.

It wasn't until I paid the cabbie and hit the pavement that I started to get nervous.

Maybe it was the way she sat, back framed in the grimy bay window, red and green neon backwashing her features like some DC comic damsel in distress. Maybe it was the window itself, which hung dripping like a plate-glass gullet. The way it displayed her.

Like bait . . .

I felt it, all right. As I hunkered over and puddle-dodged toward the door, it was there: a small, wormy gut-rush, synching with the Bud and Stroh's signs that blinked wanly behind the glass, vestige of some primal warning mechanism not entirely obliterated by the drugs. Saying: *No . . . No . . . No . . .*

It was enough to register. It was not enough to stop me. The place was a dump, all right, but I felt sure I'd seen worse. It was nestled in the middle of a block dominated by drug dealers, pimps, and pawnshops, with the occasional ratbag adult emporium tossed in for good measure. The sign above the awning read simply **BAR**, with a badly painted-over prefix that looked as though the name had changed hands so many times that they'd just given up. The grime on the big window was thick enough to carve my initials in. The street itself was mercifully void, thanks to the rain; a sole Chicano bum not too far from his teens sprawled by the doorway, oblivious to the pounding. He twitched and muttered sporadically.

I fingered the folding knife thrust deep into the right-hand pocket of my jacket, the one that I'd habitually carried since being mugged last summer. It was long and thin and very sharp; stainless-steel casing, stainless-steel blade. I had never pulled it, never even used it, and often wondered if I carried it as a kind of a talisman more than a weapon. I hoped that I wouldn't need it in either capacity tonight. The thought: *Oh shit, LeeAnn, what are you into now?* loomed forth. The only possible answer was directly ahead.

The smell of bridges burning lay behind.

The first thing that hit me was the stink, a palpable presence that grew exponentially as the door shut behind. The usual stale smoke/stale beer bouquet, yes. But something else, underneath: a vague, foul underpinning. Familiar. Like . . .

Sewage, I realized. *Great.* My stomach rolled. I grimaced and took in the layout in an instant. The interior was long and low and dark, the furthest reaches of it enshrouded in greasy shadow some forty feet back. A pseudo-oldtime finger-sign pointed down some steps near the back, one word emblazoned in large gold script:

GENTLEMEN.

The source, no doubt. This must be my night. My bladder begged to differ. It wouldn't be long before I had to hit the hopper. It was no longer an idea I relished.

I noted that the rest of the decor was strictly Early K mart: imitation-walnut paneling and formica as far as the eye could see. The bar itself was unique, hugging the wall to a point halfway down the far side. It was a large and graceless structure replete with tarnished brass hand and foot rails, and somehow managed to be constructed entirely of oak without being the tiniest bit attractive. Twin ceiling-mounted Zenith nineteen-inch TVs blasted cablevision mercilessly on either end.

The Hooter Girl adorned the center.

She looked like one of those paintings of the hydro-cephalic sad-eyed children, pumped full of silicon and estro-gen. The kind of black velvet sofa-sized monstrosities you see cranked out by the yard and offered up on abandoned gas-station aprons across America, right next to Elvis and Jesus and the moose on the mountain. Big moon eyes and tits like basketballs. Pure class. The neon color scheme had faded over the passage of smoke-filled time, leaving her once-electric tan lines merely jaundiced.

It might have been funny, under other circumstances. At the moment it was making me ill. That and every other sor-did detail from the fly-specked ceiling tiles to the screaming vids to the sodden regulars that lined the bar like crows on a barnyard fence. What the hell was I *doing* here, in this hole, at this hour?

The answer crossed the lateral distance of the room and wrapped herself around me before I could mutter a word. We stood there for what seemed a very long time. I probably would have remained in that position forever, but for the eyes that had followed her course to me. They were hungry, angry, gimlet eyes.

The hunger was for her.

The anger was all mine.

"Would you please tell me what the fuck is going on here?" I said under my breath. It came out a little more hysterical than I'd wished. *Good start, chump,* I thought. *Don't whine.*

"Thanks for coming," she whispered into my armpit. I waited for more. It did not seem to be forthcoming, but she added a squeeze for emphasis. The warm flesh of her back shuddered beneath my touch, but for all the wrong reasons.

"Hey, are you okay?" I asked, not entirely certain that I wanted to hear the answer.

She nodded and snuffled just the tiniest bit, but she didn't let go. It worried me. Very gently, I pried her arms from around my waist and started to say, "C'mon, Lee, what's going on h—"

I never finished. LeeAnn looked up.

She had a black eye. Slit-swollen. Nasty. A tiny crescent-shaped cut had congealed just under her left eyebrow. She smiled gamely, chagrined. Her right eye crinkled with little smile-lines; the left remained fixed and droopy, like a bad impression of the Amazing Melting Woman.

I don't know why I was so surprised. Maybe I wasn't. I'd seen it before. But I couldn't bear to see it again: not now, not ever. My gaze flitted spastically to my shoes, the tubes, the goons at the bar. Anywhere but her face. Her face was dangerous. Her face made *me* dangerous. I stared in red-eyed rage as twin Rambos dispensed endless all-beef lessons in how real men take care of business.

But the goons at the bar weren't watching that. They were watching us. They were watching me.

They were smiling.

It was too much. There was nowhere to turn with my anger but back to the source. The words that came were clipped and vicious, in a voice I barely recognized as my own. I didn't like it. I couldn't help it.

"Who. Did. It."

LeeAnn shook her head. "Beer first," she said. It was not a suggestion. "And we'd better sit down." Then she pulled away, turned, and strode over to her place at the window end of the bar, next to the very payphone she'd probably used to call me, and gathered up her things. She gestured to the bartender, a withered old troll in a baggy white shirt who looked as if he'd spent all his younger days on some Lower West Side dock, trundling the very same kegs he now presided over. He grunted imperceptibly, ash falling from the Lucky pinched in one corner of his lips, and began refilling her emptied pitcher with deft, wordless efficiency. She was back in control that fast. However tenuous, she was in charge. Of herself. Of me.

I stood in stunned silence, the rage draining impotently out, as LeeAnn returned. She squeezed my arm lightly, imploringly, and then walked back toward the shadowed and empty booths. I was supposed to pay; it was understood. I watched her graceful trailing trek across the room. I watched her hips. I watched her ass.

I wasn't the only one watching.

Two of the clientele, a pair of drunken dimwits interchangeable as Heckel and Jeckel, leered at her in brief, neck-craning abandon. The third, a hairball with thick gold chains and too many teeth, managed a sidelong snickering appraisal before resuming his ogling of the washed-out and weary-looking blonde to his left.

The blonde, meanwhile, was oblivious to it all: staring off into her drink as if it were a gateway to another world entirely. She was the Hooter Girl made flesh and then stepped on. Not pleasant.

I stepped up to the bar, stoned and shell-shocked, drugs and wasted adrenaline making the seamy details painfully apparent. I fished out a crinkly ten-spot and stared blankly at the wooden expanse of the counter. It was scarred and pitted, with initials and epigraphs and other vital pearls of wisdom. Ritual scarification. One stuck out like a message in a bottle: four words, carved deeper that all the rest.

TO BE A MAN.

To be a man. A bitter sneer engraved itself across my face. *To be a man.* I'd heard enough of that shit to last me a lifetime. My old man had said it. My peer group had said it. The first caveman to bludgeon his object of desire and drag her home by the hair had grunted its equivalent.

To be a man. You bet. If my mind had lips, it would have spat out the words. *Somebody got nice and manly with LeeAnn tonight. It's written all over her face...*

I looked up. The blonde was glancing at me with weak and wounded eyes. I could see every crack and sag in her features. Ten years ago or so she must have been a real looker, but that was ancient history now. That kicked-around look spilled off of her in waves: the way she hugged her vitals, as if waiting for the next blow to fall; the way she'd sort of sunken into her own carcass, as if the extra padding might help; the way her eyes kept darting to the back of the room.

I stared, waiting for the pitcher to fill. And I wondered how the hell she could have let that happen to her.

Then the men's room door squealed open like a thing in pain.

And up stomped the Mighty Asshole.

The gnarled little man with the pitcher of beer was forgotten. So were the drunks and the hairball, the blonde, the dueling idiot boxes where Rambo played out his bloodless charade. Even LeeAnn slipped from my mind for one long, cold moment, as the entire spinning universe funneled down to the behemoth pounding up the cellar stairs.

Big as life and twice as ugly, he swaggered toward the bar, fumbling absently with his fly. Arms like girders. Eyes like meatballs. Feet pounding the floorboards like an overblown Bluto in a Max Fleisher cartoon, sending shock waves up my legs from halfway across the room.

The impulse to retreat must have come on a cellular level, because I had backed into a barstool before I even knew I was moving. Connecting with teetering solid matter jostled me back to the broader reality, and I cast a nervous glance over to LeeAnn. She was watching him, too.

We were *all* watching him.

It wasn't just that he was tanked, or that he was built like one. Or even that he was bearing down on us like some angry moron-god. Rather, it was his presence: the sheer force and volume of his rage. It was as vivid as the glow around a candle's flame, and black as the dead match that first fired it up.

The Mighty Asshole thundered over to his seat next to the blonde. The terror in her eyes answered my previous question quite nicely: they were an item. Like hammer and anvil, they were made for each other. I shuddered involuntarily.

Then the troll was back, pitcher and mugs clunking down onto the bar. He grinned at me, a toothless rictus, as I handed him the money. Looking into his eyes was like staring down an empty elevator shaft and never quite seeing the bottom. He smiled as he handed back my change, smiled as I hefted the goods, and kept right on smiling as I made my way back. The Asshole shot me a beady-eyed and territorial sneer as I hustled back.

I crossed the room like the guest of honor at a firing squad. The screaming of my nerves eased up only marginally, the farther away from the bar I drew. LeeAnn was already seated, tucked into one of the half-dozen claustrophobic, dimly-lit booths that ringed the desolate rear of the room. I joined her, setting down the pitcher and mugs, peeling off my wet jacket and tossing it into a heap on the bench. The beer sat untouched on the table. I sighed, grabbed the pitcher and filled both our mugs. LeeAnn watched, I handed her one, took a swig off my own, and waited.

Nothing.

"Well?" I said. It was meant to sound level and controlled, but it came out all wrong.

LeeAnn looked away. "Finish your beer," she said. She was serious. She was miserable.

"What?"

"Your beer." She was adamant. "Finish it."

I glared at her exasperatedly, then tipped back the mug, drained it in two gulps, and banged it on the table. "There," I said. "All gone. Happy?"

"Very," she said, refilling my mug. "Have another."

"What?! C'mon, LeeAnn, this is bullshit."

"Trust me, David. Drink up."

I stared at her for a moment longer, weighing the situation. I didn't want any more beer. I really didn't. In fact, the whole situation was beginning to grate on my nerves. My clothes were wet, the night was old, my bladder ached, and my patience was wearing thin. The words *don't play games with me, dammit* flickered through my mind on their way to my mouth. I caught them just in time.

But the anger remained. It was not lost on LeeAnn; she knew who it was for. Her whole body flinched back for a microsecond. The gesture was mostly surprise; but there was no getting around the fear, iris-black and widening, at its center. I'd seen fear in her eyes before, but I'd never been its cause.

I felt like a total shit.

"Jesus, kiddo," I whispered. "I'm sorry." Now it was her turn to avert the eyes. I looked at the mug of beer before me. It wasn't that much to ask. I wondered what the fuck was wrong with me.

I drained the goddamned mug.

"Okay," I said deliberately, with as much aplomb as I could scrounge up. "The beer is drunk, and so am I. I'm sedated. I'm fine. I will not get angry.

"So tell me: was it someone you know?"

She nodded, still looking away. Her good eye glistened.

"One of your lovers?"

Another nod, with an accompanying tear; that one hurt. It wasn't phrased to hurt. It couldn't help itself.

"Who?"

No answer.

"Who?"

A small voice, barely there at all. "Martin."

For one terrible moment of silence, the world went cold and dead.

"Come again?" I said. Vacuum, voice, through a throat constricted. I knew I'd heard it right, was terrified that I'd heard it right. My temples began to thud. The bile swilled in my guts.

"Martin," she said. Louder. Defiant.

"The Martin?" I pressed. She shrank back again; inside my skull, there was thunder. "Scum-sucking douchebag Martin? Originator-of-this-whole-downhill-slide Martin? *That* Martin? Is that what you're telling me?"

"Yes." Less a word than a squeak. She was still shrinking

back, her spine flush with the booth. Retreating, now. Into herself.

"Are you serious?!"

"YES!" She screeched, her tears flowing freely.

"JESUS!!" I screamed, clapping my hands over my forehead. "You're sick!" She winced. "How could you *do* that?!"

But I already knew the answer. It was easy. She had help. *Martin.*

The first, and the worst . . .

LeeAnn had broken up with him about two years ago, right around when we first met. I'd only seen the guy once or twice, when he came by the office to meet her after work. He seemed all right enough; tall and good-looking in a yuppified way. Real confident. Real smooth. They seemed like the perfect couple, and I was crushed.

But then I started hearing the horror stories about how he constantly bullied and sniped at her; how the emotional abuse had begun to turn physical, and the physical act of love became brutal, supply-on-demand . . . until, when she finally grew sick of him and was no longer willing to offer herself, he went ahead and took her anyway.

Repeatedly.

No charges were ever filed. I hadn't really known her then, had only admired her from afar, and it wasn't my place to speak out. But I remembered seeing the bruises and hearing about the asshole ex-boyfriend following her around, making threatening phone calls and an ugly nuisance of himself.

And I remember, even then, wanting to tear his stupid throat out.

She'd been with him for almost two years: a very gradual descent into hell. She never talked about it much; I had to piece most of my knowledge together from the rumor mill and an outsider's perspective. But the bitch of it was, I think she really did love him. And that's what scarred her so badly: she cared, and she trusted him. She'd truly given him a piece of her heart. His betrayal was tantamount to a traumatic amputation; even after the shock she could still feel a twinge of the missing piece. The phantom pain, where it used to be.

And tonight she'd gone back, once again.

To find it.

I really didn't want to hear the gory details; I could fill them in well enough by rote. She was scared: of him, of

herself. She had good reason to be. It was a twisted sort of
ourobouros, the snake forever consuming its own tail, forever vomiting itself right back up; victim and victimizer,
locked in an endlessly spiraling death dance.

And for the very first time I saw her, flung head-first off
the pedestal and down into the slime. I saw her the way *they*
must.

Flawed. Vulnerable.

Pathetic.

And for one bone-chilling moment, I thought that maybe
Martin had a point.

No. The word was vehement, the voice very much my
own. *No no no NO!* The vision ran completely counter to
everything that I held dear, everything that I'd ever believed
about the nature of love and the dignity of the human spirit.
It made me crazy to think that such a thought had even entered my head . . .

*. . . but still I could see it, in psychotic Technicolor clarity:
LeeAnn, cringing before my swinging fist; the moment of glorious frisson, as flesh met surrendering flesh . . .*

WHAT THE FUCK IS WRONG WITH ME?, I silently
screamed. My eyes snapped shut. The vision vanished. I
whirled in my seat, away from LeeAnn and toward the bar,
not wanting my face to betray the merest hint of what had
just gone on inside my mind.

Then the bartender turned toward me. And nodded. And
smiled.

And the pain in my bladder went nova.

It was remarkably like getting kicked in the balls: the
same explosion of breath-stealing, strength-sapping anguish.
It doubled me up in my seat, brought my face within inches
of the table-top between LeeAnn and me. At that distance,
with the dim light etching them in massive shadow, I couldn't
help but see the four words crudely carved across its surface:

TO BE A MAN.

"What is it?" her voice said in quivering tones. Her tears
were subsiding; she was regrouping in the rubble. I dragged
my gaze up to hers with difficulty, still drowning in the pain.

"It's nothing, kiddo. Honest." I was trying to brush it
aside, to hide it. It wasn't working. My voice was even more
wobbly and wasted than hers.

"Don't bullshit me, Dave. You're in pain. Is it an ulcer?"

"I don't think so. I never had one before." But I had to
briefly consider the possibility, because, *Jesus,* did it hurt!

"You look horrible."

"Thanks a lot."

"No, I'm seri—"

"LEEANN!" I thudded my fist against the table in pain and frustration and anger. "We didn't come here to talk about *my* goddamn pain! We came here to talk about yours! Now will you stop trying to change the fucking subject for a minute!"

She was stunned. In this, she was not alone. I could no more believe what I'd said than I could what I followed it up with.

"Baby, I'm not the one who got smacked around tonight! I'm not the one who went to Martin's and asked *him* to do it, either! I didn't even ask to come here! I only came because you begged me to, and I only did *that* because . . ."

I stopped, then. It was like slamming down the brakes at 120 m.p.h. The only sound in my head was the *screeeeeeee* of rubber brain on asphalt bone. I blinked at the dust and smoke behind my eyes.

"Because why?" Her voice was soft as a whisper, warm as a beating heart. Her good eye was green and deep and inscrutable. It unnerved me, that eye, even more than its battered mate or the question that accompanied it. It scrutinized me with zoom-lens attention to every blackhead and ingrown hair on my soul.

Because I love you, my mind silently told her. *Because I'm a goddamn chump, that's why.*

I couldn't decide which conclusion was truer. I couldn't even sustain the internal debate. If I didn't get up and drag my ass down the stairs, I would let loose in my pants, and that was all there was to it. It was a matter of piss or die now, and there was no holding back.

"Excuse me a moment," I managed to mutter, rising up at half-mast and away from my seat.

But suddenly, LeeAnn didn't want to drop it. She grabbed my wrist just as I cleared the table. "David, please . . ." she said. It took everything I had to force the gentleness into my voice.

"I gotta pee, baby. Please. I'm gonna blow up if you don't let me go."

She actually smiled, then. In retrospect, were it not for the pain and embarrassment, that might have been the finest moment of my life. "I really do want to know," she said, soft as before. And her hand stayed right where it was.

I laid my free hand over it. The fingers meshed.

"Hold that thought," I whispered. Not entirely romantic; speech had gotten very difficult. Then I turned and beat a hasty retreat.

She watched me go. I could feel her eyes.

I knew what they were saying.

I will never forget.

Mark Twain once said that if God exists at all, he must surely be a malign thug. I wish it were true. It would be easier to blame God, or Fate, or the drugs, or the bar, or even LeeAnn.

But I know where the blame lays.

Right where it belongs.

I waddled away from the table with a smile on my face. The pain was still there...it kept me half doubled-over... but those last few moments had rendered it nearly insignificant. I was aglow with proximity to my heart's desire. I was aglow with impending triumph.

And that, of course, was when the Mighty Asshole chose to speak.

"Hey! Lookit the fuckin' *creampuff!*" he bellowed. "Guess you gotta go wee-wee, huh?"

There was a pause that crackled in my ears like static, dispersed by a ripple of harsh, raucous laughter. I turned to face a dozen mirthlessly-grinning eyes: the Asshole and his punching bag, the troll, and the hairball, and Heckel and Jeckel. All them watching. Most of them laughing.

The Mighty Asshole, most of all.

Something clicked inside me. The words *I don't need this* took control of my brain. Under ordinary circumstances, I might have been scared. Not now.

I stared him down for a long defiant second.

Then I smiled. And curtsied. And blew him a kiss.

"Eat shit," I said.

Crude, but effective. I felt better almost instantly. The shock on his face was a joy to behold. I turned and scuttled down the stairs before he could rally; my mind raced in mad tandem with my feet. *Never mind them,* I told myself. *You've got to get your butt back there, tell her that you love her, give her the kiss you've been dreaming about. The time has come. She WANTS you, man!*

Then the stairway ended, and my thoughts screeched to a halt.

I had reached my destination.
And the source.

The door itself was ill-hewn and splintery, lusterless and finger-smeared where the finish hadn't worn away entirely. The word **GENTLEMEN** was spelled out in eight-inch metal caps that glimmered flatly in the glare of the overhead bulb. I yanked on the handle; it was surprisingly heavy, beyond its mass. I pulled harder, and it reluctantly gave way.

I'd forgotten about the hinges, the terrible screeching sound they made. *Like a thing in pain.* The small hairs on the nape of my neck stood up like frightened sentries as the sound sawed through my eardrums and raked along my spine.

I stepped inside. The door creaked shut.

And the presence of the room assailed me.

There was the resonant *boom* that sent echoes bouncing off the filthy tiles. There was the overpoweringly ammoniacal sewage-stench, jolting up my nostrils like smelling salts. There was the dim insectoid buzz of the overhead flourescents, spackling the interior with blotches of pulsing, spasming shadow.

And there was the *size*...

Mad, twirling Christ, it was huge. I stood in stunned amazement of what lay ahead. Now, the claustrophobic crapper of any midtown Manhattan working-class watering hole is just about big enough for the average-sized man to squeeze in and out of with an absolute maximum of discomfort. By comparison, this place was a fucking castle.

Twin rows of nonfunctional, moldy sinks: ten, in all. They lined a long tiled corridor on the way to the main room, from which I could make out a solitary stall.

A solitary stall...

Its door hung lopsidedly askew, as though wrenched violently off its hinges. An enormous pool of black, fetid water extended around it in a widening berth, apparently stemming from the blockage of gray, spongy effluvium that floated in the bowl like the lost continent of Atlantis. By craning my neck I could make out a pair of urinals just around the corner, clinging for dear life to the wall beyond.

One stall. Two urinals. Ten sinks.

Under any other circumstances it would've been weird enough to ponder. At the moment, my priorities were far more basic. I groaned, surveying the terrain. There was no way around it.

Only through it.

So I started in, holding my breath, gingerly skirting one of the main tributaries. Each of the sinks had its own mirror bolted to the wall above it. Nine of them had been smashed into glittering shards, held in place by inertia and thin metal frames. The buzzing light refracted off of them, making the streamlets of the pool appear to ripple with a malignant life of their own. The last mirror, the one nearest an adult novelty dispenser proffering big-ribbed condoms in tropical colors, was intact. My reflection fought its way back through the grit and haze; it looked pasty and haggard, forlorn.

"No wonder she's crazy about you," I muttered. "You gorgeous thing."

Something burbled, distinctly, from inside the stall.

"Huh?" I sputtered, startled, and turned to see a fresh ripple of foul water expanding outward in ever-increasing concentric rings. My thoughts turned to my quality footwear and nervously gauged the odds of making it over and back unscathed. It didn't look good.

The stall belched in agreement, sending out another wave.

I peeked around the corner, into the main body of the room. It was infinitely worse: the water actually deepened, and though it could only reasonably be a few inches, it looked bottomless. Some of the floor tiles were warped enough to form a series of little dry islands.

It was my only hope. Taking a last, desperate glance at my reflection, lips curled in disdain, I began to hippety-hop from dry spot to dry spot like a little kid crossing a creek. The beer made me clumsy, the drugs hypersensitized me, and the fumes burned like lye in my eyes and nose. But I made it, awkwardly straddling the sole oasis beneath the far urinal.

The stench was incredible. I momentarily regretted leaving my jacket upstairs, where a half-pack of Merits were serving no useful purpose. The joint was there, too, as were all of my matches. There was nothing I could do to abate the smell.

Those were the facts I had to face as I, at last, unzipped my fly.

And not a moment too soon; no sooner had I freed my screaming pecker than the pee blasted out and splished against the porcelain like a runaway firehose. I sighed, a deep and vastly relieved "Ahhhhhh . . . ," and leaned forward to brace myself against the wall, feeling slightly dizzy and a vague surge of pride at having made it.

I looked at the wall, while the bladder-pain receded. There was a profusion of graffiti there; the same sort of jerk-off witticisms that probably graced the pissoirs at the dawn of time. Crudely optimistic penises pounding into yawning pudenda. Tits like udders, hanging from faceless howling female forms. Phone numbers advertising good times at someone else's expense. Initials. Dates. Dreams of seamy grandeur.

And the same four words:

TO BE A MAN.

In the stall, something big went *squish* and then sputtered. I could hear the tinkling of falling droplets, delicate as the tines of the tiniest music box as they sprinkled the surface of the pool.

My spine froze. My pissing and breathing cut off instinctively. I leaned back as far as I could and listened.

Nothing.

"This is stupid," I informed myself by way of the room at large. My paranoia burgeoned. "There's nobody in there."

Still nothing. Ripples, expanding quietly outward. I exhaled. My pissing resumed with great difficulty.

And the door to the men's room flew suddenly open.

I jerked, nearly spraying myself. From inside, the echoing screech of the hinges resounded like a billion bat shrieks in a cave. The door *screeee*ed and slammed shut like thunder. The walls boomed with the sound of amplified footsteps.

Every alarm in my nervous system went off. It was like pissing on the third rail of a subway track, a thousand volts of terror sizzling through me in the space of a second. The footsteps got closer, and I found myself wanting to get out of there very badly. *Relax,* I hissed silently, as internal organs tightened to pee faster. *You're stoned. This is stupid. Nothing's going to happen. Nothing's—*

"Well, well, well," he said, sneering. "Look it what we got here."

The footsteps came up behind me and paused. I didn't want to turn around and look.

I had to.

The Mighty Asshole stood at the edge of the swamp: arms

crossed, legs spraddled, a hideous grin on his face. He said, "Looks like we got us a live one."

Something burbled and glooped in the toilet stall.

What the fuck did he mean by that? I wondered. The images it conjured up were not very pretty. The smile that flicked across my face was meant to look cool and unruffled. It failed. I flashed it anyway, trying to hide my desperation. He grinned back at me, flat-eyed and mean as a mouthful of snakes.

The Mighty Asshole sploshed, indifferent, through the pool of rancid liquid. He came up beside me, unzipped his fly, and finagled himself into trajectory with the urinal to my left. I took a deep, nasty breath and exhaled it at once, not looking at him. His pissing chorused with mine.

A moment passed.

"You're a faggot, you know it?" he said casually. "You're a little fucking faggot."

I looked at him then, peering straight into his idiot face.

"Yeah you," he continued. "A little fucking *faggot*."

"'Zat so?" I said. "Geez. This is sure news to me." My bladder was draining, like air from a flat, and with it, the pain and the fear.

"A faggot," he repeated, as loud as before, but his sense of utter mastery had dwindled a bit. Our eyes were locked, and I could see the sudden twitching of dim-witted uncertainty there.

"'Zat a fact," I said, marking time till I was done. I didn't want to fight him, that much was for sure. My knife was upstairs, with the Merits and the joint. He wasn't all that much bigger than me, but he was blitzed and stupid; even if I jawed him, he probably wouldn't know it, and we'd end up rolling around here in the slime of the ages.

"Thass a fact, alright." He slurred it, and it took a long time to get out. Good sign. My pissing was almost done, by the time he formulated another thought, I'd be gone.

"I know a woman who'd be interested to hear that," I said. "Yessiree. She'd find that pretty goddamned funny."

He laughed. I joined him.

He stopped. I didn't.

He hit me.

It was a short, straight-armed punch, with a lot of muscle behind it. It caught me square in the side of the head, sending hot black sparks pinging through my skull. I lurched to the side, off my little island, and straight into the sludge.

Cold putrescence flooded up through the hole in my shoe.

"Shit!" I yelled. "Shit! Shit!" I splashed around to face him, waiting for my vision to clear. I could feel my ear starting to cauliflower, feel the hot trickle of blood seeping down. I thought about booting him right in the nuts, grinding his face into that same black water. I was furious. *"You stupid motherfu—"* I began.

And then stopped.

Suddenly.

Completely.

Stopped.

In the pool. In the slime.

It started with the sole of the right foot: a numbing sensation that I at first mistook for the cold. In the thin web of flesh between the first and second shafts of the metatarsus, seeping up through the sodden expanse of my gym sock, the horror took root and spread. Up along the flexor tendons, through their fibrous sheaths. Soaking into the flexor brevis digitorum. An impulse, shooting out at the speed of thought, socked into the motor nucleus at the fifth nerve of the brain.

I couldn't move.

The numbness spread.

In the grume. Where He waits. Forever and ever.

Up through fibula and tibia, dousing bone and soaking marrow. Up through muscle and sinew, tendrils snaking up arteries and conduits, putting frost in my ganglion, ice in my veins. Up through the femur and into the hip, the pelvis. Numbing my cock, my balls. Spreading down the other leg.

Ancient. Eternally crawling.

Blitzkrieg in my bladder. In my spleen. Worming a finger up through my intestines. Oozing through the superficial fascia of the abdominal wall and then outward. Seeping through the pores. Bleeding through my sweatshirt.

Eternally struggling toward form.

And taking it.

For His own.

My eyes riveted on the eyes of the man before me: moist and pulsing, the color of slugs. A spasm ran through us both, synchronized and uncontrollable. Then I was pivoted and slammed facefirst into the filthy tiles above the urinal. I couldn't feel it.

I could feel nothing.

In the stall, the burbling became violently frantic. I managed to lift my head away from the wall. The magic-marker scrawlings hovered inches from my eyes.

Then they began to shift. To change.

And He began to speak.

YOU'RE JUST A LITTLE FUCKING FAGGOT, He said. **OH YES YOU ARE.**

My eyes were glued to the words as they synched with the voice booming inside my head.

JUST A LITTLE FUCKING, CREAMPUFF FAGGOT WHO DOESN'T KNOW HOW TO TAKE CARE OF BUSINESS.

I thought about the blonde at the bar, her groveling eyes. I thought about LeeAnn. I wanted to scream.

He sensed it. It made Him happy.

LIKE HER, He said, immensely pleased. **OH YES, EX-ACTLY.**

Something slithered out of the toilet bowl and landed on the floor with a thick, wet, splutting sound. LeeAnn appeared in grotesquely animated caricature on the wall before me, silently screaming as a monstrously bloated penis plunged in and out and in and

YOU DON'T KNOW HOW TO BE A MAN. YOU'RE AFRAID TO BE A MAN.

I tried to scream. I couldn't.

YOU'RE AFRAID TO GO OUT THERE AND TAKE WHAT YOU WANT.

Sliding up my larynx, out over my tongue. Pouring into the hollows behind my eyes. Oozing into the billion soft folds of my brain. Black static, eating inward from the periphery of my vision. Blocking out everything.

But the realization.

Forever and ever.

It was crawling toward me. I couldn't see it, couldn't turn my head, but I could hear the horror revisited in the breath of the man beside me.

And I could hear it, slithering. I could feel its hunger. I could taste its boundless greed. A tiny voice in my head shrieked *it's only the drugs,* but the voice was tiny, and hollow, and fading.

Something small and moist grabbed onto my pants leg.

NOW YOU'RE GOING TO KNOW WHAT IT IS ...

Crawling up.

... TO BE A MAN ...

Coming closer.

Struggling toward form.

TO BE A MAN.

Tiny fingers clawed the base of my skull. My jaws were pried open. A caricature appeared on the wall, mocking me.

OH, YES.

And there was nothing I could do.

But let Him in.

When I came to, some ten minutes later, the Mighty Asshole was gone. I knew that I'd have no more trouble from him that night, or ever after. In fact, I could come back as much as I wished. Again. And again.

I belonged now. Completely.

He had not let us fall, cunning fuck that He was. When I came to, we were in front of the sole surviving mirror, and He was splashing freezing water in our face.

He cleaned us up: meticulously washing away the blood, smoothing back the disheveled hair. Tomorrow we'd get it cut, He informed me. Nice and short, maybe a flattop. And we'd start working out, put some meat on these bones.

A real man, He said, *always takes care of business.*

When we were nice and clean, He turned and bought us a big-ribbed condom. For later. He smiled at our face in the grimy mirror. It was a cruel smile, and infinitely calculated. His smile. The mirror grinned coldly back.

And He smashed it.

With my fist.

When we finally came up the stairs, twenty minutes had passed. LeeAnn was waiting anxiously at the table. "David?" she demanded. "What happened to you? I was really getting worried."

He lifted one finger, and told her to shush.

She obeyed.

"You're a sweetheart," He said, moving close.

Then He kissed her.

Passionately.

With my lips.

There is a book on the history of photojournalism on the endtable beside me. It was one of LeeAnn's favorites, but that's not why He keeps it around. He likes the pretty pictures.

And He likes to torture me.

Right now, it's open to the page on the liberation of the concentration camps, at the end of World War II. One photo in particular stands out, flickering in the dim light of the TV's hissing screen like footage from some long-forgotten newsreel. It's a black-and-white picture of the gate to Auschwitz. Perhaps it's even one of Margaret Bourke-White's; that would be nice, but I guess it doesn't really matter. So what if I can't make out the credit? I can make out the inscription clear enough: **ARBEIT MACHT FREI,** in huge iron letters. That's what's important.

ARBEIT MACHT FREI.

Work Makes Freedom.

I've thought about that a lot. One of the many thoughts that help me in the night, long after He's passed out in His favorite easychair, drunken and still dressed. Tonight, He didn't even get the damned field jacket off.

I'm so glad.

I'm sure that LeeAnn would be, too.

It took her over a year to tear away: thirteen months of steadily escalating madness. Oh, He was great, for the first month or so: strong and sensitive and very, very sincere. He made all the right moves, said all the right things. And she welcomed my newfound assertiveness, with an ardor that both amazed and destroyed me.

He waited with the patience of the ages, until the hooks were planted nice and deep. Until she fell for Him. Until she trusted Him. Until He could destroy her. It was amazing, how much groundwork I'd already lain. It made it infinitely easier for Him. And infinitely worse, for me.

And then, when the moment was right, He showed her His true self. Repeatedly.

I'll never forget the look of betrayal on her face.

It took her over six months to escape; we were living together by then. He tried to break her, and she fought Him. Escape cost her dearly: emotionally, mentally.

Physically.

But escape she did, and I love her for it. I've thought of her often, God knows. I've wondered how she's doing, wondered where she is.

But I don't really want to know.

And, besides, I never will.

Because every night after that, He dragged me downtown and back to the bar. The guys were all there, of course. The guys were always there. We got along famously, round after round, while the Hooter Girl sadly presided.

And every night after that, we went out in search of fresh meat. There were always women out there, waiting to be punished for something. He was always eager to oblige. He wanted me to watch. He needed me to forget. His failure. Her victory.

But I didn't, damn it.

I remembered.

Within the month, he'd found a suitable distraction: Lisa. She wasn't as sharp as LeeAnn, or as strong. But her blue eyes were bright, and her curvature dazzled, and her smile could have sold you the moon. We've been married now, the three of us, going on four years. We have kids, to my unending sorrow: Patricia, little David, Jr., and another damned soul on the way. Lisa's eyes no longer sparkle, and she hardly ever smiles. Thirty pounds of purpled padding grace the skeleton of her beauty like a shroud.

But tonight, that's all behind her.

It's taken four years. Four years of practice: at night, while He slept drunkenly on. Cell by cell. Inch by inch. Four very long years. LeeAnn would be proud.

I can move my right arm, you see.

Only when He sleeps, true, and not very much. It's not very strong, either. Yes, life is a bitch.

But it was strong enough to open the book tonight. And with a little strength to spare . . .

It'll be enough to reach the knife.

And so what if it takes me all night. ARBEIT MACHT FREI, right?

Sometimes, that's just what it takes.

To be a man.

Down in the Darkness

by DEAN R. KOONTZ

Dean Kootnz has more bestsellers than many authors have published books and is one of the true gentlemen of publishing: honest, talented, and concerned. As he mentioned in an interview in the Dean R. Koontz Special Issue of The Horror Show, *he writes emotional, not category, fiction. He never cheats his readers, always tells his story first and breathes rounded reality into his characters. Here, he writes in an older mode, in a new way...*

Darkness dwells within even the best of us. In the worst of us, darkness not only dwells but reigns.

Although occasionally providing darkness with a habitat, I have never provided it with a kingdom. That's what I prefer to believe. I think of myself as a basically good man: a hard worker, a loving and faithful husband, a stern but doting father.

If I use the cellar again, however, I will no longer be able to pretend that I can suppress my own potential for evil. If I use the cellar again, I will exist in eternal moral eclipse and will never thereafter walk in the light.

But the temptation is great.

I first discovered the cellar door two hours after we had signed the final papers, had delivered the check to the escrow company to pay for the house, and had received the keys. It was in the kitchen, in the corner beyond the refrigerator: a raised-panel door, stained dark like all the others in the house, with a burnished-brass lever-action handle instead of a conventional knob. I stared in disbelief, for I was certain the door had not been there before.

Initially, I thought I had found a pantry. When I opened it, I was startled to see steps leading down through deepening shadows into pitch blackness. A windowless basement.

In Southern California, nearly all houses—everything from the cheaper tract crackerboxes to those in the multimillion-dollar range—are built on concrete slabs. They have no basements. This is prudent design. The land is frequently sandy, with little bedrock near the surface. And in country that is subject to earthquakes and mudslides, a basement with concrete-block walls is a point of structural weakness into which all the rooms above might collapse if the giants in the earth suddenly woke and stretched.

Our new home was neither crackerbox nor mansion, but it had a cellar. The real-estate agent never mentioned it. Until now, we had never noticed it.

Peering down the steps, I was at first curious—then uneasy.

A wall switch was set just inside the door. I clicked it up, down, up again. No light came on below.

Leaving the door open, I went looking for Carmen. She was in the master bedroom, hugging herself, grinning, admiring the handmade emerald-green ceramic tiles and the Sherle Wagner sinks with their gold-plated fixtures.

"Oh, Jess, isn't it beautiful? Isn't it grand? When I was a little girl, I never dreamed I'd live in a house like this. My best hope was for one of those cute bungalows from the forties. But this is a palace, and I'm not sure I know how to act like a queen."

"It's no palace," I said, putting an arm around her. "You've got to be a Rockefeller to afford a palace in Orange County. Anyway, you've always had the style and bearing of a queen."

She stopped hugging herself and hugged me. "We've come a long way, haven't we?"

"And we're going even further, kid."

"I'm a little scared, you know?"

"Don't be silly."

"Jess, honey, I'm just a cook, a dishwasher, a pot-scrubber, only one generation removed from a shack on the outskirts of Mexico City. We worked hard for this, sure, and lots of years... but now that we're here, it seems to have happened overnight."

"Trust me, kid—you could hold your own in any gathering of society ladies from Newport Beach. You have natural-born class."

I thought: God, I love her. Seventeen years of marriage, and she is still a girl to me, still fresh and surprising and sweet.

"Hey," I said, "almost forgot. You know we have a cellar?"

She blinked at me.

"It's true," I said.

Smiling, waiting for the punch line, she said, "Yeah? And what's down there? The royal vaults with all the jewels? A dungeon?"

"Come see," I said.

She followed me into the kitchen.

The door was gone.

Staring at the blank wall, I was for a moment icebound.

"Well?" she said. "What's the joke?"

I thawed enough to say, "No joke. There was... a door."

She pointed to the outline of a kitchen window that was etched on the wall by the sun streaming through the glass. "You probably saw that. The square of sunlight coming through the window, falling on the wall. It's more or less in the shape of a door."

"No. No... there was..." Shaking my head, I put one hand on the sun-warmed plaster and lightly traced its contours, as if the seams of the door would be more apparent to the touch than to the eye.

Carmen frowned. "Jess, what's wrong?"

I looked at her and realized what she was thinking. This lovely house seemed too good to be true, and she was superstitious enough to wonder if such a great blessing could be enjoyed for long without fate throwing us a weight of tragedy to balance the scales. An overworked husband, suffering from stress—or perhaps afflicted by a small brain tumor—beginning to see things that were not there, talking excitedly of nonexistent cellars... That was just the sort of nasty turn of events with which fate too frequently evened things out.

"You're right," I said. I forced a laugh but made it sound natural. "I saw the rectangle of light on the wall and thought it was a door. Didn't even look close. Just came running for you. Now, has this new house business got me crazy as a monkey or what?"

She looked at me somberly for a moment, then matched my smile. "Crazy as a monkey. But then... you always were."

"Is that so?"

"My monkey," she said.

I said, "Ook, ook," and scratched under one arm.

I was glad I had not told her that I had opened the door. Or that I had seen the steps beyond.

The house in Laguna Beach had five large bedrooms, four baths, and a family room with a massive stone fireplace. It also had what they call an "entertainer's kitchen," which did not mean that Wayne Newton or Liberace performed there between Vegas engagements, but referred instead to the quality and number of appliances: double ovens, two microwaves, a warming oven for muffins and rolls, a Jenn Air cooking center, two dishwashers, and a Sub Zero refrigerator of sufficient size to serve a restaurant. Lots of immense windows let in the warm California sun and framed views of the lush landscaping—bougainvillea in shades of yellow and coral, red azaleas, impatiens, palms, two imposing Indian laurels—and of the rolling hills beyond. In the distance, the sun-dappled water of the Pacific glimmered enticingly, like a great treasure of silver coins.

Though not a mansion, it was unquestionably a house that said, "The Gonzalez family has done well, has made a fine place for itself." My folks would have been very proud.

Maria and Ramon, my parents, had been Mexican immigrants who had scratched out a new life in *El Norte,* the promised land. They had given me, my brothers, and my sister everything that hard work and sacrifice could provide, and we four had earned university scholarships. Now, one of my brothers was an attorney, the other a doctor, and my sister was Chairperson of the Department of English at U.C.L.A.

I had chosen a career in business. Together, Carmen and I opened a restaurant, for which I provided the business expertise, for which she provided the exquisite and authentic Mexican recipes, and where we both worked twelve hours a day, seven days a week. As our three children reached adolescence, they came to work with us as waiters. It was a family affair, and every year we became more prosperous, but it was never easy. America does not promise easy wealth, only opportunity. We seized the machine of opportunity and lubricated it with oceans of perspiration, and by the time we bought the house in Laguna Beach, we were able to pay cash. Jokingly, we gave the house a name: *Casa Sudor*—House of Sweat.

It was a huge home. And beautiful.

It had everything. Even a basement with a disappearing door.

The previous owner was Mr. Nguyen Quang Phu. Our realtor—a sturdy, garrulous, middle-aged woman named Nancy Keefer—said Phu was a Vietnamese refugee, one of the courageous boat people who had fled months after the fall of Saigon. He was one of the fortunate who had survived storms, gunboats, and pirates.

"He arrived in the U.S. with only three thousand dollars in gold coins and the will to make something of himself," Nancy Keefer told us when we first toured the house. "A charming man and a fabulous success. Really fabulous. He's pyramided that small bankroll into so many business interests, you just wouldn't believe it, all in fourteen years! Fabulous story. He's built a new house, twelve thousand square feet on two acres in North Tustin, it's just fabulous, really, you should see it, you really should."

Carmen and I made an offer for Phu's old house, which was less than half the size of the one he had recently built, but which was a dream home to us. We dickered a bit, but finally agreed on terms, and the closing was achieved in just ten days because we were paying cash, taking no mortgage.

The transfer of ownership was arranged without Nguyen Quang Phu and me coming face to face. This is not an unusual situation because, unlike some states, California does not require a formal closing ceremony with seller, buyer, and their attorneys gathered in one room.

It was Nancy Keefer's policy to arrange a meeting between the buyer and seller at the house, within a day or two of the completion of the deal. Although our new home was beautiful and in splendid repair, even the finest houses have their quirks. Nancy thought it was a good idea for a seller to walk the buyer through the place, pointing out which closet doors tended to slide off their tracks and which windows wept in a rainstorm. She arranged for Phu to meet me at the house on Wednesday, May 14.

Monday, May 12, was the day we closed the deal. And

that was the afternoon when, strolling through the empty house, I first saw the cellar door.

Tuesday morning, I returned to the house alone. I did not tell Carmen where I was really going. She thought I was at Horace Dalcoe's office, wrangling with him over his latest extortion scheme.

Dalcoe owned the small open-air shopping center in which our restaurant was located, and he was the very man for whom the word "sleazeball" had been coined. Our lease, signed when Carmen and I were poorer and naive, gave him the right to approve every minor change we made in the premises. Therefore, six years after we opened, when we wanted to remodel the restaurant at a cost of $300,000— which would have been an improvement to *his* property—we were required to give Dalcoe ten thousand in tax-free cash, under the table, for his okay. When I bought out the lease of the stationery store next door to expand into their quarters, Dalcoe insisted upon a steep cash payment for his approval. He was interested not only in large lumps of sugar but in tiny grains of it as well; when I put a new and more attractive set of front doors on the place, Dalcoe wanted a lousy hundred bucks under the table to okay that small job.

Now, we hoped to replace our old sign with a new one, and I was negotiating a bribe with Dalcoe. He didn't know it, but I had discovered that he did not own the land on which his own little shopping center stood; he had taken a ninety-nine-year lease on it twenty years ago and felt secure. At the same time that I was working out a new bribe with him, I was secretly negotiating a purchase of the land, after which Dalcoe would discover that, while he might have a stranglehold on me by virtue of my lease, I would have a stranglehold on him because of *his* lease. He still thought of me as an ignorant Mex, maybe second-generation, but Mex just the same; he thought I'd had a little luck in the restaurant business, luck and nothing more, and gave me no credit for intelligence or savvy. It was not going to be exactly a case of the little fish swallowing the big one, but I expected to arrange a satisfactory stalemate that would leave him furious and impotent.

These machinations, which had been continuing for some time, gave me a believable excuse for my whereabouts Tuesday morning. I'd be bargaining with Dalcoe at his office, I told Carmen. In fact, I went to the new house, feeling guilty about having lied to her.

When I stepped into the kitchen, the door was where I had seen it the previous day. No rectangle of sunlight. No mere illusion. A real door.

I worked the lever-action handle.

Beyond, steps led down into the deepening shadows.

"What the hell?" I said. My voice echoed back to me as if it had bounced off a wall a thousand miles away.

The switch still did not work.

I had brought a flashlight. I snapped it on.

I crossed the threshold. The wooden landing creaked; the boards were old, unpainted, scarred. Mottled with gray and yellow stains, webbed with hairline cracks, the plaster walls looked as if they were much older than the rest of the house. The cellar clearly did not belong in this structure, was not an integral part of it. I moved off the landing onto the first step.

A frightening possibility occurred to me. What if the draft pushed the door shut behind me—and then it vanished as it had done yesterday, leaving me trapped in the cellar?

I retreated in search of something with which to brace the door. The house contained no furniture, but in the garage I found a length of two-by-four that did the job.

Standing on the top step once more, I shone the flashlight down, but the beam did not reach nearly as far as it should have. I could not see the cellar floor. The tar-black murk below was unnaturally deep. This was a darkness that was not merely an absence of light but seemed to possess substance, texture and weight, as if the lower chamber were filled with a pool of oil, though it was not. Like a sponge, the darkness absorbed the light, and only twelve steps were revealed in the pale beam before it faded in the gloom.

I descended two steps, and two more steps appeared at the far reach of the light. I eased down four additional steps, and four more came into view below.

Six steps behind, one under my feet, and twelve ahead—nineteen so far. How many steps would you expect to find in an ordinary basement? Ten? Twelve? Not this many, surely.

Quickly and quietly, I descended six steps. When I stopped, twelve steps were illuminated ahead of me. Dry, aged boards. An unrusted nailhead gleaming here and there. The same mottled walls.

Unnerved, I looked back up at the door, which was thirteen steps and one landing above me. The sunlight in the kitchen looked warm, inviting—and more distant than it should have been.

My hands had begun to sweat. I switched the flashlight from one hand to the other, blotting my palms on my slacks.

The air had a vague lime odor and an even fainter underlying scent of mold and corruption.

I hurriedly and noisily descended six more steps, then eight more, then another eight, then six. Now forty-one rose at my back—and twelve were still illuminated below me.

Each of the steep steps was about ten inches high, which meant I had gone approximately three stories underground. No ordinary basement had such a long flight of stairs. I told myself that this might be a bomb shelter, but I knew that it was not.

As yet, I had no thought of turning back. This was our house, damn it, for which we had paid a small fortune in money and a larger fortune in time and sweat, and we could not live in it with such a mystery beneath our feet, unexplored. Besides, when I was twenty-two and twenty-three, far from home and in the hands of enemies, I had known two years of terror so constant and intense that my tolerance for fear was higher than that of most men.

One hundred steps farther, I stopped again because I figured I was ten stories below ground level, which was a milestone requiring some contemplation. Turning and peering up, I saw the light at the open kitchen door far above me, an opalescent rectangle that appeared to be one-quarter the size of a postage stamp.

Looking down, I studied the eight bare wooden steps illuminated ahead of me—eight, not the usual twelve. As I had gone deeper, the flashlight had become less effective. The batteries were not growing weak; the problem was nothing as simple or explicable as that. Where it passed through the lens, the beam was as bright as ever. But the darkness ahead was somehow thicker, *hungrier*, and it absorbed the light in a shorter distance than it had done farther up.

The air still smelled vaguely of lime, though the scent of decay was now nearly the equal of that more pleasant odor.

This subterranean world had been preternaturally quiet except for my own footsteps and increasingly heavier breathing. Pausing at the ten-story point, however, I thought I heard something below. I held my breath, stood motionless, and listened. I thought I heard strange, furtive sounds a long way off—whispering and oily squelching noises—but I could not be certain. They were faint and short-lived. I could have been imagining them.

Descending ten more steps, I came to a landing at last, where I discovered opposing archways in the walls of the stairwell. Both openings were doorless and unornamented, and my light revealed a short hallway beyond each. Stepping through the arch on my left, I followed the narrow corridor for perhaps fifteen feet, where it ended at the head of another staircase, which went down at a right angle to those stairs I had just left.

Here, the odor of decay was stronger. It was reminiscent of the pungent fumes of rotting vegetable matter.

The stink was like a spade, turning up long-buried memories. I had encountered precisely this stench before, in the place where I had been imprisoned during my twenty-second and twenty-third years. There, they had sometimes served meals largely composed of rotting vegetables—mostly turnips, sweet potatoes, and other tubers. Worse, the garbage that we would not eat was thrown into the sweatbox, a tin-roofed pit in the ground where recalcitrant prisoners were punished with solitary confinement. In that hole, you were forced to sit in foot-deep slime that reeked so strongly of decay that, in heat-induced delusion, you sometimes became convinced that you were dead already and that what you smelled was the relentlessly progressing corruption of your own lifeless flesh.

"What's going on?" I asked, expecting and receiving no answer.

Returning to the main stairs, I entered the arch on the right. At the end of that hall, a second set of branching stairs also led down. From the tenebrous depths, a different rancidity arose, and I recognized this one as well: decomposing fish heads.

Not just decomposing fish but, specifically, fish *heads*—like the guards had sometimes put in our soup. Grinning, they had stood and watched us as we greedily sucked up the broth. We gagged on it but were usually too hungry to pour it on the ground in protest. Sometimes, starving, we choked down the repulsive fish heads as well, which was what the guards most wanted to see. They always found our disgust—and especially our self-disgust—amusing.

I hurriedly returned to the main stairwell. I stood on the ten-story landing, shuddering uncontrollably, trying to shake off those unbidden memories.

By now, I was half-convinced that I was dreaming or that I did, indeed, have a brain tumor which, by exerting pressure on surrounding cerebral tissues, was the cause of these hallucinations.

I continued downward and noticed that, step by step, the range of my flashlight was decreasing. Now, I could see only seven steps ahead ... six ... five ... four ...

Suddenly, the impenetrable darkness was only two feet in front of me, a black mass that seemed to throb in expectation of my final advance into its embrace. It seemed *alive*.

Yet, this was not the end of the stairs, for I heard those whisperings again, far below, and the oily squelching sound that brought gooseflesh to my arms.

I reached forward with one trembling hand. It disappeared into the darkness, which was bitterly cold.

My hammering heart was seeking escape from the prison of my ribs, and my mouth was suddenly dry and sour. I let out a cry that sounded like the shrill squeal of a child and, at last, I fled back to the kitchen and the light.

That evening at the restaurant, I greeted the guests and seated them. Even after all these years, I spend most nights at the front desk, meeting people, playing the host. Usually, I enjoy it. Many of our customers have been coming to us for a decade, and they are honorary members of the family, old friends. But that night, my heart was not in it, and several people asked me if I was feeling well.

Tom Gatlin, my accountant, stopped by for dinner with his wife. He said, "Jess, you're *gray,* for God's sake. You're three years overdue for a vacation, my friend. What's the point of piling up the money if you never take time to enjoy it?"

Fortunately, the restaurant staff we have assembled is first-rate. In addition to Carmen and me and our kids— Stacy, Heather, and young Joe—there are twenty-two employees, and every one of them knows his job and performs it well. Though I was not at my best, there were plenty of others to take up the slack.

Stacy, Heather, and Joe. Very *American* names. Funny. My mother and father, being immigrants, clung to the world they left by giving all their children traditional Mexican names. Carmen's folks were the same way: her brothers were Juan and José, and her sister's name is Evalina. My name actually was Jesus Gonzalez. I had it changed to Jess years ago, though I hurt my parents. Jesus is a common name in Mexico. (The Spanish pronunication is "Hayseuss," although most North Americans pronounce it as if referring to the Christian savior. There's just no way you can be regarded as either one of the guys or a serious businessman when burdened with such an exotic moniker.) It's interesting how the children of immigrants, second-generation Americans like Carmen and me, usually give their own kids the most popular American names, as if trying to conceal how recently our ancestors got off the boat—or in this case, crossed the Rio Grande. Stacy, Heather, Joe.

Just as there are no more fervent Christians than those recently converted to the faith, there are no more ardent Americans than those whose claim to citizenship begins with them or their parents. We want so desperately to be part of this great, huge, crazy country. Unlike some whose roots go back generations, we understand what a blessing it is to live beneath the stars and stripes. We also know that a price must be paid for the blessing, and that sometimes it's high. Partly, the cost is in leaving behind everything we once were. Sometimes, however, there is a more painful price inflicted, as I well know.

I served in Vietnam.

I was under fire. I killed the enemy.

And I was a prisoner of war.

That was where I ate soup with rotting fish heads.

That was part of the price I paid.

Now, thinking about the impossible cellar beneath our new house, remembering the smells of the prison camp that had wafted out of the darkness at the bottom of those stairs, I began to wonder if I was still paying the price. I had come home sixteen years ago—gaunt, half my teeth rotten. I'd been starved and tortured but not broken. There had been nightmares for years, but I hadn't needed therapy. I had come through all right, as had many of the guys in those North Vietnamese hell holes. Badly bent, scarred, splintered—but, damn it, not broken. Somewhere, I had lost my Catholicism, but that had seemed a negligible loss at the time. Year by year, I had put the experience behind me. Part of the price. Part of what we pay for being where we are. Forget it. Over. Done. And it *had* seemed behind me. Until now. The cellar could not be real, which meant I must be having vivid hallucinations. Could it be that, after so long a time, the fiercely repressed emotional trauma of imprisonment and torture were working profound changes in me, that I had been ignoring the problem rather than dealing with it, and that now it was going to drive me mad?

If that was the case, I wondered what had suddenly triggered my mental collapse. Was it that we had bought a house from a Vietnamese refugee? That seemed like too small a thing to have been the trigger. I couldn't see how the seller's original nationality alone could have caused wires to cross in my subconscious, shorting out the system, blowing fuses. On the other hand, if my peace with the memories of Vietnam and my sanity were only as stable as a house of cards, the barest breath could demolish me.

Damn it, I didn't *feel* insane. I felt stable—frightened but firmly in control. The most reasonable explanation for the cellar was hallucination. But I was largely convinced that the impossible subterranean staircases were real, that the disconnection from reality was external rather than internal.

At eight o'clock, Horace Dalcoe arrived for dinner with a party of seven, which almost took my mind off the cellar. As holder of our lease, he believes that he should never pay a cent for dinner in our establishment. If we didn't comp him and his friends, he would find ways to make us miserable, so we oblige. He never says thank you, and he usually finds something to complain aobut.

That Tuesday night, he complained about the margaritas —not enough tequila, he said. He fussed about the corn chips—not crisp enough, he said. And he groused about the abondigas soup—not enough meatballs, he said.

I wanted to throttle the bastard. Instead, I brought margaritas with more tequila—enough to burn up an alarming number of brain cells per minute—and new corn chips, and a bowl of meatballs to supplement that already meat-rich soup.

That night, in bed, thinking about Dalcoe, I wondered what would happen to him if I invited him to our new house, pushed him into the cellar, closed and latched the door, and left him down there for a while. I had the bizarre but unshakable feeling that something lived deep in the basement . . . something hideous that had been only a couple of feet away from me in that impenetrable darkness that had devoured the flashlight beam. If something *was* down there, it would climb the stairs to get Dalcoe. Then he would be no more trouble to us.

I did not sleep well that night.

Wednesday morning, May 14, I returned to the house to walk through it with the former owner, Nguyen Quang Phu. I arrived an hour ahead of our appointment, in case the cellar door was there.

It was.

Suddenly I felt that I should turn my back on the door, walk away, ignore it. I sensed that I could make it go away forever if only I refused to open it. And I knew—without knowing *how* I knew—that not only my body and my soul was at risk if I could not resist the temptation to explore those lower realms.

I braced it open with the two-by-four. I went down into the darkness with the flashlight.

More than ten stories underground, I stopped once more on the landing with the flanking archways. The stink of rotting vegetables came from the branching stairwell to the left, the foul aroma of rancid fish heads from the right.

I pressed on and found that the peculiarly substantive darkness did not thicken as quickly as it had done yesterday. I was able to go deeper . . . as if the darkness knew me better now and welcomed me into more intimate regions of its domain.

After an additional fifty or sixty steps, I came to another landing. Again, arches offered a change of direction on both sides.

On the left I found another short hall leading to another set of stairs which descended into a pulsing, shifting, malignant blackness as impervious to light as a pool of oil. Indeed, the beam of my flash did not fade into that dense gloom but actually terminated in a circle of reflected light, as if it had fallen on a wall, and the churning blackness glistened slightly like molten tar. It was a thing of great power, enormously repulsive. Yet somehow I knew that it was not merely oil or any other liquid, but was instead the essence of all darkness; it was a syrupy distillation of a million nights, a billion shadows. Darkness is a condition, not a substance, and therefore cannot be distilled. Yet here was that same impossible extract, ancient and pure: concentrate of night, the vast blackness of interstellar space decorated until it had been rendered into an oozing sludge. And it was evil.

I backed away and returned to the main stairwell. I did not inspect the branching stairs beyond the archway on the right, for I knew that I would find the same malevolent distillate waiting down there, slowly churning, churning.

In the main stairwell, I descended only a little farther before encountering the same foul presence. It rose like a wall in front of me. I stood two steps from it, shaking uncontrollably with fear.

I reached forward.

I put a hand against the pulsing mass of blackness.

It was cold.

I reached forward a bit farther. My hand disappeared to the wrist. The darkness was so solid, so clearly defined, that my wrist looked like an amputee's stump; a sharp line marked the point at which my hand vanished into the tardense mass.

Panicked, I jerked back. My hand had not been amputated. It was still there, attached to the end of my arm. I wiggled my fingers.

I looked up from my hand, straight into the gelid darkness before me, and suddenly I knew that it was *aware* of me. I had sensed that it was evil, yet somehow I had not thought of it as *conscious*. Staring into a featureless countenance, I felt that it was welcoming me to the cellar that I had not yet reached, to the chambers below that were still countless steps beneath me. I was invited to embrace darkness, to step entirely across the threshold into the gloom where my hand had gone, and for a moment I was overcome with a longing to do precisely that, to move out of the light, down, down.

Then I thought of Carmen. And my daughters—Heather and Stacy. My son Joe. All of the people I loved and who loved me. The spell was instantly broken. The mesmeric attraction of the darkness lost its hold on me, and I turned and ran up to the bright kitchen, my footsteps booming in the narrow stairwell.

Sun streamed through the big windows.

I pulled the two-by-four out of the way, slammed the cellar door. I willed it to vanish, but it remained.

"I'm mad," I said aloud. "Stark raving mad."

But I knew that I was sane.

It was the world that had gone mad, not me.

* * *

Twenty minutes later, Mr. Nguyen Quang Phu arrived, as scheduled, to explain all the peculiarities of the house that we had bought from him. I met him at the front door, and the moment I saw him I knew why the impossible cellar had appeared and what purpose it was meant to serve.

"Mr. Gonzalez?"

"Yes."

"I am Nguyen Quang Phu."

He was not merely Nguyen Quang Phu. He was also the torture master.

In Vietnam, he had ordered me strapped to a bench and had, for more than an hour, beat the soles of my feet with a wooden baton— until each blow jarred through the bones of my legs and hips, through my rib cage, up my spine, to the top of my skull, which felt as if it was going to explode. He had ordered me bound hand and foot and had forcibly submerged me in a tank of water fouled with urine from other prisoners who had been subjected to the ordeal before me; just when I thought I could hold my breath no longer, when my lungs were burning, when my ears were ringing, when my heart was thundering, when every fiber of my being strained toward death, I was hoisted into the air and allowed a few breaths before being plunged beneath the surface again. He had ordered that wires be attached to my genitals, and he had given me countless jolts of electricity. Helpless, I had watched him beat a friend of mine to death, and I had seen him tear out another friend's right eye with a stiletto merely for cursing the soldier who had served him yet another bowl of weevil-infested rice.

I had absolutely no doubt of his identity. The memory of the torture master's face was branded forever in my mind, burned into the very tissue of my brain by the worst heat of all—hatred. And he had aged much better than I had. He looked only two or three years older than when I'd last seen him.

"Pleased to meet you," I said.

"Likewise," he said as I ushered him into the house.

His voice was as memorable as his face: soft, low, and somehow cold—the voice a snake might have if serpents could talk.

We shook hands.

He was five ten, tall for a Vietnamese. He had a long face with prominent cheekbones, a sharp nose, a thin mouth, and

the delicate jaw line of a woman. His eyes were deeply set—
and as strange as they had been in Nam.

In that prison camp, I had not known his name. Perhaps it
had been Nguyen Quang Phu. Or perhaps that was a false
identity he had assumed when he had sought asylum in the
United States.

"You have bought a wonderful house," he said.

"We like it very much," I said.

"I was happy here," he said, smiling, nodding, looking
around at the empty living room. "Very happy."

Why had he left Nam? He had been on the winning side.
Well, maybe he'd fallen out with some of his comrades. Or
perhaps the state had assigned him to hard farm labor or to
the mines or to some other task that he knew would destroy
his health and kill him before his time. Perhaps he had gone
to sea in a small boat when the state no longer chose to give
him a position of high authority and dominance.

The reason for his emigration was of no importance to
me. All that mattered was that he was here.

The moment I saw him and realized who he was, I knew
that he would not leave the house alive. I would never per-
mit his escape.

"There's not much to point out," he said. "There's one
drawer in the master bathroom cabinets that keeps running
off the track and needs to be fixed. And the pull-down attic
stairs in the closet have a small problem sometimes, but
that's easily remedied. I'll show you."

"I'd appreciate that."

He did not recognize me.

I supposed he'd tortured too many men to be able to recall any single victim of his sadistic urges. All the prisoners
who suffered and died at his hands had probably blurred into
one faceless target. The torturer had cared nothing about the
individual to whom he'd given an advance taste of hell; to
Nguyen Quang Phu, each man on the rack was the same as
the one before, prized not for his unique qualities but for his
ability to scream and bleed, for his eagerness to grovel at the
feet of his tormentor.

As he took me through the house, he also gave me the
names of reliable plumbers and electricians and air-condi-
tioner repairmen in the neighborhood, plus the name of the
artisan who had created the stained-glass windows in a couple of rooms. "If one should be badly damaged, you'll want
it repaired by the man who made it."

I will never know how I restrained myself from attacking him with my bare hands. More incredible still: neither my face nor my voice revealed my inner tension. He was utterly unaware of the danger into which he had stepped.

In the kitchen, after he had shown me the unusual position of the restart switch on the garbage disposal beneath the sink, I asked him if, during rainstorms, there was any problem with seepage in the cellar.

He blinked at me. His soft, cold voice rose slightly: "Cellar? Oh, but there is no cellar."

Pretending surprise, I said, "Well, of course there is. Right over there's the door."

He stared at it in disbelief.

I picked up the flashlight off the counter and opened the door.

Protesting that no such door had existed while he had lived in the house, the torture master moved past me in a high state of astonishment and curiosity. He went through the door, onto the upper landing.

"Light switch doesn't work," I said, crowding in behind him, pointing the flashlight down past him. "But we'll see well enough with this."

"But . . . where. . . . how . . . ?"

"You don't really mean you never noticed the cellar?" I said, forcing a laugh. "Come now. Are you joking with me or what?"

As if weightless with amazement, he drifted downward from one step to the next.

I followed close behind.

Soon, he knew that something was terribly wrong, for the steps went on too far without any sign of the cellar door. He stopped, began to turn, and said, "This is strange. What's going on here? What on earth are you—"

"Go on," I said harshly. "Down. Go down, you bastard."

He tried to push past me.

I knocked him backward down the stairs. Screaming, he tumbled all the way to the first landing that was flanked by archways. When I reached him, I saw that he was dazed and in great pain. He was making a thin keening sound. His lower lip was split; blood trickled down his chin. He'd skinned the palm of his right hand. I think his arm was broken.

Weeping with pain, cradling his arm, he looked up at me, afraid and confused.

I hated myself for what I was doing.

But I hated him more.

"In the camp," I said, "we called you The Snake. I know you. Oh, yes, I know you. You were our torture master."

"Oh God," he said. He neither asked what I was talking about nor tried to deny it. He knew who he was, what he was, and he knew what would become of him.

"Those eyes," I said, shaking with fury now. "That voice. The Snake. A repulsive, belly-crawling snake. Contemptible. But very, very dangerous."

For a moment we were both silent. In my case, at least, I was temporarily speechless because I was in awe of the profound machinery of fate which, in its slow-working and laborious fashion, had brought us together in this time and place.

From down in the darkness, a noise arose: sibilant whispers, a wet oozing sound that made me shudder. Millennial darkness was on the move, surging upward, the embodiment of endless Night, cold and deep and . . . hungry.

The torture master, reduced to the role of victim, gazed around in bewilderment, through one archway and then another, then down the stairs that continued from the landing on which he was sprawled. His fear was so great that it drove out his pain; he no longer wept or made the keening noise. "What . . . what *is* this place?"

"It's where you belong," I said.

I turned from him and climbed the steps. I did not stop or look back. I left the flashlight with him because I wanted him to see the thing that came for him.

(Darkness dwells within us all.)

"Wait!" he called after me.

I did not pause.

"W-w-what's that sound?" he asked.

I kept climbing.

"What's going to h-happen to me?"

"I don't know," I told him. "But whatever it is . . . it'll be what you deserve."

Anger finally stirred in him. He said, "You're not my judge!"

"Oh, yes, I am."

At the top, I stepped into the kitchen, and closed the door behind me. It had no lock. I leaned against it, trembling.

Apparently Phu saw something ascending from the stairwell below him, for he wailed in terror and clambered up the steps with much thumping and clattering.

Hearing him approach, I leaned hard against the door.

He pounded on the other side. "Please. Please, no. Please, for God's sake, no, for God's sake, please!"

I had heard my army buddies begging with that same desperation when the merciless torture master had forced rusty needles under their fingernails and through their clamp-held tongues. I dwelt on those images of horror that I had thought I had put behind me, and they gave me the will to resist Phu's pathetic pleas.

In addition to his voice, I heard the sludge-thick darkness rising behind him, cold lava flowing uphill: wet sounds, and that sinister whispering . . .

The torture master stopped pounding on the door and let out a scream that told me the darkness had seized him.

A great weight fell against the door for a moment, then was withdrawn.

The torture master's shrill cries rose and fell and rose again, and with each blood-curdling cycle of screams, his terror was more acute. From the sound of his voice, from the hollow booming of his feet striking the steps and kicking the walls, I could tell that he was being dragged down.

I had broken into a sweat.

I could not get my breath.

Suddenly I tore open the door and plunged across the threshold, onto the landing. I think I intended to pull him into the kitchen, to save him after all. I can't say for sure. What I saw in the stairwell, only a few steps below, was so shocking that I froze—and did nothing.

The torture master had not been seized by the darkness itself but by the hands of skeletally thin men who reached out from that ceaselessly churning mass of blackness. Dead men. I recognized them. They were American soldiers who had died in the camp, at the hands of the torture master, while I had been there. Neither of them had been friends of mine, and in fact they had both been hard cases themselves, bad men who had *enjoyed* the war before they had been captured and imprisoned by the Vietcong, the rare and hateful kind who liked killing and who engaged in black-market profiteering during their off-duty hours. Their eyes were icy, opaque. When they opened their mouths to speak to me, no words came forth, only a soft hissing and a faraway whimpering that made me think the noises were coming not from their bodies but from their souls, which were chained in the cellar far below. They were straining out of the oozing distillate of darkness, unable to escape it entirely, revealed only to the extent required to grasp Nguyen Quang Phu by both arms and legs.

As I watched, they drew him, screaming, into that thick decoction of night that had become their eternal home. When the three of them vanished into the throbbing gloom, that rippling tarry mass flowed backward away from me. Steps came into sight like sections of a beach appearing as the tide withdraws.

I stumbled out of the stairwell, across the kitchen, to the sink. I hung my head and vomited. Ran the water. Splashed my face. Rinsed my mouth. Leaned against the counter, gasping.

When at last I turned, I found that the cellar door had vanished. It had wanted the torture master. That's why the door had appeared, why a way had opened into . . . into the place below. It had wanted the torture master so badly, so intensely, that it could not wait to claim him in the natural course of events, upon his predestined death, so it had opened a door into this world and had swallowed him. Now it had him, and my encounter with the supernatural was surely at an end.

That's what I thought.

I just did not understand.

God help me, I did not understand.

Nguyen Quang Phu's car—a new white Mercedes—was parked in the driveway, which is rather secluded. I got in without being observed and drove the car away, abandoning it in a parking lot that served a public beach. I walked the few miles back to the house and later, when Phu's disappearance became a matter for the police, I claimed that he had never kept our appointment. I was believed. They were not in the least suspicious of me, for I am a leading citizen, a man of some success, and in possession of a fine reputation.

During the next three weeks, the cellar door did not reappear. I didn't think I would ever be entirely comfortable in our new dream house, but gradually the worst of my dread faded and I no longer avoided entering the kitchen.

I'd had a head-on collision with the supernatural, but there was little or no chance of another such encounter. A lot of people see one ghost sometime in their lives, are caught up in one paranormal event that leaves them shaken in doubt about the true nature of reality, but they have no further occult experiences. I doubted that I would ever see the cellar door again.

Then, Horace Dalcoe, holder of our restaurant's lease, discovered that I was secretly negotiating to buy the property that *he* had leased for his shopping center, and he struck back. Hard. He has political connections. I suppose he encountered little difficulty getting the health inspector to slap us with citations for nonexistent violations of the public code. We have always run an immaculate restaurant; our own standards for food-handling and cleanliness have always exceeded every one of the Health Department's requirements. Therefore, Carmen and I decided to take the matter to court rather than pay the fines—which was when we got hit with a citation for fire code violations. And when we announced our intention of seeking a retraction of those unjust charges, someone broke into the restaurant at three o'clock on a Thursday morning and vandalized the place, doing over fifty thousand dollars worth of damage.

I realized that I might win one or all of these battles but still lose the war. If I had been able to adopt Horace Dalcoe's scurrilous techniques, if I had been able to resort to bribing public officials and hiring thugs, I could have fought back in a way that Dalcoe would have understood, and he would no doubt have called a truce. However, although I was not without the stain of sin on my soul, I could not lower myself to Dalcoe's level.

Maybe my reluctance to play rough and dirty was more a matter of pride than genuine honesty or honor, though I would prefer to believe better of myself.

Yesterday morning (as I wrote this in the diary of damnation that I have begun to keep), I went to see Dalcoe at his plush office. I humbled myself before him and agreed to abandon my efforts to buy the leased property on which his small shopping center stands. I also agreed to pay him three thousand in cash, under the table, for being permitted to erect a larger, more attractive sign for the restaurant.

He was smug, condescending, infuriating. He kept me there for more than an hour, though our business could have been concluded in ten minutes, for he relished my humiliation.

Last night, I could not sleep. The bed was comfortable,

and the house was silent, and the air was pleasantly cool—all conditions for easy, deep sleep—but I could not stop brooding about Horace Dalcoe. The thought of being under his thumb for the foreseeable future was more than I could bear. I kept turning the situation over in my mind, looking for a handle, for a way to get an advantage over him before he knew what I was doing, but no brilliant ploys occurred to me.

Finally, I slipped out of bed without waking Carmen, and I went downstairs to get a glass of milk, hopeful that a calcium fix would sedate me. When I entered the kitchen, still thinking about Dalcoe, the cellar door was there.

Staring at it, I was very much afraid, for I knew what its timely reappearance meant. I needed to deal with Horace Dalcoe, and I was being provided with a final solution to the problem. Invite Dalcoe to the house on one pretext or another. Show him the cellar. And let the darkness have him.

I opened the door.

I looked down the steps at the blackness below.

Long-dead prisoners, victims of torture, had been waiting for Nguyen Quang Phu. What would be waiting down there to seize Dalcoe?

I shuddered.

Not for Dalcoe.

I shuddered for me.

Suddenly I understood that the darkness below wanted *me* more than it wanted Phu the torture master or Horace Dalcoe. Neither of those men was much of a prize. They were destined for hell, anyway. If I had not escorted Phu into the cellar, the darkness would have had him sooner or later, when at last death visited him. Likewise, Dalcoe would wind up in the depths of Gehenna upon his own death. But by hurrying them along to their ultimate destination, I would be giving myself to the dark impulses within me and would, thereby, be putting my own soul in jeopardy.

Staring down the cellar stairs, I heard the darkness calling my name, welcoming me, offering me eternal communication. Its whispery voice was seductive, its promises sweet. The fate of my soul was still undecided, and the darkness saw the possibility of a small triumph in claiming me.

I sensed that I was not as yet sufficiently corrupted to *belong* down in the darkness. What I had done to Phu might be seen as the mere enactment of long-overdue justice, for he was a man who deserved no rewards in either this world or the next. And allowing Dalcoe to proceed to his predestined doom ahead of schedule would probably not condemn me to perdition, either.

But who might I be tempted to lure into the cellar after Horace Dalcoe? How many and how often? It would get easier each time. Sooner or later, I would find myself using the cellar to rid myself of people who were minor nuisances. Some of them might be borderline cases, people deserving of hell but with a chance of salvation, and by hurrying them along, I would be denying them the opportunity to mend their ways and remake their lives. Their damnation would be partly my responsibility. Then, I too would be lost . . . and the darkness would rise up the stairs and come into the house and take me when it wished.

Below, that sludge-thick distillation of a billion moonless nights whispered to me, whispered.

I stepped back. I closed the door.

It did not vanish.

Dalcoe, I thought, desperately, why have you been such a bastard? Why have you made me hate you?

Darkness dwells within even the best of us. In the worst of us, darkness not only dwells but reigns.

I am a good man. A hard worker. A loving and faithful husband. A stern but doting father. A good man.

Yet I have human failings—not the least of which is a taste for vengeance. Part of the price I have paid is the death of my innocence in Nam. There, I learned that great evil exists in the world, not in the abstract but in the flesh, and when evil men tortured me, I was contaminated by that contact. I developed a thirst for vengeance.

I tell myself that I dare not succumb to the easy solutions offered by the cellar. Where would it stop? Some day, after sending a score of men and women into the lightless chamber below, I would be so thoroughly corrupted that it would be easy to use the cellar for what had previously seemed unthinkable. For instance, what if Carmen and I had an argument? Would I devolve to the point where I could ask her to explore those lower regions with me? What if my children displeased me as, God knows, children frequently do? Where would I draw the line? And would the line be constantly redrawn?

I am a good man.

Although occasionally providing darkness with a habitat, I have never provided it with a kingdom.

I am a good man.

But the temptation is great.

I have begun to make a list of people who have, at one time or another, made my life difficult. I don't intend to do anything about them, of course. The list is merely a game. I will make it and then tear it to pieces and flush it down the toilet.

I am a good man.

The list means nothing.

The cellar door will stay closed forever.

I will not open it again.

I swear by all that's holy.

I am a good man.

The list is longer than I had expected.

Haunted

by JOYCE CAROL OATES

Joyce Carol Oates is a two-time recipient of the O. Henry Special Award for Continuing Achievement in the short story, winner of the National Book Award for her novel Them, *and has received honors from the Guggenheim Foundation, the Lotos Club, and the National Institute of Arts; and with all this she is a writer not afraid of genre. Her work is often described as being in the Gothic mode, and here is a story in the central tradition of houses of horror.*

Haunted houses, forbidden houses. The old Medlock farm. The Erlich farm. The Minton farm on Elk Creek. *No Trespassing* the signs said, but we trespassed at will. *No Trespassing No Hunting No Fishing Under Penalty of Law* but we did what we pleased because who was there to stop us?

Our parents warned us against exploring these abandoned properties: the old houses and barns were dangerous, they said. We could get hurt, they said. I asked my mother if the houses were haunted and she said, Of course not, there aren't such things as ghosts, you know that. She was irritated with me; she guessed how I pretended to believe things I didn't believe, things I'd grown out of years before. It was a habit of childhood—pretending I was younger, more childish, than in fact I was. Opening my eyes wide and looking puzzled, worried. Girls are prone to such trickery; it's a form of camouflage when every other thought you think is a forbidden thought and with your eyes open staring sightless you can sink into dreams that leave your skin clammy and your

197

heart pounding—dreams that don't seem to belong to you that must have come to you from somewhere else from someone you don't know who knows *you*.

There weren't such things as ghosts, they told us. That was just superstition. But we could injure ourselves tramping around where we weren't wanted—the floorboards and the staircases in old houses were likely to be rotted, the roofs ready to collapse, we could cut ourselves on nails and broken glass, we could fall into uncovered wells—and you never knew who you might meet up with, in an old house or barn that's supposed to be empty. "You mean a bum?—like somebody hitch-hiking along the road?" I asked. "It could be a bum, or it could be somebody you know," Mother told me evasively. "A man, or a boy—somebody you know—" Her voice trailed off in embarrassment and I knew enough not to ask another question.

There were things you didn't talk about, back then. I never talked about them with my own children; there weren't the words to say them.

We listened to what our parents said, we nearly always agreed with what they said, but we went off on the sly and did what we wanted to do. When we were little girls: my neighbor Mary Lou Siskin and me. And when we were older, ten, eleven years old, tomboys, roughhouses our mothers called us. We liked to hike in the woods and along the creek for miles; we'd cut through farmers' fields, spy on their houses—on people we knew, kids we knew from school—most of all we liked to explore abandoned houses, boarded-up houses if we could break in; we'd scare ourselves thinking the houses might be haunted though really we knew they weren't haunted, there weren't such things as ghosts. Except—

I am writing in a dime-store notebook with lined pages and a speckled cover, a notebook of the sort we used in grade school. *Once upon a time* as I used to tell my children when they were tucked safely into bed and drifting off to sleep. *Once upon a time* I'd begin, reading from a book because it was safest so: the several times I told them my own stories they were frightened by my voice and couldn't sleep and afterward I couldn't sleep either and my husband would ask what was wrong and I'd say, Nothing, hiding my face from him so he wouldn't see my look of contempt.

I write in pencil, so that I can erase easily, and I find that I am constantly erasing, wearing holes in the paper. Mrs. Harding, our fifth grade teacher, disciplined us for handing in messy notebooks: she was a heavy, toad-faced woman, her voice was deep and husky and gleeful when she said, "You, Melissa, what have you to say for yourself?" and I stood there mute, my knees trembling. My friend Mary Lou laughed behind her hand, wriggled in her seat she thought I was so funny. Tell the old witch to go to hell, she'd say, she'll respect you then, but of course no one would ever say such a thing to Mrs. Harding. Not even Mary Lou. "What have you to say for yourself, Melissa? Handing in a notebook with a ripped page?" My grade for the homework assignment was lowered from A to B, Mrs. Harding grunted with satisfaction as she made the mark, a big swooping B in red ink, creasing the page. "More is expected of you, Melissa, so you disappoint me more," Mrs. Harding always said. So many years ago and I remember those words more clearly than words I have heard the other day.

One morning there was a pretty substitute teacher in Mrs. Harding's classroom. "Mrs. Harding is unwell, I'll be taking her place today," she said, and we saw the nervousness in her face; we guessed there was a secret she wouldn't tell and we waited and a few days later the principal himself came to tell us that Mrs. Harding would not be back, she had died of a stroke. He spoke carefully as if we were much younger children and might be upset and Mary Lou caught my eye and winked and I sat there at my desk feeling the strangest sensation, something flowing into the top of my head, honey-rich and warm making its way down my spine. *Our Father Who art in Heaven* I whispered in the prayer with the others my head bowed and my hands clasped tight together but my thoughts were somewhere else leaping wild and crazy somewhere else and I knew Mary Lou's were too.

On the school bus going home she whispered in my ear, "That was because of us, wasn't it!—what happened to that old bag Harding. But we won't tell anybody."

Once upon a time there were two sisters, and one was very pretty and one was very ugly. . . . Though Mary Lou Siskin wasn't my sister. And I wasn't ugly, really: just sallow-skinned, with a small pinched ferrety face. With dark almost lashless eyes that were set too close together and a nose that didn't look right. A look of yearning, and disappointment.

But Mary Lou *was* pretty, even rough and clumsy as she

sometimes behaved. That long silky blond hair everybody remembered her for afterward, years afterward.... How, when she had to be identified, it was the long silky white-blond hair that was unmistakable. . . .

Sleepless nights, but I love them. I write during the night-time hours and sleep during the day, I am of an age when you don't require more than a few hours sleep. My husband has been dead for nearly a year and my children are scattered and busily absorbed in their own selfish lives like all children and there is no one to interrupt me no one to pry into my business no one in the neighborhood who dares come knock-ing at my door to see if I am all right. Sometimes out of a mirror floats an unexpected face, a strange face, lined, rav-aged, with deep-socketed eyes always damp, always blinking in a shock or dismay or simple bewilderment—but I adroitly look away. I have no need to stare.

It's true, all you have heard of the vanity of the old. Be-lieving ourselves young, still, behind our aged faces—mere children, and so very innocent!

Once when I was a young bride and almost pretty my color up when I was happy and my eyes shining we drove out into the country for a Sunday's excursion and he wanted to make love I knew, he was shy and fumbling as I but he wanted to make love and I ran into a cornfield in my stock-ings and high heels, I was playing at being a woman I never could be, Mary Lou Siskin maybe, Mary Lou whom my hus-band never knew, but I got out of breath and frightened, it was the wind in the cornstalks, that dry rustling sound, that dry terrible rustling sound like whispering like voices you can't quite identify and he caught me and tried to hold me and I pushed him away sobbing and he said, What's wrong? My God what's wrong? as if he really loved me as if his life was focused on me and I knew I could never be equal to it, that love, that importance, I knew I was only Melissa the ugly one the one the boys wouldn't give a second glance, and one day he'd understand and know how he'd been cheated. I pushed him away, I said, Leave me alone! don't touch me! You disgust me! I said.

He backed off and I hid my face, sobbing.

But later on I got pregnant just the same. Only a few weeks later.

* * *

Always there were stories behind the abandoned houses and always the stories were sad. Because farmers went bankrupt and had to move away. Because somebody died and the farm couldn't be kept up and nobody wanted to buy it—like the Medlock farm across the creek. Mr. Medlock died aged seventy-nine and Mrs. Medlock refused to sell the farm and lived there alone until someone from the county health agency came to get her. Isn't it a shame, my parents said. The poor woman, they said. They told us never, never to pike around in the Medlocks' barns or house—the buildings were ready to cave in, they'd been in terrible repair even when the Medlocks were living.

It was said that Mrs. Medlock had gone off her head after she'd found her husband dead in one of the barns, lying flat on his back his eyes open and bulging, his mouth open, tongue protruding, she'd gone to look for him and found him like that and she'd never gotten over it they said, never got over the shock. They had to commit her to the state hospital for her own good (they said) and the house and the barns were boarded up, everywhere tall grass and thistles grew wild, dandelions in the spring, tiger lilies in the summer, and when we drove by I stared and stared narrowing my eyes so I wouldn't see someone looking out one of the windows—a face there, pale and quick—or a dark figure scrambling up the roof to hide behind the chimney—Mary Lou and I wondered was the house haunted, was the barn haunted where the old man had died, we crept around to spy, we couldn't stay away, coming closer and closer each time until something scared us and we ran away back through the woods clutching and pushing at each other until one day finally we went right up to the house to the back door and peeked in one of the windows. Mary Lou led the way, Mary Lou said not to be afraid, nobody lived there any more and nobody would catch us, it didn't matter that the land was posted, the police didn't arrest kids our ages.

We explored the barns, we dragged the wooden cover off the well and dropped stones inside. We called the cats but they wouldn't come close enough to be petted. They were barn cats, skinny and diseased-looking, they'd said at the county bureau that Mrs. Medlock had let a dozen cats live in the house with her so that the house was filthy from their messes. When the cats wouldn't come we got mad and threw stones at them and they ran away hissing—nasty dirty things, Mary Lou said. Once we crawled up on the tar-paper

roof over the Medlocks' kitchen, just for fun, Mary Lou
wanted to climb up the big roof too to the very top but I got
frightened and said, No, no please don't, no Mary Lou
please, and I sounded so strange Mary Lou looked at me and
didn't tease or mock as she usually did. The roof was steep,
I'd known she would hurt herself. I could see her losing her
footing and slipping, falling, I could see her astonished face
and her flying hair as she fell, knowing nothing could save
her. You're no fun, Mary Lou said, giving me a hard little
pinch. But she didn't go climbing up the big roof.

Later we ran through the barns screaming at the top of
our lungs just for fun for the hell of it as Mary Lou said, we
tossed things in a heap, broken-off parts of farm implements,
leather things from the horses' gear, handfuls of straw. The
farm animals had been gone for years but their smell was still
strong. Dried horse and cow droppings that looked like mud.
Mary Lou said, "You know what—I'd like to burn this place
down." And she looked at me and I said, "Okay—go on and
do it, burn it down." And Mary Lou said, "You think I
wouldn't? Just give me a match." And I said, "You know I
don't have any match." And a look passed between us. And
I felt something flooding at the top of my head, my throat
tickled as if I didn't know would I laugh or cry and I said,
"You're crazy—" and Mary Lou said with a sneering little
laugh, *"You're crazy,* dumbbell. I was just testing you."

By the time Mary Lou was twelve years old Mother had
got to hate her, was always trying to turn me against her so
I'd make friends with other girls. Mary Lou had a fresh
mouth, she said. Mary Lou didn't respect her elders—not
even her own parents. Mother guessed that Mary Lou
laughed at her behind her back, said things about all of us.
She was mean and snippy and a smart-ass, rough sometimes
as her brothers. Why didn't I make other friends? Why did I
always go running when she stood out in the yard and called
me? The Siskins weren't a whole lot better than white trash,
the way Mr. Siskin worked that land of his.

In town, in school, Mary Lou sometimes ignored me
when other girls were around, girls who lived in town, whose
fathers weren't farmers like ours. But when it was time to
ride home on the bus she'd sit with me as if nothing was
wrong and I'd help her with her homework if she needed
help, I hated her sometimes but then I'd forgive her as soon

as she smiled at me, she'd say, "Hey 'Lissa are you mad at me?" and I'd make a face and say no as if it was an insult, being asked. Mary Lou was my sister I sometimes pretended, I told myself a story about us being sisters and looking alike, and Mary Lou said sometimes she'd like to leave her family her goddamned family and come live with me. Then the next day or the next hour she'd get moody and be nasty to me and get me almost crying. All the Siskins had mean streaks, bad tempers, she'd tell people. As if she was proud.

Her hair was a light blond, almost white in the sunshine, and when I first knew her she had to wear it braided tight around her head—her grandmother braided it for her, and she hated it. Like Gretel or Snow White in one of those damn dumb picture books for children, Mary Lou said. When she was older she wore it down and let it grow long so that it fell almost to her hips. It was very beautiful—silky and shimmering. I dreamt of Mary Lou's hair sometimes but the dreams were confused and I couldn't remember when I woke up whether I was the one with the long blond silky hair, or someone else. It took me a while to get my thoughts clear lying there in bed and then I'd remember Mary Lou, who was my best friend.

She was ten months older than I was, and an inch or so taller, a bit heavier, not fat but fleshy, solid and fleshy, with hard little muscles in her upper arms like a boy. Her eyes were blue like washed glass, her eyebrows and lashes were almost white, she had a snubbed nose and Slavic cheekbones and a mouth that could be sweet or twisty and smirky depending upon her mood. But she didn't like her face because it was round—a moon face she called it, staring at herself in the mirror though she knew damned well she was pretty—didn't older boys whistle at her, didn't the bus driver flirt with her?—calling her "Blondie" while he never called me anything at all.

Mother didn't like Mary Lou visiting with me when no one else was home in our house: she didn't trust her, she said. Thought she might steal something, or poke her nose into parts of the house where she wasn't welcome. That girl is a bad influence on you, she said. But it was all the same old crap I heard again and again so I didn't even listen. I'd have told her she was crazy except that would only make things worse.

Mary Lou said, "Don't you just hate them?—your mother, and mine? Sometimes I wish—"

I put my hands over my ears and didn't hear.

The Siskins lived two miles away from us, farther back the road where the road got narrower. Those days, it was un-paved, and never got plowed in the winter. I remember their barn with the yellow silo, I remember the muddy pond where the dairy cows came to drink, the muck they churned up in the spring. I remember Mary Lou saying she wished all the cows would die—they were always sick with something—so her father would give up and sell the farm and they could live in town in a nice house. I was hurt, her saying those things as if she'd forgotten about me and would leave me behind. Damn you to hell, I whispered under my breath.

I remember smoke rising from the Siskins' kitchen chim-ney, from their wood-burning stove, straight up into the winter sky like a breath you draw inside you deeper and deeper until you begin to feel faint.

Later on, the house was empty too. But boarded up only for a few months—the bank sold it at auction. (It turned out the bank owned most of the Siskin farm, even the dairy cows. So Mary Lou had been wrong about that all along and never knew.)

As I write I can hear the sound of glass breaking. I can feel glass underfoot. *Once upon a time there were two little princesses, two sisters, who did forbidden things.* That brittle terrible sensation under my shoes—slippery like water—"Anybody home? Hey—anybody home?" and there's an old calendar tacked to a kitchen wall, a faded pic-ture of Jesus Christ in a long white gown stained with scarlet, thorns fitted to His bowed head. Mary Lou is going to scare me in another minute making me think that someone is in the house and the two of us will scream with laughter and run outside where it's safe. Wild frightened laughter and I never knew afterward what was funny or why we did these things. Smashing what remained of windows, wrenching at stairway railings to break them loose, running with our heads ducked so we wouldn't get cobwebs in our faces.

One of us found a dead bird, a starling, in what had been the parlor of the house. Turned it over with a foot—there's the open eye looking right up calm and matter-of-fact. *Me-*

lissa, that eye tells me, silent and terrible, *I see you.*

That was the old Minton place, the stone house with the caved-in roof and the broken steps, like something in a picture book from long ago. From the road the house looked as if it might be big, but when we explored it we were disappointed to see that it wasn't much bigger than my own house, just four narrow rooms downstairs, another four upstairs, an attic with a steep ceiling, the roof partly caved in. The barns had collapsed in upon themselves; only their stone foundations remained solid. The land had been sold off over the years to other farmers, nobody had lived in the house for a long time. The old Minton house, people called it. On Elk Creek where Mary Lou's body was eventually found.

In seventh grade Mary Lou had a boyfriend she wasn't supposed to have and no one knew about it but me—an older boy who'd dropped out of school and worked as a farmhand. I thought he was a little slow—not in his speech which was fast enough, normal enough, but in his way of thinking. He was sixteen or seventeen years old. His name was Hans; he had crisp blond hair like the bristles of a brush, a coarse blemished face, derisive eyes. Mary Lou was crazy for him she said, aping the older girls in town who said they were "crazy for" certain boys or young men. Hans and Mary Lou kissed when they didn't think I was watching, in an old ruin of a cemetery behind the Minton house, on the creek bank, in the tall marsh grass by the end of the Siskins' driveway. Hans had a car borrowed from one of his brothers, a battered old Ford, the front bumper held up by wire, the running board scraping the ground. We'd be out walking on the road and Hans would come along tapping the horn and stop and Mary Lou would climb in but I'd hang back knowing they didn't want me and the hell with them: I preferred to be alone.

"You're just jealous of Hans and me," Mary Lou said, unforgivably, and I hadn't any reply. "Hans is sweet. Hans is nice. He isn't like people say," Mary Lou said in a quick bright false voice she'd picked up from one of the older, popular girls in town. "He's . . ." And she stared at me blinking and smiling not knowing what to say as if in fact she didn't know Hans at all. "He isn't *simple,*" she said angrily, "he just doesn't like to talk a whole lot."

When I try to remember Hans Meunzer after so many

decades I can see only a muscular boy with short-trimmed
blond hair and protuberant ears, blemished skin, the shadow
of a moustache on his upper lip—he's looking at me, eyes
narrowed, crinkled, as if he understands how I fear him, how
I wish him dead and gone, and he'd hate me too if he took
me that seriously. But he doesn't take me that seriously, his
gaze just slides right through me as if nobody's standing
where I stand.

There were stories about all the abandoned houses but
the worst story was about the Minton house over on the Elk
Creek Road about three miles from where we lived. For no
reason anybody ever discovered Mr. Minton had beaten his
wife to death and afterward killed himself with a .12-gauge
shotgun. He hadn't even been drinking, people said. And his
farm hadn't been doing at all badly, considering how others
were doing.

Looking at the ruin from the outside, overgrown with
trumpet vine and wild rose, it seemed hard to believe that
anything like that had happened. Things in the world even
those things built by man are so quiet left to themselves . . .

The house had been deserted for years, as long as I could
remember. Most of the land had been sold off but the heirs
didn't want to deal with the house. They didn't want to sell it
and they didn't want to raze it and they certainly didn't want
to live in it so it stood empty. The property was posted with
No Trespassing signs layered one atop another but nobody
took them seriously. Vandals had broken into the house and
caused damage, the McFarlane boys had tried to burn down
the old hay barn one Halloween night. The summer Mary
Lou started seeing Hans she and I climbed in the house
through a rear window—the boards guarding it had long
since been yanked away—and walked through the rooms
slow as sleepwalkers our arms around each other's waists our
eyes staring waiting to see Mr. Minton's ghost as we turned
each corner. The inside smelled of mouse droppings, mildew,
rot, old sorrow. Strips of wallpaper torn from the walls, plasterboard exposed, old furniture overturned and smashed, old
yellowed sheets of newspaper underfoot, and broken glass,
everywhere broken glass. Through the ravaged windows
sunlight spilled in tremulous quivering bands. The air was
afloat, alive: dancing dust atoms. "I'm afraid," Mary Lou
whispered. She squeezed my waist and I felt my mouth go
dry for hadn't I been hearing something upstairs, a low per-

sistent murmuring like quarreling like one person trying to convince another going on and on and on but when I stood very still to listen the sound vanished and there were only the comforting summer sounds of birds, crickets, cicadas; birds, crickets, cicadas.

I knew how Mr. Minton had died: he'd placed the barrel of the shotgun beneath his chin and pulled the trigger with his big toe. They found him in the bedroom upstairs, most of his head blown off. They found his wife's body in the cistern in the cellar where he'd tried to hide her. "Do you think we should go upstairs?" Mary Lou asked, worried. Her fingers felt cold; but I could see tiny sweat beads on her forehead. Her mother had braided her hair in one thick clumsy braid, the way she wore it most of the summer, but the bands of hair were loosening. "No," I said, frightened. "I don't know." We hesitated at the bottom of the stairs—just stood there for a long time. "Maybe not," Mary Lou said. "Damn stairs'd fall in on us."

In the parlor there were bloodstains on the floor and on the wall—I could see them. Mary Lou said in derision, "They're just waterstains, dummy."

I could hear the voices overhead, or was it a single droning persistent voice. I waited for Mary Lou to hear it but she never did.

Now we were safe, now we were retreating, Mary Lou said as if repentant, "Yeah—this house *is* special."

We looked through the debris in the kitchen hoping to find something of value but there wasn't anything—just smashed chinaware, old battered pots and pans, more old yellowed newspaper. But through the window we saw a garter snake sunning itself on a rusted water tank, stretched out to a length of two feet. It was a lovely coppery color, the scales gleaming like perspiration on a man's arm; it seemed to be asleep. Neither one of us screamed, or wanted to throw something—we just stood there watching it for the longest time.

Mary Lou didn't have a boyfriend any longer. Hans had stopped coming around. We saw him driving the old Ford now and then but he didn't seem to see us. Mr. Siskin had found out about him and Mary Lou and he'd been upset—acting like a damn crazy man Mary Lou said, asking her every kind of nasty question then interrupting her and not believing her anyway, then he'd put her to terrible shame by going over to see Hans and carrying on with him. "I hate them all," Mary Lou said, her face darkening with blood. "I wish—"

We rode our bicycles over to the Minton farm, or tramped through the fields to get there. It was the place we liked best. Sometimes we brought things to eat, cookies, bananas, candy bars; sitting on the broken stone steps out front, as if we lived in the house really, we were sisters who lived here having a picnic lunch out front. There were bees, mosquitoes, but we brushed them away. We had to sit in the shade because the sun was so fierce and direct, a whitish heat pouring down from overhead.

"Would you ever like to run away from home?" Mary Lou said. "I don't know," I said uneasily. Mary Lou wiped at her mouth and gave me a mean narrow look. "I don't know," she said in a falsetto voice, mimicking me. At an upstairs window someone was watching us—was it a man or was it a woman—someone stood there listening hard and I couldn't move feeling so slow and dreamy in the heat like a fly caught on a sticky petal that's going to fold in on itself and swallow him up. Mary Lou crumpled up some wax paper and threw it into the weeds. She was dreamy too, slow and yawning. She said, "Shit—they'd just find me. Then everything would be worse."

I was covered in a thin film of sweat and I'd begun to shiver. Goose bumps were raised on my arms. I could see us sitting on the stone steps the way we'd look from the second floor of the house, Mary Lou sprawled with her legs apart, her braided hair slung over her shoulder, me sitting with my arms hugging my knees my backbone tight and straight knowing I was being watched. Mary Lou said, lowering her voice, "Did you ever touch yourself in a certain place, Melissa?" "No," I said, pretending I didn't know what she meant. "Hans wanted to do that," Mary Lou said. She sounded disgusted. Then she started to giggle. "I wouldn't let him, then he wanted to do something else—started unbuttoning his pants—wanted me to touch *him*. And . . ."

I wanted to hush her, to clap my hand over her mouth. But she just went on and I never said a word until we both started giggling together and couldn't stop. Afterward I didn't remember most of it or why I'd been so excited my face burning and my eyes seared as if I'd been staring into the sun.

* * *

On the way home Mary Lou said, "Some things are so sad you can't say them." But I pretended not to hear.

A few days later I came back by myself. Through the ravaged cornfield: the stalks dried and broken, the tassels burnt, that rustling whispering sound of the wind I can hear now if I listen closely. My head was aching with excitement. I was telling myself a story that we'd made plans to run away and live in the Minton house. I was carrying a willow switch I'd found on the ground, fallen from a tree but still green and springy, slapping at things with it as if it were a whip. Talking to myself. Laughing aloud. Wondering was I being watched.

I climbed in the house through the back window and brushed my hands on my jeans. My hair was sticking to the back of my neck.

At the foot of the stairs I called up, "Who's here?" in a voice meant to show it was all play; I knew I was alone.

My heart was beating hard and quick, like a bird caught in the hand. It was lonely without Mary Lou so I walked heavy to let them know I was there and wasn't afraid. I started singing, I started whistling. Talking to myself and slapping at things with the willow switch. Laughing aloud, a little angry. Why was I angry, well I didn't know, someone was whispering telling me to come upstairs, to walk on the inside of the stairs so the steps wouldn't collapse.

The house was beautiful inside if you had the right eyes to see it. If you didn't mind the smell. Glass underfoot, broken plaster, stained wallpaper hanging in shreds. Tall narrow windows looking out onto wild weedy patches of green. I heard something in one of the rooms but when I looked I saw nothing much more than an easy chair lying on its side. Vandals had ripped stuffing out of it and tried to set it afire. The material was filthy but I could see that it had been pretty once—a floral design—tiny yellow flowers and green ivy. A woman used to sit in the chair, a big woman with sly staring eyes. Knitting in her lap but she wasn't knitting just staring out the window watching to see who might be coming to visit.

Upstairs the rooms were airless and so hot I felt my skin prickle like shivering. I wasn't afraid!—I slapped at the walls with my springy willow switch. In one of the rooms high in a corner wasps buzzed around a fat wasp's nest. In another room I looked out the window to breathe thinking this was my window, I'd come to live here. She was telling me I had better lie down and rest because I was in danger of heat-stroke and I pretended not to know what heatstroke was but she knew I knew because hadn't a cousin of mine collapsed haying just last summer, they said his face had gone blotched and red and he'd begun breathing faster and faster not get-ting enough oxygen until he collapsed. I was looking out at the overgrown apple orchard, I could smell the rot, a sweet winey smell, the sky was hazy like something you can't get clear in your vision, pressing in close and warm. A half mile away Elk Creek glittered through a screen of willow trees moving slow glittering with scales like winking.

Come away from the window, someone told me sternly.

But I took my time obeying.

In the biggest of the rooms was an old mattress pulled off rusty bedsprings and dumped on the floor. They'd torn some of the stuffing out of this too, there were scorch marks on it from cigarettes. The fabric was stained with something like rust and I didn't want to look at it but I had to. Once at Mary Lou's when I'd gone home with her after school there was a mattress lying out in the yard in the sun and Mary Lou told me in disgust that it was her youngest brother's mattress—he'd wet his bed again and the mattress had to be aired out. As if the stink would ever go away, Mary Lou said.

Something moved inside the mattress, a black glittering thing, it was a cockroach but I wasn't allowed to jump back. Suppose you have to lie down on that mattress and sleep, I was told. Suppose you can't go home until you do. My eye-lids were heavy, my head was pounding with blood. A mos-quito buzzed around me but I was too tired to brush it away. Lie down on that mattress, Melissa, she told me. You know you must be punished.

I knelt down, not on the mattress, but on the floor beside it. The smells in the room were close and rank but I didn't mind, my head was nodding with sleep. Rivulets of sweat ran down my face and sides, under my arms, but I didn't mind. I saw my hand move out slowly like a stranger's hand to touch the mattress and a shiny black cockroach scuttled away in fright, and a second cockroach, and a third—but I couldn't jump up and scream.

Lie down on that mattress and take your punishment.

I looked over my shoulder and there was a woman stand-ing in the doorway—a woman I'd never seen before.

She was staring at me. Her eyes were shiny and dark. She

licked her lips and said in a jeering voice, "What are you doing here in this house, miss?"

I was terrified. I tried to answer but I couldn't speak.

"Have you come to see me?" the woman asked.

She was no age I could guess. Older than my mother but not old-seeming. She wore men's clothes and she was tall as any man, with wide shoulders, and long legs, and big sagging breasts like cow's udders loose inside her shirt not harnessed in a brassiere like other women's. Her thick wiry gray hair was cut short as a man's and stuck up in tufts that looked greasy. Her eyes were small, and black, and set back deep in their sockets; the flesh around them looked bruised. I had never seen anyone like her before—her thighs were enormous, big as my body. There was a ring of loose soft flesh at the waistband of her trousers but she wasn't fat.

"I asked you a question, miss. Why are you here?"

I was so frightened I could feel my bladder contract. I stared at her, cowering by the mattress, and couldn't speak.

It seemed to please her that I was so frightened. She approached me, stooping a little to get through the doorway. She said, in a mock-kindly voice, "You've come to visit with me—is that it?"

"No," I said.

"No!" she said, laughing. "Why, of course you have."

"No. I don't know you."

She leaned over me, touched my forehead with her fingers. I shut my eyes waiting to be hurt but her touch was cool. She brushed my hair off my forehead where it was sticky with sweat. "I've seen you here before, you and that other one," she said. "What is her name? The blond one. The two of you, trespassing?"

I couldn't move, my legs were paralyzed. Quick and darting and buzzing my thoughts bounded in every which direction but didn't take hold. "Melissa is *your* name, isn't it," the woman said. "And what is your sister's name?"

"She isn't my sister," I whispered.

"What is her name?"

"I don't know."

"You don't know."

"—don't know," I said, cowering.

The woman drew back half sighing half grunting. She looked at me pityingly. "You'll have to be punished, then."

I could smell ashes about her, something cold. I started to whimper started to say I hadn't done anything wrong, hadn't hurt anything in the house, I had only been exploring—I wouldn't come back again...

She was smiling at me, uncovering her teeth. She could read my thoughts before I could think them.

The skin of her face was in layers like an onion, like she'd been sunburnt, or had a skin disease. There were patches that had begun to peel. Her look was wet and gloating. Don't hurt me, I wanted to say. Please don't hurt me.

I'd begun to cry. My nose was running like a baby's. I thought I would crawl past the woman I would get to my feet and run past her and escape but the woman stood in my way blocking my way leaning over me breathing damp and warm her breath like a cow's breath in my face. Don't hurt me, I said, and she said, "You know you have to be punished—you and your pretty blond sister."

"She isn't my sister," I said.

"And what is her name?"

The woman was bending over me, quivering with laughter.

"Speak up, miss. What is it?"

"I don't know—" I started to say. But my voice said, "Mary Lou."

The woman's big breasts spilled down into her belly. I could feel her shaking with laughter. But she spoke sternly saying that Mary Lou and I had been very bad girls and we knew it her house was forbidden territory and we knew it hadn't we known all along that others had come to grief beneath its roof?

"No," I started to say. But my voice said, "Yes."

The woman laughed, crouching above me. "Now, miss, 'Melissa' as they call you—your parents don't know where you are at this very moment, do they?"

"I don't know."

"Do they?"

"No."

"They don't know anything about you, do they?—what you do, and what you think? You and 'Mary Lou.'"

"No."

She regarded me for a long moment, smiling. Her smile was wide and friendly.

"You're a spunky little girl, aren't you, with a mind of your own, aren't you, you and your pretty little sister. I bet your bottoms have been warmed many a time," the woman

said, showing her big tobacco-stained teeth in a grin,
". . . your tender little asses."

I began to giggle. My bladder tightened.

"Hand that here, miss," the woman said. She took the
willow switch from my fingers—I had forgotten I was holding it. "I will now administer punishment: take down your
jeans. Take down your panties. Lie down on that mattress.
Hurry." She spoke briskly now, she was all business. "Hurry,
Melissa! *And* your panties! Or do you want me to pull them
down for you?"

She was slapping the switch impatiently against the palm
of her left hand, making a wet scolding noise with her lips.
Scolding and teasing. Her skin shone in patches, stretched
tight over the big hard bones of her face. Her eyes were
small, crinkling smaller, black and damp. She was so big she
had to position herself carefully over me to give herself
proper balance and leverage so that she wouldn't fall. I could
hear her hoarse eager breathing as it came to me from all
sides like the wind.

I had done as she told me. It wasn't me doing these things
but they were done. Don't hurt me, I whispered, lying on my
stomach on the mattress, my arms stretched above me and
my fingernails digging into the floor. The coarse wood with
splinters pricking my skin. Don't hurt me O please but the
woman paid no heed her warm wet breath louder now and
the floorboards creaking beneath her weight. "Now, miss,
now 'Melissa' as they call you—this will be our secret won't
it . . ."

When it was over she wiped at her mouth and said she
would let me go today if I promised never to tell anybody if I
sent my pretty little sister to her tomorrow.

She isn't my sister, I said, sobbing. When I could get my
breath.

I had lost control of my bladder after all, I'd begun to pee
even before the first swipe of the willow switch hit me on the
buttocks, peeing in helpless spasms, and sobbing, and afterward the woman scolded me saying wasn't it a poor little
baby wetting itself like that. But she sounded repentant too,
stood well aside to let me pass, Off you go! Home you go!
And don't forget!

And I ran out of the room hearing her laughter behind me
and down the stairs running running as if I hadn't any weight

my legs just blurry beneath me as if the air was water and I
was swimming I ran out of the house and through the cornfield running in the cornfield sobbing as the corn stalks
slapped at my face. *Off you go! Home you go! And don't
forget!*

I told Mary Lou about the Minton house and something
that had happened to me there that was a secret and she
didn't believe me at first saying with a jeer, "Was it a ghost?
Was it Hans?" I said I couldn't tell. Couldn't tell what? she
said. Couldn't tell, I said. Why not? she said.

"Because I promised."

"Promised who?" she said. She looked at me with her
wide blue eyes like she was trying to hypnotize me. "You're a
goddamned liar."

Later she started in again asking me what had happened
what was the secret was it something to do with Hans? did he
still like her? was he mad at her? and I said it didn't have
anything to do with Hans not a thing to do with him. Twisting my mouth to show what I thought of him.

"Then who—?" Mary Lou asked.

"I told you it was a secret."

"Oh shit—what kind of secret?"

"A secret."

"A secret *really?*"

I turned away from Mary Lou, trembling. My mouth kept
twisting in a strange hurting smile. "Yes. A secret *really,*" I
said.

The last time I saw Mary Lou she wouldn't sit with me on
the bus, walked past me holding her head high giving me a
mean snippy look out of the corner of her eye. Then when
she left for her stop she made sure she bumped me going to
my seat, she leaned over to say, "I'll find out for myself, I
hate you anyway," speaking loud enough for everybody on
the bus to hear, "—I always have."

Once upon a time the fairy tales begin. But then they end
and often you don't know really what has happened, what
was meant to happen, you only know what you've been told,
what the words suggest. Now that I have completed my story,
filled up half my notebook with my handwriting that disap-
points me, it is so shaky and childish—now the story is over
I don't understand what it means. I know what happened in

my life but I don't know what has happened in these pages.

Mary Lou was found murdered ten days after she said those words to me. Her body had been tossed into Elk Creek a quarter mile from the road and from the old Minton place. Where, it said in the paper, nobody had lived for fifteen years.

It said that Mary Lou had been thirteen years old at the time of her death. She'd been missing for seven days, had been the object of a countywide search.

It said that nobody had lived in the Minton house for years but that derelicts sometimes sheltered there. It said that the body was unclothed and mutilated. There were no details.

This happened a long time ago.

The murderer (or murderers as the newspaper always said) was never found.

Hans Meunzer was arrested of course and kept in the county jail for three days while police questioned him but in the end they had to let him go, insufficient evidence to build a case it was explained in the newspaper though everybody knew he was the one wasn't he the one?—everybody knew. For years afterward they'd be saying that. Long after Hans was gone and the Siskins were gone, moved away nobody knew where.

Hans swore he hadn't done it, hadn't seen Mary Lou for weeks. There were people who testified in his behalf said he couldn't have done it for one thing he didn't have his brother's car any longer and he'd been working all that time. Working hard out in the fields—couldn't have slipped away long enough to do what police were saying he'd done. And Hans said over and over he was innocent. Sure he was innocent. Son of a bitch ought to be hanged my father said, everybody knew. Hans was the one unless it was a derelict or a fisherman—fishermen often drove out to Elk Creek to fish for black bass, built fires on the creek bank and left messes behind—sometimes prowled around the Minton house too looking for things to steal. The police had records of automobile license plates belonging to some of these men, they questioned them but nothing came of it. Then there was that crazy man, that old hermit living in a tar-paper shanty near the Shaheen dump that everybody'd said ought to have been committed to the state hospital years ago. But everybody knew really it was Hans and Hans got out as quick as he could, just disappeared and not even his family knew where unless they were lying which probably they were though they claimed not.

Mother rocked me in her arms crying, the two of us crying, she told me that Mary Lou was happy now, Mary Lou was in Heaven now, Jesus Christ had taken her to live with Him and I knew that didn't I? I wanted to laugh but I didn't laugh. Mary Lou shouldn't have gone with boys, not a nasty boy like Hans, Mother said, she shouldn't have been sneaking around the way she did—I knew that didn't I? Mother's words filled my head flooding my head so there was no danger of laughing.

Jesus loves you too you know that don't you Melissa? Mother asked hugging me. I told her yes. I didn't laugh because I was crying.

They wouldn't let me go to the funeral, said it would scare me too much. Even though the casket was closed.

It's said that when you're older you remember things that happened a long time ago better than you remember things that have just happened and I have found that to be so.

For instance I can't remember when I bought this notebook at Woolworth's whether it was last week or last month or just a few days ago. I can't remember why I started writing in it, what purpose I told myself. But I remember Mary Lou stooping to say those words in my ear and I remember when Mary Lou's mother came over to ask us at suppertime a few days later if I had seen Mary Lou that day—I remember the very food on my plate, the mashed potatoes in a dry little mound. I remember hearing Mary Lou call my name standing out in the driveway cupping her hands to her mouth the way Mother hated her to do, it was white trash behavior.

" 'Lissa!" Mary Lou would call, and I'd call back, "Okay, I'm coming!" *Once upon a time.*

In the Memory Room

by MICHAEL BISHOP

Mike Bishop is a Nebula Award winning novelist (No Enemy but Time), *whose dark fantasies are collected in* One Winter in Eden. *Like famed anthropologist Ashley Montagu, he sees much of what is inherent in man through language and custom. And he knows our lives are written not as guidebooks for the vacationing visitor, but in each individual's universal experiences. The past is ever with us, for we each dwell in the memory room.*

"This isn't my mother!" Kenny repeats, staring down at the dead woman in the Memory Room.

Kenny has a lumberjack's beard. His glasses magnify his eyes to the size of snowballs. His belly is so big that he cannot pull his maroon leather car coat tight enough to button it.

"I don't care what you guys say," Kenny tells the other eight members of Gina Callan's family arrayed behind him. "This . . . this *manikin* isn't my mother!"

"Just who the hell you think it is, then?" white-haired Uncle Sarge Lobrano asks him. "Queen Elizabeth?"

Aunt Dot, Gina's sister, rebukes her husband: "Sergio!"

"This is the wrong woman they got in here! The wrong goddamn woman! My mother was beautiful, and this person —she looks like she's hurting. Still hurting."

"Kenny, it was a painful death," Aunt Dot tries to explain. "Your mama's kidneys failed. She was retaining fluid. That's why her cheeks and jowls are so puffy."

217

The hostess who ushered Gina's family into the room says, "We did our best. I worked very hard to make her lifelike."

"My mother always wore glasses. We gave 'em to you. What the hell did you do with 'em?"

"Items to help make the likeness true are received at the desk, Mr. Petruzzi," the hostess tells Kenny. "Nobody passed her glasses on to me."

Kenny struggles to free his wallet from the hip pocket of his tent-sized trousers. From the wallet he extracts a photograph. "Didn't you get a picture, then? Here's the way my mother ought to look—beautiful."

He thrusts the photo at the hostess, a smart-looking, fortyish woman wearing slacks and a bulky fishnet sweater. Then, gesturing hugely, he declares again, *"That's* not my mother."

Vince—Uncle Sarge and Aunt Dot's son, a high school football coach in Colorado Springs—takes his cousin's elbow. "Of course that isn't your mother, Kenny. It's only her body. Your mother's real self—her soul—is in heaven."

"I *know* where she is. But she doesn't look like *that.*" Kenny flaunts the wallet photo. "This is how she looks, and this is the way I'll always remember her."

"That picture's five years old," Uncle Lyle says. "You can't expect your mother to look today the way she looked five years ago when she was in nearly perfect health."

"I can expect these bums to put the glasses we gave 'em on her, can't I?"

The hostess turns to Uncle Lyle, Gina's brother. "Mr. Sekas, I never received a photo of Mrs. Callan. Or her glasses. They never got to me."

"What you've done here," declares Kenny, "is a disgrace."

The hostess colors. But to preserve her professional dignity, she purses her lips and lowers her head.

Aunt Dot squeezes forward and puts her hand on the edge of the casket. "It's not just the glasses," she tells everyone. "Gina's not wearing earrings. Sis'd never dress up in such lovely clothes without putting on her earrings."

Claudia, Vince's nineteen-year-old sister, seconds her mother: "That's right, Gina isn't Gina without her earrings."

"Gina isn't Gina because these goofballs lost the picture we gave them. And her glasses, too."

"Mr. Petruzzi," the hostess says, the Memory Room

seeming to contract about her, "If you gave us a photo and some glasses, we'll find them. But no one passed them on to me, and I had to make do as well as I could without them."

"It wasn't very good, was it?"

"Get this bugger out of here," Uncle Sarge directs Vince and Frank. Frank is Uncle Lyle and Aunt Martha's son, a pharmacist in Kenny's hometown, Gunnison.

Then Sarge turns to the hostess. "Kenny's upset—we're all upset—and you just gotta excuse him, ma'am. He depended like crazy on his mother. Even after he was this big grown man you see hulking here, he couldn't stop grabbing at her apron strings."

Like a couple of tugboats flanking the *Queen Mary,* Vince and Frank take Kenny's arms. Their huge, goggle-eyed cousin does not resist them. Instead he begins to blubber:

"She . . . she did everything for me. Loaned me money. Bought me clothes. Even if I came home at two in the morning, she'd crawl out of bed to fix me something to eat."

"She was that way to everybody," Claudia assures Kenny.

"And not just simple sandwich stuff, either. Gourmet doings. Omelets. Polenta and gravy. Steak and eggs."

Vince and Frank maneuver their cousin, the adopted son of Gina and the late Ernesto Petruzzi, toward the parlor beyond the Memory Room. Out of the pale of his dead mother's aura.

"She was my intercessor!" Kenny cries over his shoulder. "My champion when nobody else gave a damn!"

Alone with the dead woman, the hostess perches near the casket doing some careful repair work on the masklike face of Gina Sekas Petruzzi Callan. In the hermetic, off-white room, she feels again that she is inhabiting the remembered life of the deceased.

Frank Sekas's wife Melinda Jane has gone out into the February cold with Dorothy and Claudia Lobrano to buy some earrings.

All the other mourners—Uncle Sergio, Cousin Vincent, Uncle Lyle, Aunt Martha, Cousin Frank, and the distraught Kenny—have retired to the parlor, where they sit on lumpy divans or pace the worn carpet. A peculiar odor of lilies, nostalgia, and embalming fluid permeates the Memory Room.

It seems to the hostess that her subject is listening intently to her family's muted conversation.

Sergio Lobrano is saying, "It doesn't have to be open-casket, Kenny. You know that, don't you?"

"Aunt Dot wants it open."

"Now, look, let's get this straight. Your aunt's not bossing this business, and I don't want you saying afterwards that it was open-casket because that's how Aunt Dot wanted it, and your mother didn't look like herself, and blah blah blah."

"Uncle Sergio, I'm not—"

" 'Cause that'd be a cheap trick, Kenny. It wouldn't be fair to your Aunt Dot and it wouldn't be fair to yourself."

"Wait a minute," Uncle Lyle objects, and Aunt Martha chimes in, "Sarge, you haven't given Kenny a chance to—"

"I don't want him blaming his aunt for making a mockery of his mother at her own funeral, that's all."

Kenny's high-pitched, indignant voice startles the hostess: "I love my Aunt Dot, Uncle Sergio! I'd never do anything to hurt her—any more'n I'd ever do anything to hurt my own mother. So what the hell're you talking here?"

"Well, I—" his uncle begins, audibly abashed.

"You didn't let me finish. I'm only saying that whatever aunt Dot wants, *I* want. And if we both want it, how could I ever trash her for something I've okayed myself?"

"Yeah," Sarge feebly confesses. "That's different."

"You didn't let me finish."

"Kenny, I'm sorry."

"It's okay," Kenny says. "Just don't try to tell me I'd ever do somethin' to hurt Aunt Dot."

"I won't. Believe me, I won't."

Conversation lapses, and the hostess, studying Kenny's photo of his mother, makes an unobtrusive adjustment to the lines bracketing Gina Callan's mouth. A familiar claustrophia menaces her.

Then she hears Vince say, "I wouldn't want some stranger trying to get my body presentable."

"Shhh," Aunt Martha tells him. "Not so loud."

"I want to be cremated. I want my ashes scattered on the wind over the Great Sand Dunes National Monument. It's in my will."

Sarge makes a disgusted noise.

"Can you do that?" Kenny asks. "Can you have your ashes thrown out on federal land like that?"

"Who's going to stop you?" says Vince. "You just get somebody who's willing to go out there and do it."

"It won't be me or your mother," Sarge says. "What the hell's a punk like you doing with a will?"

"Be proud of him, Sarge," Martha says. "All most young people think about today is new cars or their next skiing trip."

"Not our Vince. He thinks about becoming a pullutant in some goddamn government showcase for sand."

"What's wrong with that?" Frank asks. "I'd like to be cremated myself. Dead's dead, and it's a helluva lot cheaper than a fancy-pants show like this."

In the ever-contracting Memory Room, the hostess imagines Frank rolling his eyes at the parlor's cut-glass chandelier.

"Gina wanted a Catholic funeral," Lyle intones. "Which is why we're doing our best to give her one. Her marrying Wesley Callan, a joker with two divorces, didn't make it all that damn easy to set up, either. I had to talk to half a dozen different priests before Father McFahey agreed to it."

"And that silly fart Callan isn't even coming," Sarge grouses.

"Are you sure?" Martha asks. "I told him over the phone he'd live to regret not coming up here."

Kenny says, "Yeah, well, he told *me* he wasn't going to listen to a bunch of R.C. mumbo-jumbo. He and his holier-than-everybody cronies in Gunnison's gonna put on some sort of memorial service of their own."

"Mumbo-jumbo?" Martha says.

"Yeah, 'mumbo-jumbo.' So I said, 'You've got your own sort of mumbo-jumbo to listen to, don't you, Wes?'"

Sarge laughs. "What'd he say to that, Kenny?"

"He didn't like it. But if you treat people lousy, it stands to reason you're gonna get treated lousy back."

"Those goddamn Jehovah's Witnesses drive me bats," Frank says. "'Live Forever on Paradise Earth.' 'Blessed Are the One Hundred and Forty-Four Thousand.' 'Jesus Is Actually the Archangel Michael in Disguise.' Etcetera, etcetera. Aunt Gina was a saint to put up with three years of that malarky. A bona fide saint."

"And beautiful," Kenny murmurs. "Always beautiful."

"Wes may be a Witness," Martha declares, "but when he tucks it in, they'll cremate him—hear that, Vince?—and put his ashes in a jar and stick him on a shelf right across from Gina's vault in the Tower of Memories."

"But what about me?" Kenny asks. "Where am I gonna

go? They saved no place for me, Aunt Martha."

Kenny's complaint reduces everyone else to silence.

In the Memory Room, the hostess makes a tiny incision in
Gina's neck, swabs the vulcanized flesh around it, and seals
the cut with a special mortician's adhesive. It seems to her
that, now, she and her subject are straining hard enough to
hear the snow whirl out of the overcast. It clings to their
turn-of-the-century building like Colorado cotton, rectangles
of frozen flannel.

The door opens, and a teenage girl comes into the room
with a small manila folder and a leather glasses case.

"I found these things upstairs," she says, giving them to
the woman on the stool.

"Wonderful."

"What's wrong, Mrs. Dennis?"

"They'd've been a lot of help yesterday." Mrs. Dennis,
the hostess, opens the envelope, removes the glossy photo,
and tilts it to compare its likeness to the face undergoing
renovation.

"But I wasn't here yesterday. I couldn't—"

"Never mind, Heather. Get on back upstairs."

The girl hesitates, collects herself, and leaves, going
through the smoke-filled parlor past Kenny Petruzzi, the Se-
kases, and the Lobranos. Mrs. Dennis gets only a glimpse of
the family before the door drifts shut again and she must
return her attentions to the dead woman in the casket.

—Forgive my Kenny, the corpse implores her. Ernesto
and I spoiled him when he was little.

He isn't little now, Mrs. Dennis rejoins.

—His thoughtless behavior isn't really his fault. He never
learned any responsibility.

Why the hell didn't he?

—I couldn't have children so we adopted. We were so
glad to get Kenny that we went overboard to prove it. Ernesto gave him a diamond ring when he was six. He lost it
the next day.

Mrs. Dennis merely stares at the dead woman.

—Kenny was the only thing Wes and I ever argued about,
Gina Callan continues. Except for Wes's new religion.

Aloud, Mrs. Dennis says, "Same old story. Child won't
accept original parent's choice of stand-in spouse."

—It wasn't that, the corpse informs her. Kenny was almost thirty when Wes and I married. Ernesto'd been dead since Kenny was nine, and Kenny *liked* Wes. Or he did before the Witnesses got to him.

Then I had it backward, thinks Mrs. Dennis, still working on her subject's throat: It was Wes who didn't like Kenny.

—Wes liked him as a person, only he couldn't put up with him being so flighty. When we got married, Kenny was just back from Vietnam. His wife had run out on him while he was over there, and he didn't want to do nothing but play the dogs in Colorado Springs and Pueblo.

And Wes didn't approve of gambling?

—Oh, before he got converted, Wes'd play the dogs, too. It was Kenny's losing and borrowing money that drove him buggy.

But Wes loaned him money, anyway? Betting money?

—No, I loaned Kenny the money. Sometimes I just handed it to him. Sometimes he'd ask me for something to pawn. Jewelry, maybe, or silverware, and I'd give it to him so he could play his "system" and try to win back what he'd already lost.

Thinks Mrs. Dennis, No wonder Wes went buggy, Mrs. Callan. You were feeding Kenny's habit.

—It *was* a habit. A habit and an obsession. He had computer printouts and three-by-five cards about them damn dogs all over our house in Gunnison. His room downstairs . . . it looked the way an embassy looks when they have to shred their files. He was working out his "system"—A system to make him rich.

And you fell for that?

—Well, sometimes, just occasionally, he'd win. When he did, he wouldn't think to pay us back for staking him. But he'd go out and buy me a color TV set or Wes some expensive hunting equipment. That'd stick him in a hole deeper than his evening's winnings, and Wes'd start ranting about Kenny being a numbskull and a moocher and a baby. A three-hundred-pound baby.

Painstakingly relining Gina Callan's eyes, Mrs. Dennis murmurs, "Seems like an accurate character assessment to me."

—No, wait. A month before I went into Fitzsimmons, he quit the dogs cold. Stopped going to the track. Wouldn't let his old betting buddies talk him into giving it another go. Even Wes was impressed. Even Wes.

Observes the hostess, But Wes isn't here.

—That's because my family's Catholic, and I wanted to be put to rest like a Catholic, and being a Witness has made it impossible for Wes to think about my religion without getting angry. It's got nothing to do with Kenny.

Except Kenny's Catholic, too. And hates your husband for his pious intolerance. And resents him for not being here.

—Kenny's *not* Catholic. After Wes and I married, he quit us. Now he's a Unitarian or something. Kenny hates the Catholics for refusing to let me take communion because I fell in love with and actually married a guy who'd been married twice already.

"Wheels within wheels," Mrs. Dennis tells the ceiling.

Reminisces Gina Callan:

—Our first years together, Wes had no faith but pro football. About four years ago, though, a doctor at Fitzsimmons botched the prostate surgery he needed. Wesley nearly died. These Witnesses got to him while he was suffering, talked to him, studied with him, poured their propaganda on him. He was down so far he bought it. Kenny says if only the Buddhists or the Hare Krishnas had reached him first, Wesley'd be that today instead. I wish they had.

I guess Wes was easier to take as a Denver Bronco fan than as a religious zealot?

—You bet. He wouldn't celebrate birthdays or Christmas. He wouldn't even buy me a stupid Valentine. He was afraid one of the brothers or sisters would call him "frivolous." That's when Kenny started to get fed up with *him*.

"I'm almost finished, Mrs. Callan." Mrs. Dennis leans back on her stool, studies her subject, and then removes the dead woman's glasses from their leather case and sets them on her nose, snugging the ear struts into her bouffant hairdo.

—I went into the hospital terrified, the bespectacled Gina Callan tells her hostess. I remembered how one of their lousy doctors nearly killed Wes, and *I* was afraid to die, afraid they'd push me to it the way they'd almost done him.

I suppose it's a cliché, Mrs. Callan, Mrs. Dennis rejoins, but there are worse things than dying.

—Fear's one, admits the dead woman. And when I was really hurting, retaining water and so on, one of those army dorks . . . Wes called 'em *dorktors* right to their face, but they always seemed just to think he talked funny . . . came into my room and said, "Mrs. Callan, you're dying. I think you should know. You've probably only got a few more hours."

He didn't ask Wes, he didn't ask Kenny, he just took it upon himself to tell me.

My God, thinks Mrs. Dennis, genuinely appalled.

—That did it. That whomped the heart right out of me. Maybe some people'd be grateful to be told, but not me. I was thinking I'd make it, but what he said was absolutely chilling. I was . . . well, the only word that says it is *horror-struck*.

Mrs. Callan, I can imagine.

—They'd been taking me on and off various monitors and kidney machines, and sticking me with needles, and running plastic tubes in and out of me, and, well, I didn't last till morning. Kenny and Wesley sat there helpless beside me as I passed on. And being dead hasn't been half so bad as going terrified into the hospital and being told by some army quack—that *dorktor,* as Wes'd call him—that I was dying.

To herself, not to the woman's corpse, Mrs. Dennis thinks, How much more of this am I going to be able to stand?

—Know what terrifies me now? What ruins the death snooze I'm entitled to after sixty-seven years working and worrying?

No, ma'am. What?

—Wes'll be okay. He's got his religion to fall back on. But what's to become of Kenny?

Thinks Mrs. Dennis consolingly, He'll be okay, too.

—No. No, he won't. He never learned any responsibility. It was my fault, mine and Ernesto's, but poor Kenny's gonna be the one to pay for it. He's a baby. Still a baby . . .

Aunt Dot, Cousin Claudia, and Melinda Jane return from their shopping expedition. Mrs. Dennis and her subject can hear them coming down the carpeted stairs. The menfolk rise to greet them, while Aunt Martha blurts, "Those are wonderful, Dot. Those are Gina, all right. They're unquestionably Gina."

The women come crowding in, warning Kenny, Sarge, Lyle, Vince, and Frank to stay put. This is a female matter, cosmeticizing Gina, and Kenny and the guys will be allowed to look at her again only when Aunt Dot says she's presentable. Mrs. Dennis consents to their invasion—even though she cannot help feeling that they are barging into a torture chamber, not merely coming home with bangles with which to adorn their dead.

Melinda Jane shuts the door behind them.

"Ta da," says Claudia. She holds up a pair of beaten-brass earrings, with artificial pearls in the center of each clip.

"Thank God you got clip-ons," Mrs. Dennis tells her. "I know she had pierced ears, but the holes've closed up."

"Clip-ons, schlip-ons," Claudia replies. "All that matters is for 'em to look like her. These do."

"Big and jangly," says one of the aunts.

"Gina through and through," says the other.

Everyone in the Memory Room stares down at the dead woman. The hostess realizes that her subject, who stopped transmitting at the first sound of the women's return, is basking in their approval. For the first time since entering the mortuary, Gina Callan feels good about herself.

"Okay," says Aunt Dot, taking a deep breath and wiping her eyes with her sleeve. "Get Kenny in here."

Someone opens the door. The men bunch up, squeeze through, and approach the casket. Kenny shoulders his way to the front.

"Whaddaya think?" Martha asks. "Isn't that more like it?"

For a moment, Kenny merely stares. His bug eyes dart from his mother's hands to her rouged face and back again. Then he turns and, locating Mrs. Dennis, reaches out and grabs her hands.

"This is my mother," he tells her. "You goofballs finally got it right."

"Thank you. Your relatives helped."

"She's beautiful again—as beautiful as I remember."

"Thank you," repeats the hostess.

"You found her glasses. Her picture, too."

"One of our employees found them. Heather Thompson."

"Heather Thompson deserves a raise," Kenny cries. "I'm gonna buy her a box of candy. You, too. Both of you."

He releases Mrs. Dennis, turns again to the casket, and lifts his arms in a dramatic gesture of thanksgiving.

"This is my mother," he proclaims. "God bless everybody here for giving me back my mother."

Alone again with the bereaved dead woman, Mrs. Dennis sits down wearily on her stool.

—Wes never came, Gina Callan tells her. And Kenny's gonna be lost without me. Absolutely lost.

"Shut up!" the hostess shouts, trying to reclaim her room. "Do you think you're the only goddamn stiff whose troubles I've got to listen to? Is that what you think?"

Gina Sekas Petruzzi Callan ceases to transmit.

"That's better," Mrs. Dennis whispers, cupping her face in her hands. "Who the hell do you guys think you are, anyway?"

Tales from the Original Gothic

by JOHN M. FORD

John M. Ford, winner of the World Fantasy Award for his novel The Dragon Waiting, *also has the marvelous ability to lead readers by the hand through the incomprehensible to harsh enlightenment. Here, Ford juggles metaphor and yarn, tradition and cliché into a terrifying gestalt whirlwind, and traps the unwary by saying, "It's just a story, just another of my tales from the original gothic."*

It was six-oh-nine ay em out on Long Island Sound, and foggy, and cold. We were technically representing the National Center for Short-Lived Phenomena. Boudreau and I were Center, observational, him video, me still, you Jane. Clement and Phail were M.I.T., hardware jockeys. Ormsby was spooky—we didn't know which agency, and they're all under orders to lie about that these days; spreads the blame around. Father Totten was direct from the Archdiocese of New York, something about eminent domain. He told me he was a qualified exorcist. I told him I was working on my biceps. He laughed the way you do when you've heard it once too often.

We had a van full of equipment: spectrometers and chromatographs, magnetometers and scintillation counters, shotgun mikes and hand-held radar. We had a real live robot, a little tank-tracked wire-guided sample-snatcher known variously as Stupid, That Piece of Shit, and Danger Will Robinson. We had, oh, lots of good stuff and lead-lined steamer trunks in case we found anything worth taking home. Per-

sonally, I had five Hasselblads with two dozen assorted camera backs, long lenses, filters like a *Playboy* shooter might
only dream of, slow fine film and insanely fast film and infra-
red and X-ray and Polaroid and you don't care what else. If
the damn house showed up I was going to get a picture of it
or, by God and George Eastman, know the reason why not.

There were two TV trucks, one from the network pool
and one indie, and a helicopter of uncertain parentage, but if
you said Air America at them they might smile back. The
house wouldn't dare not show.

This was the seventh apparition, best that we could tell.
First three were anecdotal (to wit: nobody believed a word of
it), fourth independently confirmed (to wit: eighty witnesses
in Grant Park, Chicago), fifth confirmed and documented
(to wit: television mobile crew looking for background shots
in Golden Triangle Park, Pittsburgh), sixth confirmed and
tagged for active response (to wit: two Senators whose morning field lecture on the need for direct intervention against
you know who, you know where, was upstaged by the ap-
pearance behind them).

The data points went into a big computer designed to ex-
trapolate impact points and fallout patterns, and the computer drew a map and posted a time. So here we were (to
wit: to woo).

Six-eleven. See, all that nattering only took a couple minutes. Time is all relative when you're freezing your butt off
waiting for a supernatural manifestation to manif. The computer said six-fifteen, but time was the loosest part of the
prediction, because nobody had reported exactly seeing the
thing appear: they just looked up and—

There it was.

Shit, we gasped, or maybe, Gasp, we shat. The house
surprised us. How do you think that looks on your resume,
Once ambushed by a house?

I fumbled my fingers onto my shutter switches and started
tripping the light. Boudreau spun up a standard and a high-
speed film camera, pressed his eye to his video rig. Clement
and Phail played their instruments like dueling jazz drum-
mers. Ormsby did something—I assume what he was supposed to do. (When he joined the party he said, "Good
morning, I've been attached to your unit." Makes you think
of a lamprey, right? Ormsby the Sucker, Yup.)

Oh, and Father Totten made the sign of the Big X.
Thanks, Father, for sharing that with us.

It was three stories high, Victorian, high-floored and gabled, maybe sixty feet from porch to peak, and with that Victorian vertical style that made it look even taller. There was gingerbread all over, spindles and doily-edging. Mansard roof, hexagonal shingles. Thin windows with shutters. A great portico in front, with thin white pillars going up to the second floor. We'd seen the Pittsburgh videotape, and it looked like that, but—but that was *videotape*, a comb-filtered picture on a tin box. This was live, wide-screen. I almost said palpable, but that wouldn't be right. It was there, but not quite real yet.

It was very gray. The fog was still heavy, and muted everywhere, but the house was a deep, slaty, shifty color, as if the fog itself had condensed and gelled to make it, which was at the time just as good a guess as anybody's. The wood trim was white, and there was some green-painted ironwork, but that too had the grayness. The house wasn't more than fifty yards away from us, but it might have been miles; the moon through a cloud.

"Is it real?" Ormsby said. Terrific question, Ormsby.

"We got it on the radar," Phail said.

"I want contact," Ormsby said, and I looked up and Clement looked up; nobody'd quite properly explained to us that what Ormsby wanted made any special difference, but the way he talked and looked, you could tell that it did and he knew it. "Is the robot ready?"

"Ready as it'll ever be," Clement said, and picked up the control box. "What do you *want* it to do?"

"Physical contact first. Run it right up to those stairs and see if it hits anything."

"Okay, Stupid," Clement said, to the robot, sort of, and pushed the sticks. The robot whined and started crawling toward the porch, trailing its cables behind it.

Then the front door opened, and the woman came out. Shit, gasp, in spades. Clement nearly dropped his controls; the robot veered over and went crash-bump against the steps. Contact.

She came down the stairs, seeming not to see the robot. I grabbed a long lens to look at her; she didn't seem to see anything at all, but God her eyes were beautiful. Her face was beautiful, lineless as new porcelain, framed in dark hair. My hand wobbled too badly to watch her through the telephoto.

She was wearing a nightgown, smoke-gray, like the house

not a precise color but shifting, and she was carrying a long silver candlestick. The second report had mentioned this, but, like I said, nobody paid any attention to the second report. Oh, and one other thing, I looked up. There it was: one light shining from the attic window.

Now do you see why the early reports got shitcanned? We don't all live within stone walls of canker'd reason, but there are limits, and the cover of a paperback romance showing up in downtown Spokane is damn it one of them.

Ormsby said, "Is she solid?"

Phail said, "Huh?"

"On the radar."

"I . . . don't know. She might not show up, so close to the house."

"What can you use on her?"

"Uh . . . the spec unit's lasers."

"Okay, do it. Clement, get the robot over to her."

I snapped frames as fast as my motor drives would hum. Boudreau had it easy: all he had to do was stare with his trigger finger down. The priest was saying something in Latin, I didn't know what.

Clement got the robot backed up. "Come on, junkheap," he muttered. "Nice and slow now."

The woman was down the steps now, walking across the soft ground, more or less toward us. Her gown drifted on the air, mist on mist: it seemed light as spidersilk, but was remarkably opaque for all that. Her arms were bare, and there was a vague hint of cleavage. She should have been shivering like a birch in a hurricane. I blew out a cloudy breath and realized that hers wasn't fogging.

Clement had the robot a couple of steps behind her now, and started working the manipulator. It wasn't a very sophisticated arm, just a one-joint with a clamp on the end. It stretched up toward the woman's gown like a lecherous metal midget.

Then it stopped. Short. Clement struggled with the control sticks for a moment—and then his arms spasmed and he gagged and fell down, twitching like a stunned steer. The robot was smoking, and the cable, and Clement.

Phail shouted and started for him. Ormsby straight-armed Phail in the chest. "Don't touch him," Ormsby said. He didn't share the advice with the priest, who crouched and rolled Clement over.

Clement groaned. His gloves were burned nearly

through, and when Totten pulled them off the skin below was scorched, but Clement said, "I'm all right—I got a shock," (yeah, us too) and got up. "What did she do?" That was a couple of kinds of good question, because she was gone.

Boudreau had been watching, taping. (He hadn't turned to look at Clement steaming and screaming. No comment.) "She took off into the woods. That way."

Ormsby got out a walkie-talkie, and the helicopter spun up its rotors, presumably to chase Our Heroine across the frozen woods. "Okay," Ormsby said to us, "we're going inside."

"Could I remind you," Clement said, as Phail wrapped his hands in gauze, "that in the previous sightings the house disappears within half an hour? What happens if we're inside when it goes?"

"Then we go where it's going," Ormsby said, and that was it, because we all knew when we took this job that we were going inside the house when it showed up, if it showed up, if it had an inside to go into. Clement was just expressing a little manly high spirit, common among the nearly electrocuted. So I took my number-one camera and thirty-pound equipment vest, Boudreau switched to battery power, Clement and Phail took up their portable gear. Father Totten clutched his prayerbook and Ormsby put on his hardest expression.

As we approached, the house seemed to get taller still, like a mountain that looks like nothing from a distance but is scraping cloud by the time you reach its foothills. The grayness didn't change as we grew near. When you walk through the fog, things are supposed to get clearer, it says so right here on the label; this didn't, inspring thoughts of classical tortoises that can cover half the distance till doomsday but never all of it, so much for your damned slow and steady (do Zeno and Aesop sit around in the first circle of Hell swapping turtle stories, A to Z?).

We all got into what I would suppose one might call ready positions, and Phail pushed open the door. It swung wide and silently. There was a hall beyond: exactly the sort of hall you would expect to find behind that sort of door, with a red carpet and an umbrella stand. We went in.

There was a grand stairway at the end of the hall, going up into genuinely total darkness. And there was a large arch, opening onto a bay-windowed parlor.

The parlor was full of wheelchairs, all of them occupied,

and there was a woman in a starched white dress. They were
all looking out the windows.

"Hey," Ormsby said.

No one paid attention to him. Bad move with Ormsby.

"What the hell is that?" Ormsby said. Once, before I
died, I would have liked to hear Ormsby answer a question
even half as stupid as the ones he asked. No such luck.

"The book," I told him.

"What book?"

"The book we just walked into the cover of."

There is a version of the story in which the house has
been converted into a hospital for wounded Allied pilots at
the height of the Battle of Britain: if you look into the mist
you may see the lights of the R.A.F. aerodrome nearby. She
has been sent from London for safety's sake, but as the aerodrome is in danger from German raids—perhaps the house
as well, as who can measure the depravity of the Hun—there
is no safety. And she is surrounded daily with the smells of
disinfectant, of human fluids, of death, and with the pilots
themselves, blind, burnt, broken. There are jobs for the injured in this desperate hour, but none for them, and so they
know that they are useless, shall perhaps always be useless:
these are *men who flew* and now are wrecked, a Victorian
hall of Icarii.

Outside, half seen through the taped windows and the
trees, there was a crash and a fireball rolling up. A bell
began to toll, and of course we asked who for. "The chop-
per," Ormsby said, and drew the gun that how could he have
doubted he would be carrying, it looked so natural on him,
and went to the window, thinking that a helicopter had
crashed on the other side of the window, but wrong craft,
wrong tale, wrong earth. The smoke comes from a burning
Spitfire, shot down in the Bloody April of 1940.

Ormsby turned from the window and saw her, standing
not ten steps away from him in her severe whites and her
nurse's cap, looking out at the wreck and hoping that it is not
him, not *him* in the twist of metal and flaming petrol, before
she turns back to the men in her charge.

She stared at the roomful of eyeless men, limbless men,
physical metaphors of the more fundamental incapacity.
Though most can still speak, they cannot speak their need
for her, to arouse them from slumber, to absorb their seed
and return it as children, strong sons who will learn the ways
of the split-S and the Immelmann turn, who will learn the

arcana of the Norden bombsight, men who will learn, as their fathers did not, that they must avert their eyes from the falling pregnant bomb.

She must acquiesce, they must do this. It is the only way they can continue to fight the war.

Ormsby still didn't see, though the room is full of ravaged men. Of course not, how could we have been so foolish, he has a purpose here and they are not part of it. Visitations. Apparition. Troop movements. From those wonderful folks who brought you helicopter-borne assaults, a new sort of borning: the First Ectoplasmic Infantry. Having mastered the delivery of Hellfire, they have sent Ormsby to discover the remaining secrets of the damned, coming soon to a theatre of war near you. He saw the veterans, all keloid and the stumps of limbs, he saw them clearly enough. But he looked straight through them, for he knew their secrets already.

He took hold of her, pinning down the lass he grasps, and demanded of her what has happened to the helicopter.

She understands, though he does not. She knows what he has lost in the fall of his machine. She sponges his manly brow, she absorbs his curses, his demands for the missing part of himself. She knows where the rest of Ormsby is, buried in a concrete tomb without the codes to launch.

Ormsby began to panic as she tended to him. He waved his pistol. This should excite him, always has. At least it should produce some response from her that will excite him. But no. There is a war on, and loose lips sink ships.

Ormsby yelled something that Adam probably yelled at Eve and certainly yelled at Lilith, and ripped her white dress open.

There came (oof) the roar of Rolls-Royce Merlin engines, the flash of a propeller—an airscrew, the British call it—switch on, contact. Airscrew. Contact. Loose lips rip zips. Ormsby screamed (like a woman, he would say if it were another man making the noise) as the white blades ground his bone. Littering the past, he gasped.

Ormsby danced hither and yon, as if trying to gather his guts for the journey home, shock trooper bundling his chute. Hold still, Ormsby, how shall they find your pieces on the judgement day? Down he goes. Pigeon under glass at last. She stares at him. The wheelchairs circle round.

Suddenly there is nothing but Ormsby in the room, crumpled on the floor in a puddle of himself.

And we . . .

Well, picture it. Here we were, gang of scientists confronted by the new phenomenon, ready to analyze it to destruction. Everything dies if you turn enough light on it. Those of you who are familiar with the history of astronomy will recall how the immensely complex theory of epicyclic motion was created to explain those celestial movements that a sun-centered system put into much more elegant order. Once it became accepted that buildings and their contents might manifest out of the clear blue (Rayleigh scattering—oh excuse me) then a thousand small mysteries of life, from the slowness of urban mail delivery to the theft of cable television service, would at once fall into systematic place.

As if systems or sensibility had anything to do with it. The dark closes in. You push it back, using what cleverness you can hold onto in your crab-crawling terror to make light.

Mind makes tools, tools dispel madness, madness, oh, *oh*.

Rock breaks scissors, scissors cut paper, paper smothers rock.

We ran.

Clement smashed through a glass door. We hadn't seen it, and yes we were so looking. I doubt it was there, doesn't matter, wasn't there anymore anyhow. Clement was on his knees in a garden, green and mossy and crystalline with broken glass.

Phail was there in an instant. Their hands touched, and instantly I knew why Ormsby had not permitted them contact in his sight. Clement seemed all right, the gauze wrapping his hands had prevented much further damage.

"Are we outside?" Clement asked, looking around at the fog, the peat, the vines and trees.

"This is Spanish moss," Boudreau said, not touching it. "Spanish moss doesn't grow up here. Besides," he added, ever the camera-eyed observer, "if we're outside, where's the sun?"

She came around a moss-shrouded tree, and we turned to see her, dressed in her white, with her pale smile.

Clement took a step toward her, a little unsteady on the soft soil, and said, "Who are you?"

"Please," she said, or I thought I heard her say, her lips didn't seem to move, those thin lips like a shallow wound. "Help me, I need you," the wound said.

Clement must have heard. He went to help her. Any way he could.

There is a version of the story in which the house has

stood for centuries with the same mistress, in which all pleasure and all need are reduced to a single bittersweet act.

She was determined, but the determination was not the
courage of the living but the implacable advance of the walking dead. Beauty must age and die, you see, that's the way
things work; if beauty survives, then it must be by some terrible and unnatural means. She has been roused from her bed
in her bedclothes by the scratch of Hell beneath the thin
earth: she has been driven from her grave barefoot in her
shroud by the hunger for salt blood.

But she will settle for whatever Clement has.

He shriveled as she touched him; he did not pull away,
though it was a long, long moment until her fingers were
actually around his throat; seeing that, computing that, sci-
entifically analyzing that, led to only one conclusion about
why he did not pull away. Why Ormsby took hold of his
apparition with such definite intent. It didn't speak well for
the rest of us; fear we had, desire we had, strength, well,
Totten and I held Phail by the arms as Clement was pulled
into the soil, and Boudreau's finger was on the camera trigger; Clement was a film of skin on blackening bones by the
time he was breast-deep, but he didn't seem to be fighting.
He didn't seem to be having a bad time at all, not nearly as
bad as Phail was having. You know the song of the Lorelei,
as she draws men to die on the stones: a kiss on the hand
may be quite continental, but diamonds . . .

Suddenly Clement's eyes looked up—they were loose
marbles in a skull, now—and his tongue rattled in what
might have been a scream had there been any air to drive it,
fluid to wet the system. And he was gone.

"There is a light this way," Father Totten said, pretty obvious from the way it lit up the fog, but there wasn't anywhere else to go, was there?

"I'm all right now," Phail lied, and we let him go and
walked toward the glow, feeling for glass walls that might
suddenly pop up. Instead we came to double doors, and a
room beyond.

The lights were very bright in here, and copper cookware
hung on racks, and stainless steel countertops ran every
which way.

There is a version of the story in which she is a scullery
maid, trapped in the kitchen kept insanely ordered by a head
cook who is certainly a sadist, probably a lesbian, no question incompetent at food preparation—you never see the

maiden preparing tournedos Rossini or medaillions de veau
or even brutalizing a defenseless carpaccio, do you? It's
always "Stir the stew" and "Scour out the roasting pans."
She can cook, of course, though Cook bushels her light, until
by happy accident her midnight snack reaches the late-night
plate of the master of the house, who will, presented with
this clear example of genetic superiority, elevate her to master of the house's mistress (lawfully, of course) where she will
never again have to slice onions or scour a pot, and Cook will
be horsewhipped and sent away, and God alone knows what
the household will eat after that.

Phail looked around nervously at the boiling cauldrons,
the crackling griddles. Suddenly he raised his hand, stared at
it: I expected the flesh to be medium well with diagonal grill
marks, but there was only a film of white lard on his fingers.
Or something like lard. It certainly upset Phail. He scrubbed
at it with his other hand, but that only coated the both of
them. Towel, towel, who's got a towel? Next he wiped it on
his jacket, then on his trousers. His face began to itch, he
twitched it, he nearly touched it—but oh no, realization set
in. It won't go away, not by washing. It was in his secret
places now. Are you washed in the mint sauce of the lamb?
(How about that, Father Totten? Have you spent time
among the lepers outcast unclean, or is it all their own fault?
Tell me, Father Totten, when exactly did God decide to wash
his hands of Sodom?)

It isn't death we fear, you know, we can out brief candle
all the livelong day; it is the bad procedures of death, the
mashing of meat and bone, the struggling of the heart against
the ribs of its cage, the physical scream of the steel in the
skin, the disease that hides and waits and digs itself in.

Phail stood in the kitchen, but his sustenance and his life's
hope had just died outside, leaving nothing but his fears. O
little lamb, did he who made the spirochete make thee? As if
to answer, things like purple corkscrews came drilling their
way out of Phail, and his blood mingled with the white
grease frosting him. Suppurations stitched his skin. His left
eye popped, a little beak snapping down the bits from within.
There was no longer a Phail, only a Phail-shaped disease, an
infection casting a man's shadow. Totten gabbled a prayer.
Boudreau threw up, and I watched the spew for signs of life,
but it was only honest man's vomit, coffee and danish and an
Egg McMuffin. It fried up crisp on the spotless floor.

Then Phail's belly split open, and something white and

shiny and crablike leapt out, skittering on the floor; it had a dozen cylindrical legs and a long ropy tail uncoiling slowly from Phail.

Boudreau pulled out Ormsby's gun (I guess it was brave of him to get the thing, at least) and fired at the white crab, once, twice, three times. He hit it each time, hell it was only two yards away, blasting glossy bits from it. Curiously, no guts spill, no blood sprays. The white thing was apparently solid whatever-it-was. It quit moving.

As we hustled out of the kitchen I finally recognized the thing. "Congratulations," I said to Boudreau. "You just shot the world-record specimen of the Dalkon Shield."

"You gotta be fucking kidding."

"John Carpenter's *The Thing,*" I labeled his quote, and said, "Not in the least. We keep calling this a manifestation, why haven't we thought about what it's manifesting?"

Boudreau capped his camera lens with his hand—he did that to think better—and it started to develop for him (twenty seconds in the tray, then stop bath and fixer). "It's the cover of a Gothic novel, my *wife* reads—oh my God—"

And then lightning lit the room and took our breath away.

The panorama was definitely breathtaking. Bolts of blue energy arced between pitted copper spheres, casting high shadows against the vaulted stone ceiling. Relays clattered, sparking. There was the steady maddening heartbeat of vacuum pumps. A computer, a huge console resembling a theatre organ with triode tubes instead of pipes, occupied most of one wall.

In cells of curved glass bound with steel, things pulsed and quivered and flopped. One had tiny hands, pink and baby-like.

She came wandering in, in a modernistic straight-lined gown of slick white satin. The creatures in the flasks have not yet frightened her, because she barely understands what it is she is seeing. The chamber is beautiful, in the manner of functional art, gray sheeny steel, liquid black Bakelite, indicator lamps brilliant points of primary color. The twitching things might almost be spaniels, crouched before the actinic fire, the master's slippers in their fangs, little pets with scales, with chitin, with cilia.

And all of them have blue eyes, just like her husband's.

In this version of the story, you see, her scientist (biologist? physicist? TV repairman?) husband has been making these things out of, well, the essences of matter and spirit,

right? You get the idea? (Okay. Jizz and voltage.) Only, instead of potential Notre Dame quarterbacks, he gets these
Pekingese from Hell. Finally, having mixed up Scientific Spe-
cialties Man Was Not Meant to Interface, the interdisciplin-
ary idiot wakes up one morning, smacks his forehead (quite
painful that, because his researches have given him an immensely strong and furry right hand) and says, "Of course!
Ova!" (Like all scientists, he breakfasts solely on glazed
donuts and coffee.) Following a few comic-relief episodes of
trying to buy the finished product, he decides he ought to go
to the source, and wines and dines and weds and beds (once,
experimentally) a goose of his very own. Warning her.
Never. To go. In. The. Lab.

We gaped, but didn't move. Wrong audience, don't you
see, this is a James Whale picture for Universal, Dr. Pre-
torius's homunculi in jars (as I thought that, the scene faded
to panchromatic black and white, and she turned to show
white lightning streaks in her madly ratted hair, and hissed).
It's a pretty laboratory, it must be given that, it's a place any
of us would have been willing to work, but we do work in
real workshops day in day out and (where are the moldy
coffee cups? the radio blaring FM rock? the *Playboys?*) Charlie, *this ain't it.*

The film broke, pocketa pocketa sound, glare of white
light, purple phosphenes, and there we were in the hall
again, Totten, Boudreau, me. Nobody else. Sometimes when
you win you get your marbles back. Maybe best of seven?

Totten sighed. Boudreau leaned against a wall, then his
eyes snapped open and he pushed away: but it was just a
wall, William Morris paper and vertical wainscot.

There still weren't any doors: more corridors, all dark and
absorbent, and the staircase. We could go in, we could go up.
We could not go down, how very odd.

Boudreau's camera looked at me. Below it, the muzzle of
Ormsby's gun looked just as blank. "I'm going upstairs,"
Boudreau said. "There might be a window. If we can't jump,
maybe we can signal."

Jump to where, signal to whom? But Boudreau was
frightened (so what are we, chopped liver? Well, maybe we
are at that). Usually he gets drunk when he is frightened, but
no such luck. Up we go, then.

Boudreau took a step, and then another, pointing camera
and gun into the darkness overhead. Mind makes tools, tools
dispel madness, paper smothers brain—

There was a screech, like that of a bluejay or a furious crow, and the huge taloned feet of a bird thrust down from the dark. The claws entered Boudreau's shoulders like can openers, with a wet hiss of compressing flesh, escaping blood, and a crunch as his camera crumpled. He fired a shot, generally upward, and then the gun fell. Above him was the sound of flapping wings, and he was lifted off his feet for a moment, but he seemed too heavy for the creature and it settled him down again. The shock drove the claws deeper into his body, and he howled.

Toward the top of the stairs, I could make out a rippling pattern of dark feathers, and then the pale flash of a pendulous breast. The harpy's face was invisible above. It could stay there, I would not protest. It was rending Boudreau, the only one of these men I had known for more than this morning, it was crushing him to jelly, and still I would not protest or ask to see any more of the monster's nature. Because, you see, I also knew Boudreau's wife (no, not in that sense, I am very dreadfully frightened, but why will you call me mad?) and I was too certain of the hidden face, I knew those talons much too well.

The priest chanted something about neither fearing the terror by night, and I wanted to punch his face in, but he put a foot on the stairs and walked up them, careful while treading through Boudreau's blood, and I followed. It beat drinking alone.

It was no longer dark at the top of the stairs. Candles were lighted on the walls, in iron candelabra. I felt inexpressibly sad that the holders were not grasped in human hands, but this wasn't my fantasy after all, at least not quite, not yet.

A stone archway beckoned to us, figuratively I mean. Father Totten looked through to the room beyond, said, "What on earth . . . ," making two errors in three words.

I could hardly believe he needed a gazeteer. Here we had the iron maiden, here the suspended cages, here the rack, that bed with options. Around the walls, the usual assortment of ironmongery. The budget evidently would not support Poe's pendulum, but then of course it is not so readily metaphorical.

There is a curiously popular version of the story in which the house is built on crypts containing the private torture chamber rec room and wet bar of a prominent Inquisitor. Sometimes the tale is historical, with much hot Spanish blood staining black Spanish lace, swordplay, and fairly naked Anglican commentary on the habits of those wretched Papists, and how do you feel about Ulster, Father Totten? In other editions, the evil former owner has a descendant who drools on his copy of *Philosophy in the Bedroom* and longs to keep the old family tradition alive and screaming. A ghost or ghosts may be added to taste. There are inevitably many thrilling and detailed scenes in which they use phrases such as "no mercy" and "spare her nothing" as if they were in the habit of sparing a woman anything; they call for the iron boot, the fire and the ice, when twenty minutes in the birthing room would have any of them, Cardinals on down, in a dead faint.

Father Totten said, "I don't understand," and I was rather glad for him, but not so very glad because I only half believed him, and if you had seen his face you might not have managed half.

And there she was, but oh dear, something was very wrong here, she should have been wide-eyed with terror, abject, helpless (run that word over a few times, why don't you, it's so popular, helpless, helpless, never overmatched, never even outwitted, which you'd think would be okay, no: helpless it has to be, without strength or, gulp, cunning, the stupid twit never stood a chance, *help*less, oh it has such a slick sound off the tongue, *helpless*, I want to stop but I can't I'm . . . oh God).

As if to speak of whom, Father Totten held up a cross. Didn't help Clement, but then we were all new at this death thing, and besides maybe she was Hindu or something. However, I *was* watching carefully, after all any old piety in a storm. And it's usual in these things, of course, that after blockheaded old soulless science has gotten its nose bloodied, the men of faith step in and show us the way to the light, or safety, or San Jose.

She was looking at us, smiling in her long white dress, which was actually not much more than a long strip of fabric hanging down fore and aft, a white cord belting it; and the candlestick, of course. She set the candle at the head of the rack. She lay down on the wood. She stretched her long arms up, teased the shackles with her fine wrists.

Helpless, helpless.

But then again, you know, perhaps not so feeble as that; I took a step. I heard the chains rattle and the locks click. Another step, and there was a creak as the windlass tightened. Another step, and the creak this time was from her joints. She sighed.

I touched the crank (the windlass, that is) and wound it tighter still.

"What are you *doing?*" the priest said.

"Enjoying myself," I said, not really at him. Then suddenly the handle spun under my hands as the chains wound up; there was nothing stretched between them any longer.

Lysisfuckingstrata cuts both ways, you know. You can't make me play if I don't wanna.

We went back out into the hall. Plain little hall, no doors, no stairs, windows all of cloudy glass.

There was a closet, however.

And Father Totten, and I.

There is in every man's soul a desire to confront the Devil, and a firm unfounded knowledge that the Devil can be beaten face to face: sometimes it's chance, sometimes clever argument (logic's chiefest end, as Faust said), sometimes the right lawyer (Daniel Webster comes highly recommended), but whatever the out we all want the showdown. Haven't we all looked long and hard at photographs of Belsen, of the Ripper's Whitechapel, of the nuclear mushroom? It would be terribly reassuring to have no doubt of Hell. Perhaps if we knew we could stop doubting Heaven.

Surely Father Totten didn't doubt Heaven, surely goodness and mercy he didn't doubt Hell, but why would that stop him? After all, St. Thomas's doubt was indulged to the depth of the wounds. Christ was a man. He understood these things.

Totten pulled open the closet.

There was a high rackety rumble, and there fell upon the priest a great wave of garter belts, of fishnet stockings, of spike-heeled shoes, of boned corsets, of leather and black lace and spandex and red satin and buckskin fringe and torn sweaty denim.

The pile was still, and I thought he might be dead beneath it, perhaps the shoe heels had gotten him, but then a corset stirred and a padded bra was thrust aside, and he stood up. Lace and nylon clung to him. He turned his head.

And turned, and turned, and *turned* his head, until his collar was right way round.

Totten's mouth opened, and a hand reached out, a slender knobby hand with black hair sprouting from its back, and blood-red nails. The hand flopped around, and then it pushed at Totten's upper jaw, stretching his lips until they tore, making room for another red-nailed hand to wriggle out. The two hands clawed his jaw apart, burst his throat. They tossed aside most of his head like a monkey throwing a coconut. The hands unseamed Totten's body, tossing sheaths of boneless meat aside with grand abandon and remarkable facility (do you not recall how, when you first undressed for an audience, even your socks were uncooperative?)

The escapee was perhaps a yard high, hairy goat legs ending in little hooves, the hands too big, the head too big, the hair insufficient to cover, yes, too big too. The little satyr looked around at the kinky riches spilled from the closet, and began selecting a wardrobe.

Somehow or another there was still a camera round my neck, fitted with an SCR strobe that could have lit Mount Rushmore. I punched the charge button, and it whined, an unpleasant noise to me, worse to the satyr: he clapped his red-clawed hands to his ears.

And that was how I shot him.

He screamed and started for me, stumbling on his half-donned garter belt. I shot him again. I had SCR recharge and a German motor drive. Flash flash flash. It worked for Jimmy Stewart in *Rear Window*, but then the cops were on their way to save him. Flash *whirr*flash*whirr*flash.

As I shot the thing, capturing its ugly self on Kodak VR 1000 for posterity (if any, as Paul Frees said while the Martian war machines advanced), it began to shrink. Flash*whirr*flash. A foot high now, too stupid to realize what was happening to it, or maybe too egotistical to turn away from the camera. Flash*whirr*flash went the killer *paparazzi*, peeling guilt off the thing in 35-millimeter strips, and what substance did it have but guilt? There was a pop of air and a whiff of dead goat, and it was gone.

Just me now. I wondered if I'd won. Whatever that meant.

There was a narrow stairway that hadn't been there before. A faint golden light shone on its polished wooden treads. The Light From the Attic Window, filtering down to me.

The steps creaked as I climbed them. At the top was a little room, an attic room with sloping ceilings, butter-colored light washing its wooden walls. There were brass candlesticks all around the walls.

In the center was a four-poster bed, clothed in down and satin and clean wool.

I looked back down the stairs. They were still there, but they looked rickety, and there was a hint of red to the darkness at their foot that I can't say I liked very much.

I sat down on the edge of the mattress. Soft, soft, all feathers. I hadn't slept on a featherbed since I was a kid. When you're a kid, beds are great, beds are playgrounds, magic ships. All the fooling around later, the trick architecture, heart-shapes and vibrators and waterbeds, that's got nothing to do with seduction; if it did, no bedroom would be without the rear bench seat from a '58 Chevy; no, it's all an attempt to make the bed fun again. When you're a kid, you don't know how much you'll need the fun. You don't know what it's going to mean to be alone.

My right wrist wouldn't rise from the bed. First I thought it was just buried in the feathers, but I looked down and saw the attachments, the ligaments twined down into the springs, the arteries coupled and pulsing. I jumped a little, sight of your own blood does that even when the blood's contained, and felt it somewhere past my fingertips, so the nerves were linked too.

Well. My right hand was attached to the bed, too attached to leave it, and I was too attached to the hand to leave it either. I leaned back and was accepted, taken, absorbed.

I'm not certain how long the process took, but it's just about done now, all but the brain (How do I know? Snide, aren't we? I think therefore there is still brain. *Somewhere*) and its stepchildren the eyes. I can still see the room very clearly; the light is still soft and sweetly gold, but the candles are burning low. It won't be long now.

Brain and eyes, that's all, and I cannot be certain where the brain is. But then are we ever? Wittgenstein had a problem with this.

But the eyes I know. My eyes are resting upon the pillow. Resting lightly if you please.

A tremor of the candle flames tells me of her footsteps on the stairs. What shall I do, I wonder, *sans* tongue, *sans* touch, *sans* everything? Drink to her only with mine eyes, I suppose, and she will—

The door as it opens makes a sweeping shadow on the wall, a dark scythe with a mothglow behind. I wonder if the house is still sitting, never flitting, on the pallid plot of Long Island; what are they thinking out there, how long have we been gone? Perhaps no time at all. It occurs to me that not one of us scientists checked his watch for movement, and now too late to check my watch at all. Oh my ears and whiskers.

What will they do when the house appears in Russia, in China, in the Middle East? Do you remember when we were told, with a straight face and an upraised rifle, that wearing the *chador* was a revolutionary act? Do you remember, surely you must, how often we were told that those who made peaceful revolutions impossible would inevitably bring —no, you never believed that. Well. I have seen a revolutionary act. I have become a revolutionary act, physical graffiti on the psychouterine wall, o men read me and weep.

You must, for I am past tears. In a moment she will be here, with her blazing candle, and put me past it all.

Love should, as they say, be blind.

The House That Knew No Hate

by JESSICA AMANDA SALMONSON

Jessica Amanda Salmonson is a champion of the small presses and a defender of historical perspective in the fantasy field. She is a groundbreaker, both as an editor (Tales by Moonlight) and in her own writing. The best in any art always shine in the extremes. Whitman in sonnets and free verse; Burton in Shakespeare and in improvisation. Here's another.

"It's lovely," said Nona in her quietly sincere manner, gazing upward at the three-story house, gabled and dormered and with bay windows. It looked altogether Victorian to her untrained eyes. It was handsome at all events. She took Donald's arm and said, "It's really ours."

He grinned at her bright face, amazed that an old house could make a woman in her late forties look suddenly years younger. The place made him feel invigorated as well. The sunlight reflected off the face of the big house in a way that made the whole structure glow, as might some heavenly palace. The light reflected into the wild, neglected garden where Donald and Nona stood gazing, she at the house, he at her; and that light made them angelic, too.

"It's every bit as beautiful as the photographs," she said.

"Don't get your hopes up *too* high, love. My uncle put a new roof on it a couple years before he died, but before that, he'd let the whole place go rather too long. We'll have to put up new plaster-board before it's habitable."

247

"I'm prepared for all that, Donald," she said. "Quite prepared. But let's look at it from here a moment more, okay? The light makes it look, well, so *new* in a way."

That was true enough, and odd. The bathing sunlight came over the trees, striking the face of the house. Instead of showing up the need for paint, the brightness made it look freshly whitewashed. It was a peculiar sensation standing together on the lawn unmowed for years, between masses of rose bushes gone wild (but no less beautiful for that), a warm wind kissing their cheeks. Eerie. Eerie. Donald couldn't place why he felt strange about it. "Nostalgia," he thought. For he had lived in this house as a boy. The house and the land around it was full of echoes of childhood.

He'd actually inherited the property years before, but let an uncle live in it as caretaker—foolishly perhaps, since the codger accepted the free rent but not the responsibility of keeping the place fit. It had been Donald's and Nona's dream to settle in the big house as soon as he was able to retire and get inland from the coast. At an age when many couples thought of selling their big houses to buy into condominiums, he and Nona were embarking upon the adventure of renovating a veritable mansion.

As he looked at his wife's profile, he was able to superimpose his memory of the young woman she'd been when they were married: no lines about the hazel eyes nor at the corners of her lips. How good it was that both of them were still dreamers when so many years had passed! She turned her bright face slowly to face his, then gave a pleasantly startled laugh. "Donald!" she said. "How young you look!"

He smiled. They even thought alike after so many years. "It's the house," he said. "We should be daunted by it, I suppose; but the thought of fixing it up is rejuvenating."

"I'm glad," Nona whispered, kissing his cheek, "that you always kept it in the family. Remember when I tried to convince you to sell it? Hard times in those days. How far we've come!"

"Yes," he said. "How far." And suddenly his own smile felt forced and brittle. "Let's look inside. It was supposed to be cleaned for us, but I'm sure it's a wreck."

Before she joined him on the walkway to the front door, she plucked a rose from the wild brambles. "Those were planted before I was born," said Donald.

"No!" she said in mild disbelief, smelling the petals before joining him on the step.

"I'll dig out the pictures of when I was little as soon as our things arrive, if I can remember what they're in. Those roses were prize-winning hybrids when I was a tot. Now they've completely reverted—virtual weeds instead of flowers!" He fumbled the old-fashioned skeleton key into the door, hardly knowing how to work anything but a deadbolt.

"They're not weeds at all," Nona protested, butting in to work the key for him. "We'll get the trellises back up and they'll be real beauties. Nothing wrong with wild roses."

Donald noticed that the rose had pricked his wife's finger. Why didn't she wipe away the blood?

"You've hurt yourself," he said.

"Have I?" The door swung inward. She removed a hand-kerchief from a pocket and wrapped it around her thumb. "It's nothing," she said; and they stepped inside.

It was indeed a mess. They'd arranged for a clean-up and paid stiffly for the service, but some things would take a lot more than suds and water. The linoleum was cracked and warped; Donald kicked at a loose piece in the hallway. "Pretty bad," he said.

"What's under it? Oak, you think?"

"Fir, I'm afraid."

"Well, no matter. We'll have tile or carpets."

"Can't have everything at once."

"Floors and walls at least," she said high-spiritedly.

There were missing pieces of plasterboard; the cleaning troop had apparently hauled away the loose fragments. The wall had a weird, ugly pattern of growth on it—mildew years and years old. "That goddamned Uncle Morton."

"Now, Donald."

Donald almost touched the moldy part of the wall, then changed his mind. At least the roof was fixed now. He hoped there wasn't any dry rot in the beams or rafters. They'd know soon enough, when they pulled down what was left of the plasterboard.

Other walls had not gotten wet, but Uncle Morton had lived as much as possible without heat, so that the wallpaper was damp and loose. Donald patted his forehead and went a bit red in the face. "Rather more to it than I warned you," he said.

"Nonsense. We knew it needed interior walls top floor to bottom."

"We'll have to hire a crew," he said. "We can't do it ourselves. Not at our age."

"I feel we could," said Nona. "But I guess we'd be too slow. Why so worried about cost?"

He laughed at himself. They weren't exactly poor nowadays; hadn't been for years. He'd been successful in his business. More than that, the ink was almost dried on the sale of their home on the coast. When that money came through, they could do a lot to this old place, never touching their sizable savings.

"Don't get weak-kneed now, Donald. We said we'd live in one or two rooms if we had to, until major repairs could be done for us. All we're seeing now is that that's exactly what we'll have to do. As a matter of fact, I don't think it's nearly as bad as our worst scenario for the place."

"I guess not. Looks better from the outside, though. The place needs light."

"You said it was inspected. We only need to have the electricity turned on. Donald! Look at this stairway!"

"What? What's wrong with it?"

"Nothing's *wrong* with it," she said. "It's *walnut*. Are you sure the floors are fir?"

"Oh, I vaguely recall my grandfather got the staircase as salvage when the third floor was added. The place was heavily renovated before the war."

Nona threw her arms around her husband and said, "It's full of surprises, this place is. For every run-down problem, there'll be a surprise like this old staircase."

"You really like the place?"

"Haven't seen upstairs yet," she said. "But...I love the house; I can tell I do. It has a good...*feeling* to it."

That was what he needed to hear. The place was a wreck and they both knew it. But it was full of his memories. He felt as though he'd spent his whole life away from home and for the first time as an adult he was back where he belonged, wreck or not. His concern had been chiefly that someone as fastidious as Nona would be horrified by the idea of living in a couple of mildewy rooms while waiting for repairs and for the majority of their possessions to be shipped. She was the sort to say exactly what she thought. And she'd said she loved the place. He was relieved.

There were more discoveries to be made. On the third floor, which was smaller than the two main floors, having only four large rooms, the cleaning crew had crowded most of the remaining furniture that Uncle Morton hadn't sold over the years. These unsold items included some rare antiques, in need of refinishing or reupholstering, but potentially fine pieces. "This was my great-grandma's," said Donald. "She brought it from England." It was a sofa in need of re-covering, but with fabulous carving on the arms, legs, and back. "I used to jump on it as a tot," he said. "Got yelled at."

His mom and dad hadn't lived in the place. After their divorce, his father disappeared, and his mother raised him for a while on the coast, through hard times and estrangement from her parents. Then for a while, when poverty was at its worst for him and his unhappy mother, he'd been sent to live with his grandparents. He'd stayed with them for several years, rarely seeing his mother during that time. They were the best years of his life, to tell the truth. He'd loved his mother and wouldn't speak ill of the dead, but fact was, she was a mite rough on him. Took her frustrations out. The time with Grandma and Grandpa—and with Great-grandma while she was alive, holding court in a big part of the second floor—these were the days of joy in his formative years. The rest, well, he'd blocked a lot of it from his mind: dragged from apartment to apartment, staying as long as it took landlords to get them evicted. His mother's endless array of boyfriends either pretended to like him or didn't even pretend . . . well, no need to recall them. He should just absorb the pleasant vibrations of this old house! But good memories invariably reminded him of the bad.

"You want to live with your grandparents again, do you!" His mother was livid. "They were tyrants! They always wanted to control me! And now they've got my son!" She threw herself on the bed and wept, filling his heart with her tears. "I didn't mean it!" he shouted in an agony of guilt and sadness. "I didn't mean it! I want to stay here with you!"

And all his life, in business, in everything, it had been like that. "I like my job, sure." "I enjoy puttering around our rambler home, yeah." But he was never happy, really, and he wanted to be back in this old house. That was the fool fact of it. And now he was here. Home to roost. It was fine with him; it really was. It was like taking off all the burdens of his life and being a child again.

They had to stay in a motel that night, but the next day they met the electrician at the door to get the old place's lights back on. The phone man came later in the day. "We'll square away the kitchen—and the dining room will serve as bedroom for a while," was Nona's suggestion.

The kitchen alone was big enough to live in. It'd be pretty fancy camping out, at least. They struggled down the staircases with a big, thick, chunky table and set it in the kitchen against the wall. Leaning on it, sweating, Donald said, "Grandma used to mix cookies and mincemeat on this table. I remember it as being even bigger than this!"

He opened one of the kitchen cupboards and breathed from the past. From within, he snatched out a round cookie jar. It was a faded shade of yellow with a big smiling face, and around the base stood a laughing dog, a fiddling cat, and a dish running along with a spoon. "I remember this!" He blew dust out of the inside.

"Is there anything else in there?" asked Nona.

"This is it. It used to have a lid with a cow for a handle."

"Maybe it'll turn up. Lots of old cupboards and crannies in this house."

"Grandma made good cookies," said Donald.

Nona began to giggle, then covered her mouth, not wanting to embarrass her husband.

"I'm funny?" he asked.

"You're just a kid, that's all."

"Yeah. A kid pushing fifty."

He set the full-moon cookie jar on the table.

"Come on, hon. Let's see what we can do about setting up the dining room as a temporary bedroom."

She started down the hallway to the staircase, offering a mild complaint to whatever unknown person decided the scant furnishings belonged on the top floor. On the third stair she stopped and called back, "Don?"

A few steps more, she stopped again, looking over the banister.

"Don?"

He stood in the empty dining room, paralyzed by a painful nostalgia, unable to answer. In another moment she repeated, "Donald, you coming?"

"A . . . a minute," he stammered. "Do you smell anything?"

"Cleaning chemicals."

"No . . ."

"What?"

"Cookies."

"What?" she called again.

"Yes, I'm coming," he said more loudly, moving into the hall, from which Nona was visible on the wide walnut staircase. He looked back through the dining room and into the kitchen, its door ajar.

They spent their first night in the house. They found out soon enough they needed everything, positively everything, and after a feeble look around the kitchen, Nona decided to drive out for some picnicking stuff. "No use filling the refrigerator until we get it cleaned better than that," she said, disgusted by the odor. "But I'll pack the freezer compartment with instant dinners for the time being."

"No, bring milk and stuff; I'll have it clean before you get back."

Thus Donald was alone in the house for the first time since childhood.

He walked about the premises as a man lost in a dream, searching for something his conscious mind could not specify. It led him back to the kitchen, ostensibly to clean out the small refrigerator, though something other than that had beckoned him there. He stood with head turned to one side, looking at the big, thickly hewn table. For a moment, at the edge of his vision, he thought he saw an iron stove-oven where the range actually stood; he closed his eyes against the vision—or to preserve it. He smelled the warm pastry and his heart went out, the past calling to him in a way that hurt. He opened his eyes and watched the sunlight on the wooden table, watched the bright window-shape edge toward him, across the table's top.

His legs felt weak and he was dreaming, "Grandma, Grandma," and the moving square of light reached the table's end and began to drip onto the floor.

When Nona returned home, he barely heard her, barely heard the door.

"Donald?"

He barely heard.

"Don? You here?"

Barely heard.

Time had passed without his moving—or had he moved? Guilt smote him: the refrigerator! He hadn't cleaned it! He had stood in one place so long, his knees were about to give way. Where was he? What was his dream? His vision had not strayed from the tabletop, and momentarily he saw two big bags of groceries plopped down, saw his wife in the kitchen with him. When she had put down the hefty load, she turned suddenly, gasped with a moment's fright, and said, "Donald! You frightened me! I thought you were outside somewhere."

How could she have entered the kitchen without seeing him in the doorway? "Oh Nona, I was daydreaming, but it won't take long to finish cleaning the refrigerator."

He thought his voice had echoed as through a tunnel, but Nona heard nothing funny. Or had she? Her brow wrinkled in a puzzled way and she said:

"What have you got in your hand?"

"This?" He looked at his half-eaten prize and answered with an almost banal matter-of-factness, "It's a cookie."

"I know it's a cookie. Where'd you get it?"

Fortunately she turned her attention to the piles of groceries before he had to answer; for he could not have begun to think of a reply. He turned his attention instead to scrubbing the inner walls of the old fridge.

They lived in the house off and on for the next three months. Sometimes it was too dusty from workmen and they had to clear out for differing lengths of time. But nothing went over schedule, though some things certainly cost more than expected. In a few weeks the walls had been replastered and the floors bared and sanded. Almost last of all, they hired a pair of young women who swedished floors, and the stink of the process was unbearable. But when it was completed, the house was theirs from then on—no more motel, no more eating the same boring couple of dishes available in the town's lamentable restaurants.

And through this time there was so much to worry about, so much to keep an eye on, so much coming and going of laborers and craftspersons, that Donald had scarcely a moment to himself in the house, and the uncanny odors of the past only occasionally assailed him. When memories did spring snares, and then only for the odd moment, he might feel pleasantly disoriented, but unable to hold onto these strange sensations long enough for identification.

After they were really settled in, their possessions scattered among the rooms, some useless things sold to neighbors at a lawn sale, the rest to a junk dealer for almost nothing, there remained a lot to do to the place, but only one more critical item, and that at least was outside. The illegal cesspool had to be replaced by a real septic tank, another shocking expense incurred while the north part of the backyard was torn to pieces.

Nona marked off the areas she did not want the tractors spoiling, for she had taken a fierce liking to the old rose bushes and wasn't even sure she wanted them much pruned, let alone crushed by workmen and tractors skirting the house day after day.

But when all was said and done, and despite the huge amount of money spent on the improvements, and the innumerable arguments with workers who did not wish to complete work on their own promised schedules, it was all foolish worry, for the sale of their coastal home combined with Donald's investments to make them more than commonly well-off. Neither would ever have to work for a living. There was no mortgage over their heads; their major financial problem for the future would be, quite simply, juggling their tax situation so as not to be totally devoured by the government's demands.

They'd come to the place in the glorious spring with the wild gardens in full bloom. They'd camped alternately in the house and in a motel through the dusty, torn-up summer. Come autumn, with the wind tearing the leaves from the yellowed poplars along the lane and from the maples on the far back property, the house was truly theirs. Additional work was planned for the coming spring, but could be put off indefinitely if they desired. The house was more than habitable. It was a wondrous comfort.

One night, having sat at the same moment on opposite sides of their bed, with moonlight glinting into their second-story bedroom, Donald said, "Are you still certain, Nona? Do you want to live here?"

She looked at him askance, as though he had offered a joke so feeble it didn't even deserve a polite chortle. As she threw herself back onto her pillow she saw his expression and knew he was deeply serious. "How can you ask it?" she said gravely. "You can't be having second thoughts! The worst is over, Donald. We're home!"

"Yes," he said, and lay back quietly. "Home."

In the backyard were apple trees planted by Donald's great-grandparents, on the southern edge of the land. These gave fruit in autumn. Two of the trees had tiny, hard apples of a species nobody could identify. They looked like dwarf Romes, perfectly formed, bright red and gorgeous. These, as

Donald was to explain to Nona, would still be clinging to the branches at the height of winter.

"Obviously a type no longer grown," said Nona. "Too small for commercial value," she said.

"And a great pity," he added. "They don't drop from the limbs until spring, so we'll have a natural storehouse of fresh apples anytime we want. Even my grandparents couldn't name them, as I recall."

Beyond the small orchard were the woods consisting largely of maples and a few scattered firs. Occasionally a raccoon would be seen moving about, or a possum. At night an owl hooted.

Nona had taken a fancy mainly to the front gardens which, though a tangle of thorns, she was intent on preserving in a tastefully wild state. She was raking poplar leaves every other day or so, pruning minimally for the plants' winter rest, and making idle repairs to rockeries and the like. The backyard with its fruit trees became Donald's province. Hence, when they were outside together, they were not, strictly speaking, together at all, but parted by the house. Donald found it disturbingly symbolic: *parted by the house.* Yet didn't Nona love the house as much as he? Didn't she feel the generations of familial love with the same intensity? There might be a particular personal element he could not fully share, the remembrance of those years of peace amidst formative years otherwise tumultuous; but there was no cause to consider this a division between Nona and himself. Was there?

Donald split lengths of wood that had been delivered in two large loads at the north edge of the back property, dumped unfortunately into the mud left by the septic tank installers. His muscles ached marvelously most of the time. Days went by during which he and Nona seemed never to speak to each other, though they were getting along as well as ever—they had always gotten along—and Nona was happy. But with the settling of winter, there was a colder space between them than ever in their lives. Didn't she notice it too? He didn't think she did.

Was it because Donald kept secrets? He'd never kept secrets before. Now he did. It was because he didn't wish to sound foolish. For instance, once, while splitting wood, he caught sight of two old rabbit hutches nearby. When he looked about the area with a careful sweep of his vision, there were no hutches. When he investigated the area, all he found, among the weeds at the edge of the maples, was a section of wire that might or might not have been part of one of Grandpa Nathan's rabbit hutches.

Then a real snow came. It was not a bad winter. It was pleasant, and the heating bill was kept minimal by Donald's fascination with and soon-skillful handling of the fireplace that he'd had fitted with an airtight liner. It gave off a tremendous amount of heat in the living room, but was rarely too hot for comfort because much heat was able to escape straight up the walnut staircase to their bedroom. The extra rooms on the second floor, and the entire top floor, were mostly shut off to conserve fuel, but not so completely as to ever become damp.

The dining room off the living room got its heat from two sides, since Nona had reverted to her early interest in gourmet cooking (a lack of proper restaurants and other urban distractions might have been the cause of that). She was often in the kitchen preparing something or other, and became a baker with a vengeance. Donald never mentioned how, all too often, Nona's bread smelled like cookies baking.

Small secrets, harmless secrets, but there were many of them.

Did Nona have secrets too?

Were they drifting apart in such comfort as they had fashioned?

One evening he was sitting before the fireplace, the fire a pale ghost behind the dark mica of the airtight's door. Nona came down from an upstairs room that she had already cluttered with sewing and hobby matter. She brought a book, plumped down nearby, and began to read. He remained silent. Then Nona looked up from the book with a sigh. "Donald, I'm very happy." And it was a relief for him to hear it, because he wasn't sure anymore what happiness was, if he'd ever been happy; this lost sense was something he'd imagined Nona must be feeling too. But the house could scarcely be expected to awaken *her* childhood memories. It was a new world for her, an older way of living that she had not known previously. She was enormously comfortable. She'd always been comfortable, but never idyllically. For Donald, the idyll was too reminiscent of an earlier peace in his life, an island against turmoil, an island that once before had been washed away. The things he felt were uncanny. He kept expecting to encounter his great-grandma on the stairs, to hear her gentle demands of Grandpa and Grandma: "Oh, how am I ever going to get to the dimestore today?" and of course Grandpa would volunteer. Or to see Grandma in the kitchen—baking cookies or apple pie or one of her blessed casseroles. Or to see that big table spread out even bigger with its extra leaves, covered with some holiday feast—Thanksgiving or Christmas—the house crawling with relatives of all ages, from three states around, since "the upstairs matriarch," Great-grandma Bess, was the center of the clan until the day she died.

Always absent from the premises was his mother. Never in his nostalgic reminiscences did he see her in this house. She had grown up here, but left early, all but outcast or at least self-exiled, too wild a girl for that conservative time and place. But in Donald's time, his mother was apart from the family, apart from the house, and nothing in it reminded him of her. He loved his mother so much, yet she had disliked her own parents out of some rebelliousness unexplained to him, blamed them for the mistakes she had made in her own life, resented that they had taken care of her son at a time when she could scarcely take care of herself but would accept no charity in her own behalf. A stubborn woman, and the only thing stronger than her unhappiness was her pride, injured by the confession that she needed help for her son's sake if not her own. And after that time, right up to the present time, he hated to think about his mother. How he *had* to think about her, as penance for not wanting to! How close he came to hating himself for loving the memories of this house more than any memory he could uncover with his mother in it . . .

But Nona, it would seem, suffered none of these conflicts. She smiled across the top of her book at Donald's quiet fire and said, "Isn't it like a dream?"

It was.

"There's something warm and wonderful in the walls," she said. "It should be drafty, but it never is. Isn't it magical, Donald?"

"It's very nice."

But he'd wanted to say, "Yes, magical. It's very magical. Frankly, it's supernatural."

"Nice," he said.

There was gray in Nona's hair, for she never dyed it, and she had a matronly beauty even with hair tousled or when wearing her frumpiest dress. Donald's hair was grayer still.

Yet he had thought they'd both been getting *fewer* gray hairs as the weeks went by in the old house.

And how he loved Nona! The only woman he had ever loved more was his mother—who he hated to think about.

"There must have been an incredible amount of love in this house for it to hold that feeling for so long," said Nona. "Weren't there ever disagreements in your family?"

"Yes," he said. "But not many. It's hard for me to remember anything bad."

"I envy you," she said, bright eyes smiling. "Families don't love each other the way they once did, do they? How long has it been since we've seen my sister Sharon?"

"She's awful busy with kids and grandkids," said Donald, and then bit his tongue. Now he saw it: the shadow lurking behind Nona's eyes, the secret she kept too. She didn't envy his memories of family life in this house, she *resented* those remembrances! He and Nona had never had children, their own family was each other—each had become the other's family of one. They hadn't seen Nona's sister in years, though occasionally they talked on the phone—Christmas usually; it was almost time to do it again. Sharon had grown children, and the children had children. What did Nona have? She had Donald. That was all. But Donald had a magical past. He'd brought Nona to live in the echo of his childhood. What had he given her to balance that?

Her eyes fell upon the book in her lap.

For days to follow, the weather was uncommonly pleasant for winter. Snow melted into patches, revealing brittle brown maple leaves in the backyard. He leaned over the back porch rail, a brisk wind ruffling his hair and bringing him scents that tugged at yesterdays. He squinted nearsightedly across the clearing that led to the orchard and the woods. He tried to imagine the backyard as it had looked when he was a child—and found the exercise shockingly easy.

A rope-swing with wooden seat hung from one of the maples at the yard's edge. There were rabbit hutches nearby. Rabbits stomped the floors of their cages when Buff—an old, half-blind English spaniel—came too near. Then Buff pranced like a pup, despite his rheumatism, out into the woods.

A vegetable garden lay fallow; a crucifix hung with Christmas bells stood in the middle of the garden where, in the growing season, the ringing was supposed to keep birds away. A black crow of winter sat preening on the cross, shaking the bells with one foot then the other, not in the least scared of the sound. There was a stone-lined path from the porch to the garden. Between the rocks were brittle remnants of Grandma's flowers. He heard chickens in the henhouse around the corner, beyond sight.

Overcome with pointless inspiration, little Donny ran along the rock-lined path, shouting at the crow, as though its presence mattered in a garden fully harvested weeks before and spotted with snow. The crow complained and the cross-of-bells replied musically as the black bird sped toward the tops of leafless maples. Donny hopped over the fallow rows and went to check if the rabbits had enough feed and to make sure their water bowls weren't too iced.

He stood before a hutch, watching the pink eyes of a doe watch him. White breaths issued from her opening-and-closing nostrils. Buff wasn't anywhere to be seen, so the rabbits were placid. Donny opened one of the cages, pulled a rabbit out by the scruff. It hung in his grasp, dangling limp and unconcerned. He put the big doe on the ground, intending to stroke her soft fur, but something startled her and she took off, kicking up slush and snow with big hind feet.

He ran after her, slipping and getting the knees of his pants dirty, but finally caught the dodging doe. It took all his strength to hold her at arm's length while she kicked and kicked. Finally she calmed down and he held her near, bracing her back legs so she wouldn't think she was falling. "Nice rabbit," he said. "Good doe."

From the porch, an old lady with an apron, hair in a bun, dish-towel in hand, shouted with feigned anger, "Donald! You get that rabbit right back in the hutch where it belongs!"

Donald reeled on the porch and looked at the closed screen door. He could have sworn he actually heard his grandma reprimanding him. Of course there was no one there. He puzzled over the realism of his own imagination, then looked at his shirt, on which were a few white strands of fur, and at his knees which were inexplicably sodden.

That night, Donald lay close to his wife, closer than for many days. He clung to her and she misread his attentiveness, responding easily, and they made love though that hadn't been his initial intent. In her arms, it was always spring or autumn, never a hot summer or a chilly winter. Her breath was the cool autumn breeze. Her hair was a field of gently blowing grass. Her flesh was the lure of the sea, dan-

gerous and sweet. Silly. Silly that he should ponder as a poet
—an inadequate poet, but still a poet—at his age and after
so many years together. It was unlike him, too. And he
thought he recognized, at the heart of this emotion, a familiar sense of loss rather than togetherness. People we have
lost are the ones we most idealize. Donald's were the senti-
ments of a widower, blind to the faults of a buried wife. How
pathetically morbid! On the other hand, wasn't it better to
have these feelings, these insights, *before* it was too late to
embrace, to whisper in the night, "I love you, Nona."

"I love you, too," she murmured sleepily, still with the
musk of their lovemaking about her. She snuggled closer,
sighed heavily, and grew still.

"It's haunted," he whispered, after a long silence, and in a
mild tone that suggested the continuance of some previous
conversation. Nona opened her eyes though half in slumber,
and answered, "I know; but haunted in a nice way."

"I'm not so sure," he said. The act of freeing his arm from
under her shoulders woke her more fully; or was it his seri-
ousness of tone that made her attentive? "Is it ever right that
the past haunts the present?"

"It's a fine, fine house, Donald. It was built by your
grandfather and great-grandfather with loving hands, kept by
your grandmother with loving heart, uniting a family that
loved one another so deeply it still glimmers from the foundation to the rafters. A good house, a house that has not
known hatred."

Was that true? Had there never been hatred in this
house? We always idealize the dead.

"Poetry," he said softly. "Yours is better than mine."

"It's a good haunting," she said, and Donald remembered
some fragment of Rupert Brooke and said to Nona:

> *"So a poor ghost, beside his misty streams,*
> *Is haunted by strange doubts, evasive dreams,"*

then kissed her and said no more. He let her fall into slumber
while he lay awake with his continuing uneasiness. Living in
the past, no matter how fine a past, was not the rational
thing. It worried him. Even now, every atom of his being felt
that the years were calling him back, calling him back . . .

"Donny," Grandma whispered.

"Yes, Grandma," he answered, screwing his eyes with his
knuckles.

"It's time for breakfast. Come quietly. Granny Bess isn't feeling well and we want her to sleep a bit longer. Don't rub your eyes, Donny."

"Yes, Grandma."

He slipped quietly from between the sheets, dressed, tiptoed down the stairs, feeling that any untoward noise would break some uncomprehended spell upon the house.

From the kitchen window he saw Grandpa Nathan out by the hutches. Grandpa's breakfast dishes were already cleaned and on the draining board. Donny felt an aching disappointment. He loved Grandpa Nathan and wished to rush outside and take hold of the old man's overalls and not let go of him.

Fried mush and salt pork weren't his idea of a spectacular breakfast, but he enjoyed it more than usual, almost relished it. Grandma seemed amazed he didn't complain as the mush was in fact a bit dark around the edges. He was usually such a finicky lad.

Buff was under the table, wagging his tail, begging in a way Grandma mightn't detect. Donny was the old dog's conspirator in matters of salt pork, sneaking rinds and some fat to him whenever Grandma wasn't looking, and burnt edges of fried mush. A stray cat leapt up from the porch and clung with sharp claws to the screen door, looking right into the kitchen, mewing boldly.

Grandma had a pie in the oven; the aroma was overwhelming and wonderful. Donny ate a lot of breakfast, but tried to save room for the hot piece of cinnamon-sugared pie-dough that was right beside the baking pie, waiting for him, and for a lump of fresh-churned butter.

"Grandma?"

"Hmm."

"Why am I here?"

She looked down at him through wire-rimmed bifocals and asked, "Why, what sort of question is that?"

He wasn't sure.

"Oh. I like to be here. I love you and Grandpa and Granny Bess. But I'm not supposed to be here, am I?"

"Would you rather go home?"

"I don't know. Isn't this my home? I like it here."

Grandma kissed him on the cheek, smelling of pastry flour and witch hazel. "You go home anytime you like," she said. "It's up to you."

* * *

Donald rolled over in bed, trying to piece together the strange conversation of his dream. He'd wanted to go home. But had he wanted to go home to his mother in another state or back here to Nona? He wasn't sure if in the dream he meant he didn't belong there as a little boy or if it was his old guilt-of-happiness telling him his mother needed him, that it was somehow wrong for him to be with his grandparents and forgetting about his mom. Try as he might, he couldn't make any clear sense of the dream. It faded from him though he tried to hold onto it.

What with one thing and then another, he'd never gotten around to fixing the attic door that wouldn't open. In so big a house, with rooms they hadn't conceived a use for yet, there had been little reason to explore beneath the gables. It was an unfinished attic behind that special door, and as he recalled it had never even been used for storage.

Yet as he lay there, he was thinking of that door, of that attic. He sat up, put feet in slippers, grabbed a robe, and went out into the hall. The flight of steps leading to the third floor, newer than the rest of the house, was not nearly as wide as the walnut staircase from the main floor to the second. His slippered feet made no sound upon these narrower stairs, as though no weight was placed upon them.

The door leading to the space beneath the gable was an antique affair, part of Grandpa Nathan's salvaging operation, put in this odd spot because there was no place else for it. It was grandly carved with gryphons and mice—a motif that fascinated him as a child and still had a curious charm. The rarity of the door was one reason he and Nona decided not to force it; they might have damaged the antique workings of the handle and lock.

The knob was itself cast with intricate Celtic symbols.

For some reason, Donald felt he had to look up there. The only fear was of waking Nona. She'd think him daft, breaking down that beautiful door in the early dawn, in his robe and slippers.

But the door opened without so much as a squeak of its hinges. Had it really been unlocked the whole time? Perhaps it had come unstuck on account of the changing temperatures of the wood. Donald had a dreamy uneasiness and wondered, even now, if he was imagining things.

At the top of the narrow, rickety stairwell, festoons of cobwebs clinging to his hair and shoulders, Donald stood gazing into the darkness under the gable. The exposed beams of the ceiling below had had a few warped boards laid across them to walk on and some plywood on which sat a few boxes, one with faded, dusty Christmas decorations poking through the flaps.

"Donny, where are you?" called Granny Bess, her voice feeble but insistent. "Donny, come talk to your mother on the phone. Don't be like this!"

"Is he up here?" called Grandpa Nathan.

Donny hugged his knees and sat quietly at the top of the stairs.

"He must have gone outside," said Grandpa, and Great-grandma added, "Maybe. The poor boy. Is she going to come and get him?"

"Dunno. Ma's talking to her now. He *is* her boy."

A tear tracked Donny's face.

He and Nona had lunch in town. It'd been a few weeks since they'd been to the little restaurant, but when they first moved to town, they had been daily customers, so were handsomely greeted. Away from the influence of the house, Donald felt rational once more, nothing tugging horridly at his heart, though his intellect remained uneasy.

"You're so serious lately," said Nona, her soft round face compassionate. "Why so much brooding?"

"Don't know really," he admitted. "Haven't you felt any . . . any *distancing* between us lately?"

She reached over the table and touched his hand. "After what we did last night?" And she blushed from eyebrows to throat.

"Do you ever miss the coast at all? The city?" He lowered his voice, so as not to insult the waiter-cook-owner of the present establishment, and added, "The restaurants?"

She looked at him with gentle, hazel eyes that seemed almost to pity. But why should she feel pity? He must have imagined it. "You were never fond of the city," she reminded him. "Don't tell me you're homesick."

"Home?" He laughed at the irony. "I just thought you might be bored."

"If you need to get away from the weather," said Nona, "we could take a trip to Miami."

"What if we went to visit your sister?"

"Sharon?" She almost laughed, but then scowled and said in a low, almost miserable tone: "I don't think so, Donald. No, it wouldn't do."

"Do you ever think about when you and she were little?"

"Of course."

"Weren't you close?"

"I guess we were—then. The world moves beneath us, Donald. Things never come back again."

"If things could come back," he said, not realizing he was still clutching her hand when their lunch orders came. She had to almost pry him loose so that the restaurant-keeper could put their plates on the table. When he'd toddled off, Donald leaned forward and said, "If you could recapture those years of closeness with your sister, with your parents when they were living, would you do it? Would you go back?"

"I have you, Donald. What good is such a speculation?"

"Would you go back *if you could?*"

"No, Donald. No."

"Nona."

"What, Donald?"

They stared at each other, both with puzzled faces. Suddenly he lost his nerve and fell to eating from the plate— tasting nothing. They ate in silence. Afterward they went shopping, still barely speaking, though there was no anger between them. When they started home, Donald kept to himself his feeling of desperate horror.

The mild winter gave birth to an early spring, with Nona constantly fussing in the front yard, preparing the beds of flowers and the flowering shrubs with an expectation of producing a paradise of blossoms to mark the anniversary of their arrival. Donald fussed less consistently in the backyard, splitting wood, building a hen-house for the three hens he'd purchased and which presently ran loose through the orchard, and recreating his grandmother's vegetable garden with scant realization that he was doing so.

While hoeing a row for carrots, he dug up an old brass bell stuffed with dirt. He sat beside an outside faucet cleaning the bell with water and prying finger. The clapper was gone.

The bell reminded him of the uninspected boxes of Christmas decorations stored under one of the gables. He hurried into the house on a quest for further bells, intent upon his sudden idea of making a bell-tree to keep birds from his vegetables.

He half ran to the second floor, but went somewhat more

slowly to the third after stopping at a landing to press palm to chest and take deep breaths. When he obtained the third floor he walked dizzily along the hall, toward the antique door of gryphons and mice.

The combined exertion of the long morning's labors and the quick flight through the house had conspired against him. He was totally winded. When he reached the attic door, it was all he could do to push it open. The dusty well leading upward into darkness was menacing and unreal. He gasped, opening and closing his hand, numb from hoeing or from splitting wood, he expected.

He sat on the bottom stair until he felt better, then took the stairs slowly, like an old man. He tugged the light, brittle cardboard box down the steps and into the hallway, as though it were a heavy chest. Inside were tree ornaments from his childhood, cheap things but fragrant as apples with the scent of memory.

Among all the junk he found steel jester's bells from England and several small brass bells made in India and Japan.

Through much of the early afternoon he was on the back porch with a rustic cross made from gray scrap lumber, attaching the bells one by one. He hung them from the cross-arm by means of varying lengths of thin copper wire from an old spool. How slowly, how methodically he worked at it! It was like an odd ritual, the magic of which would be spoiled by too much haste.

Only once did he look up from this loving work, and thought about making a couple of hutches, getting some rabbits to place just there by the edge of the wood. Yes, that was a good idea.

Nona found him about three o'clock, unconscious at the foot of the porch steps, the bell-tree in his hand like a shaman's wand. He awoke that evening under heavy sedation and to the news of a bad heart.

It was carefully explained to him that after a heart attack, there was often a severe depression brought on more by physiological conditions than by objective dangers or compromises he must face. He was warned and counseled. With blood pressure maintenance under the guidance of a physician, with a little care about exertion, with a careful diet, there was no reason to believe he couldn't regain, the doctor said, "As much as eighty percent of the heart's capacity."

When he was home, Nona was cheery to the point of

lunacy, boning up on low-carbohydrate, no-salt, no-fat gourmet cookery. He felt a great fuss was being made over him on the chance that he might feel discouraged. But he really never felt the depression coming on, until it arrived without warning, triggered by the stair-elevator installed a week after he came home. Nona was cheery about that, too, though it made her beloved walnut staircase look a horror. "Now you needn't sleep in the living room!" she beamed. He rode the contraption up the curve of the staircase. And somewhere between the bottom and the top, he began to despair. He'd *liked* chopping wood. He'd *liked* hoeing in the garden. He enjoyed building that henhouse and had looked forward to making some rabbit hutches. What was he supposed to do now? The thing most couples did at that age: sell a big house and move into a condo. . . .

Nona had walked beside him as he rode the chair-elevator on its trial run. She had watched the change come over his expression and the tears welling in his eyes. It didn't matter to her that the installers were standing there. She fell to her knees when they reached the topmost stair, she took hold of Donald, and they wept together. "Oh Donald," she said; "Oh, honey," wondering why no one had ever counseled her about *her* possible depression.

As summer neared, he sat more and more often on the front porch, watching Nona in the gardens. She was always watering things, wanting the flowers to last even through the height of summer when the world beyond the lane was brown and dusty. He didn't doubt she could manage so small a miracle.

She would come onto the porch from time to time and tuck blankets around him. He actually liked that.

"Shouldn't I have a rocker?" he said, his smile either half-hearted or wry.

"Maybe," she said. "And you could learn to knit."

Then she was back in the garden, weeding, wandering, vanishing behind the gigantic spray of wild roses in full bloom. He never made any fuss about his vegetables; Nona was interested only in flowers. But sitting there, he couldn't help but feel badly that *his* garden was going to seed. "Give it until spring," the doctor suggested. "You'll be chipper enough for hoeing if you really must. A little exercise is good. But don't hurry it, old boy." And the doctor slapped his shoulder.

"Nona?"

She'd vanished behind that blossoming hedgerow some moments earlier.

"Nona?"

He sighed and let his eyes close, let the perfume of the gardens envelop him. *The perfume,* he thought: *perfume.* When he opened his eyes again, the wild roses looked smaller. Or, rather, the bushes themselves were well-pruned and vastly more domesticated. The blossoms were much larger. Grandpa Nathan was having his picture taken beside some of the bushes. Donny threw the blanket off his lap and ran out to be in the picture, too. "You all right, sonny?" asked Grandpa, mussing the boy's pale hair. "Don't wanna spread your cold now, do you?"

It was no cold but rheumatic fever. He was almost well but not supposed to exert himself. For some reason they kept calling it a cold. Everyone called it that. But the doctor said rheumatic fever.

"No, Grandpa Nathan. But I want my picture took."

On the front porch, Donny's grandmother appeared with unnatural suddenness, dithering nervously back and forth across the top of the steps as though fearful of testing a single stair. She didn't want to upset Grandpa while the flower judges were taking photographs, but she had to do it. It was an emergency. "Pa! Pa, come quick! It's Granny Bess. Oh, Pa!"

"Did you call me?" asked Nona, peeping through a break in the hedgerow.

Donald was colorless. His mouth and eyes opened at the same moment, but he couldn't speak. "Donald!" Nona came rushing through the hedge though the opening was almost too small to let her through, and she scratched her arms. She was at his side in a moment, fumbling in his pocket to get at the bottle of nitrite. His eyes peeled back and looked at her horribly as she placed the pellet in his mouth and closed it for him.

Then she sat hard beside his chair, flat on the wood of the porch, and couldn't control her emotions. She rocked her head in her hands and wept aloud, "I can't face it. No, I can't, can't face it." Donald's prematurely palsied hand gently touched her hair. And he noticed how the gray was completely gone from it. She looked up at him with wet, wet eyes and forced an apologetic smile. And her face was young, so young. "Nona," he said softly, lowering his head in meek submission. "Nona."

He read up on heart conditions and soon convinced himself it was much worse than they were telling him. This invalid treatment was a bit antiquated, unless things were really bad. It no longer seemed a choice between Nona and his childhood. It was a choice between living or dying. Yet he wanted to be with her, even more now that he felt he could escape forever. The house was being good to her. The house loved her. But it couldn't take her back with him; it couldn't give her his memories. It had different gifts for different people, that was the fact of it. The house stood between them—not willfully, but nonetheless.

Yet there were other possibilities in this, including the big one, that he was mad, had been mad all along. He didn't quite believe that, but did the mad ever think of themselves as such? Nona had felt the mystic touch of the house, and they couldn't both be mad. Nona had said there was nothing sinister in the haunting. And hadn't she gotten younger? It seemed as though she had. It seemed so. It had begun that way for him, too, but something else had happened instead —his memories. Had he made that choice? Had the house made that choice?

Had this house ever known hate?

He knew he was thinking of some escape that would part him from Nona, and intentional or not, it struck him as sinister after all. It all seemed calculated by some entity outside himself. His memories beckoned him. Some*one* or some*thing* in those memories or in the house wanted him and was calling for his return. He didn't like it. The choice wasn't *quite* good enough.

There was still something he wasn't facing, something . . . perhaps . . . unnecessarily cruel in his situation. He didn't know why he felt it, but he felt *there was someone to blame.* People in trouble often sought others to blame, and Donald had never been like that. He certainly oughtn't blame anyone else for his physical condition. Yet, maybe there *was* someone he should blame. Maybe it was no coincidence things had come to so terrible a pass.

Nona had gone out for a while, shopping he thought, he hadn't paid attention. His memory had been jumbled up by the strokes. He remembered the long ago much better than the present afternoon. He found himself alone in the house, neatly dressed and a comforter on his lap, books and a radio at hand. Nona had placed the phone beside him and promised not to be long. That was already more than an hour ago. He got up and took a careful stroll around the house, rode the elevator-chair to the second floor, stood at the bottom of the next staircase gazing wistfully at the third floor that was now effectively off bounds to him. He stroked the walls, as warm as flesh. He placed a cheek to a cool window and looked out over the gardens. He saw, coming down the drive between the wind-blown poplars, a row of black automobiles—vintage, every single one of them, their headlights on though it was day.

Donald backed away from the window. He looked himself up and down. He was still a man of fifty; he didn't know whether or not to feel relieved about that. He looked from the window once more and saw nothing unusual.

Two of the unused second-floor rooms had belonged to Granny Bess. Donald walked toward those rooms, his heels clicking on wood, echoing in a manner he thought peculiar. The door was open and he saw that the main room was full of flowers and a coffin. He pressed himself against the wall beside that door so he could not see in. He touched his own cheeks, felt that they were cold and wet; and his fingers were cold, cold and almost blue. His head was throbbing but nowhere else was there pain.

Bracing himself emotionally, he looked around the corner into the room.

There were only a few boxes Nona had stored there.

He heard a car entering the drive and wondered if it was another mourner, or Nona coming home. Careless of himself, he hurried to the walnut staircase and looked down. There were a lot of people in the foyer. Grandma and Grandpa were greeting them tearfully. Donald meant to sit on the stair-elevator, but it was gone. There weren't even holes in the wall where it had been installed. He took his hand out of his pocket, holding the bottle of nitrite, and it slipped from his grasp, pellets scattering down the steps.

He looked toward the foyer again and saw Nona with two boxes in her arms, trying to manipulate the door. She looked up at the clatter of pills but saw no one.

"Come out from there, Donny," said Grandpa Nathan. "Don't you want to say good-bye to your Granny Bess?"

He heard Grandpa pushing at the door carved with gryphons and mice.

"There ain't nothing to be afraid of, son. Death is just a natural thing."

But Donny hadn't hidden from Granny Bess. It was his mother. His mother was going to be in the house. Everyone had come to see Granny Bess off to heaven—absolutely everyone because it was that important—and the house was full of every relative from near and far, full of strangers too. Even in their mourning they could not contain the whispered gossip of that *girl* someone saw at the train depot. Someone had said, "Well it's about time she showed a little shame and a little respect for this house," and someone else, "She ain't done nothing but soil a good family's name."

His mother was coming and Donny was hiding. But Grandpa Nathan saw him go up the stairs.

"What you got jammed up against the door, boy? There ain't no lock on that side."

He'd set a row of Christmas bells along the bottom edge of the door, and they held it fast like teeth.

"Ah, boy, what you want to go and hurt your Grandpa Nathan that way for?"

How could he answer that? He didn't want to hurt his grandpa. He scooted down the steps one at a time, getting years of dust on the butt of his best suit, and when he reached the bottom he moved the row of little bells aside and let Grandpa push the door open.

"Nona," Donald said, as he staggered into the hallway from the dark stairwell.

"Good lord, Donald, why are you up here? *Donald!*" She moved forward, loose nitrite pills in her hand.

Donny rushed into his Grandpa Nathan's arms. "It's okay, boy. Ain't nobody going to hurt you now."

"Donald, open your mouth! Damn you, Donald, open your mouth!" He had fallen to his knees, and Nona was pulling at his lips, pinching at the hinge of his jaw, trying to get him to take a pill.

"I'm sorry, Nona," he said, and the pill was in at once. He didn't try to spit it out. He knew it was too late to help. The heart attack had started more than half an hour before. "I'm leaving, Nona. I'm going to miss you, but I'll be all right, and you'll be all right too."

"Donald!"

"Donny!" His mother stalked up the stairs and down the

hall. Her bright red lipstick showed right through her black veil. Even in mourning she looked like a whore. "Donny! Come here to mother, Donny."

Guilt. Fear. Hatred. Love. He hadn't seen her in a long time. He forced himself to let go of Grandpa Nathan's trousers and went to greet his mother. She lifted her veil and placed a red smear on his face. "Let's you and me go say good-bye to Granny Bess, okay, Donny? She left you a lot of money, you should know. And your mommy's come to take you home."

"Home," said Donny, walking with his mother through the flower-scented house, the color drained from his complexion. "Home."

Afterword: Houses of the Mind

KATHRYN CRAMER

Horror fiction should not so much scare the reader as allow the reader to be scared, releasing tensions caused by any number of things in the real world. By invoking the fantastic, horror allows us access to hordes of things that are too painful to perceive directly, things that would only leave us numb rather than evoke an authentic response if represented in the ordinary light of realistic fiction.

By this point in the book, you have read about old houses, new houses, barns, bathrooms and basements, a hospital, a mortuary, a round house, and a ghostly house that disappears—each house different. In these stories, particularly in Ramsey Campbell's "Where the Heart Is," the architectural details of a house form a structure—literally a building—whose parts have a physical and mechanical relationship, and so the meaning of these individual architectural details—the stain on the wall, the peeling paint in the back of the closet—related through the physical structure of the house, form a structure of metaphor which, in comparison to simpler metaphors, is capable of much more elaborate meaning.

Horror fiction is about fear, and so as contemporary life becomes more complex, the things we fear are also more complex and sometimes are identifiable only as systems. From Nazism to nuclear weaponry, the cause and effect relationships within contemporary evil become increasingly difficult to discern. So although many of the traditional thing motifs—the witches, the werewolves, the occasional slug— continue to be used to good effect, in order to understand the dark issues of the twentieth century, which we ultimately

273

must to survive our newfound technological capabilities, we must come to an understanding of systems, perhaps through systemic metaphor, and perhaps even through contemplation of the house.

In this book there are stories on a number of complex themes. Karl Wagner's "Endless Night" addresses the psychology of blame: what does it mean to hate someone for doing a job? Gene Wolfe's "In the House of Gingerbread" raises questions about the source of evil. Does evil reside in people or in the crazy and malign structure of a situation? Wolfe weaves a familiar fairy tale into his story, a technique often used by contemporary German authors when writing about Germany's dark history. Robert Aickman takes on the vast question of determinism, showing us with painful clarity a man unable to escape a destiny dictated by his peculiar childhood. "The Fetch" is thematically similar to H. P. Lovecraft's "The Rats in the Wall," giving words to fear of losing control, fear of being taken over by dark and primal forces from within, fear of reverting to barbarism or worse. But unlike Lovecraft, Aickman handles it with the gentlest of touches.

In "Tales from the Original Gothic," by John M. Ford, the narrator is absorbed by the bed, becoming part of the furnishings of the house, becoming a passive observer deprived of all freedom to take action. This story is reminiscent of Charles Loring Jackson's "An Uncomfortable Night," a tale about a young man who stays overnight in a house haunted by the ghost of a passionate woman who tries to make love to him through the furniture. And there are other stories in this book about the fear of being corrupted, consumed, or enslaved by evil in the form of a house. Scott Baker's "Nesting Instinct" and Dean Koontz's "Down in the Darkness" both come to mind. John Skipp and Craig Spector's "Gentlemen" is another example, using architecture to examine the structure of contemporary sexual politics. In Joyce Carol Oates's "Haunted," abandoned houses are the locus of forbidden and potentially lethal sexual knowledge. In Jack Dann's "Visitors" the stage after adolescence *is* death. Both stories express an adolescent's battle to keep hold of identity in the face of hormonal changes and adult pressures.

Almost everyone lives in a house or apartment building during the formative years of childhood, and architecture, unlike ghosts, goblins and vampires, is all around us. Events are lost in time, but we preserve their memory by associating them with their settings, sometimes so much so that the events come to dominate: Woodstock, Watergate, Waterloo, Hiroshima, the Alamo, Pearl Harbor, Viet Nam. One event can haunt our perception of a place for a long time. In Campbell's "Where the Heart Is," memory and the house are so intertwined that the character's memories can be altered by remodeling the house. In Charles L. Grant's "Ellen, In Her Time" the presence of a dead woman prevails within her widower's house. In Jessica Amanda Salmonson's "The House That Knew No Hate," a story firmly within the tradition of Henry James's "The Turn of the Screw," the protagonist ultimately loses himself within the house's overwhelming past.

Three stories in this book—Michael Bishop's "In the Memory Room," Joseph Lyons's "Trust Me," and Ramsey Campbell's "Where the Heart Is"—question our notions of the very nature of reality. "In the Memory Room" employs one of the more subtle properties of architecture and one of the most firmly entrenched in the metaphors of ordinary speech: containment relations. The story features a talking corpse à la William Faulkner's *As I Lay Dying* and is carefully balanced between the viewpoints of living and dead. There is an implied ultimate viewpoint in the language of fiction, and by grasping architectural metaphor and using it consciously as a tool, Bishop calls the viewpoint of the live characters into question, suggesting that perhaps we are all here for the benefit of the dead, a most unsettling idea, especially when considered from a genetic point of view. "Trust Me" shows, through the language of metaphor, that the absurd fears raised by tales of terror are in some sense real, a notion that might be considered one of the axioms of this anthology. In Campbell's story, the distinction between the natural and the supernatural, between sanity and insanity, is blurred by twisting our comfortable notions of causality and the possible into Escheresque, impossible objects that must then be rejected in favor of radical doubt.

The architecture of fear is indeed the central horror of life in the twentieth century, an Escheresque castle in which evil has been loosed repeatedly, uncontained, has invaded our secure places and left us emotionally deadened and in doubt of both the reality and the nature of the actual horrors. Horror fiction can provide insight into nonfictional horrors and, more important perhaps, awaken emotional response through the mirror of art.

A Guide to Significant Works of Architectural Horror

The following list of stories, covering more than two centuries, is meant to give the reader some idea of the extensive range of works related to architectural horror. This list is by no means comprehensive, but indicates the variety of structures involved, from single rooms, to houses and monasteries, to landscapes.

"The Hospice" by Robert Aickman
"Meeting Mr. Miller" by Robert Aickman
"The Empty House" by Algernon Blackwood
"The Hungry House" by Robert Bloch
"The Haunters and the Haunted, Or, The House and the Brain" by Edward Bulwer-Lytton
The Doll Who Ate His Mother by Ramsey Campbell
The Incarnate by Ramsey Campbell
The Nameless by Ramsey Campbell
"The Haunting" by Susan Casper
Dorothea Dreams by Suzy McKee Charnas
"The Secret Sharer" by Joseph Conrad
"House Taken Over" by Julio Cortázar
"Camps" by Jack Dann
The House of the Seven Gables by Nathaniel Hawthorne
The Turn of the Screw by Henry James
The Haunting of Hill House by Shirley Jackson
The Sundial by Shirley Jackson
We Have Always Lived in the Castle by Shirley Jackson
Salem's Lot by Stephen King
The Shining by Stephen King
Phantoms by Dean R. Koontz

The House by the Churchyard by J. Sheridan Le Fanu
Our Lady of Darkness by Fritz Leiber
Gad's Hall by Norah Lofts
The Case of Charles Dexter Ward by H. P. Lovecraft
"The Rats in the Walls" by H. P. Lovecraft
"No Way Home" by Brian Lumley
Burnt Offerings by Robert Marasco
Fevre Dream by George R. R. Martin
Hell House by Richard Matheson
Blackwater by Michael McDowell
The Elementals by Michael McDowell
"The Fall of the House of Usher" by Edgar Allan Poe
"The Tell-tale Heart" by Edgar Allan Poe
"The Miraculous Cairn" by Christopher Priest
Maynard's House by Herman Raucher
The Uninhabited House by Mrs. J. H. Riddell
"Valie" (or "The House of Sounds") by M. P. Shiel
The House Next Door by Anne Rivers Siddons
Shadowland by Peter Straub
"Shottle Bop" by Theodore Sturgeon
Sweetheart, Sweetheart by Bernard Taylor
Finishing Touches by Thomas Tessier
The Black House by Paul Theroux
The Other by Thomas Tryon
"Sticks" by Karl Edward Wagner
The Castle of Otranto by Horace Walpole
Peace by Gene Wolfe
Hotel Transylvania by Chelsea Quinn Yarbro